SURVIVING

A KENT STATE MEMOIR

PAULA STONE TUCKER

Paula Stone Tucker

SUNBURY
PRESS
Mechanicsburg, PA USA

Published by Sunbury Press, Inc.
Mechanicsburg, Pennsylvania

SUNBURY
PRESS

www.sunburypress.com

For information about special discounts for bulk purchases, please contact Sunbury Press Orders Dept. at (855) 338-8359 or orders@sunburypress.com.

To request one of our authors for speaking engagements or book signings, please contact Sunbury Press Publicity Dept. at publicity@sunburypress.com.

ISBN: 978-1-62006-319-4 (Trade paperback)

Library of Congress Control Number: 2019948926

FIRST SUNBURY PRESS EDITION: September 2019

Product of the United States of America
0 1 1 2 3 5 8 13 21 34 55

Set in Bookman Old Style
Designed by Crystal Devine
Cover by Terry Kennedy
Cover photo by John Filo
Edited by Lawrence Knorr

Continue the Enlightenment!

This book is dedicated to the survivors and victims of May 4, 1970. May they and their families find peace.

Paula at Kent State University, spring 1968

AUTHOR'S NOTE

This is a true story. The names of the living have been changed, except for those of historical figures.

ACKNOWLEDGMENTS

This book has been fifty years in the making. Thank you to those who helped me along the way:

Thank you to the many people in my writing critique group, the Writers of The Villages: Christie Seiler Boeke, Larry Chizak, Dwight Connelly, Doug Cravens, Jenny Ferns, Tom Hannon, Bona Hayes, Millard Johnson, Julie Johnson, Rene Leonhard, Larry Martin, and Barb Rein.

Thank you to my mother, Jane Courtney Stone, for reading to me every night of my childhood.

Thanks to my editor, Marsha Butler, for her many helpful corrections, suggestions, and insights; to John Filo for the use of his historic photograph, and to Lawrence Knorr, Crystal Devine, and Terry Kennedy of Sunbury Press

Finally, thanks to my first and best editor, John Olesky Jr., to my son, Pat, for inspiring me, and to my family for helping me survive.

1

May 4, 1970

The Commons bell was irresistible. I heard the clanging at 11:30 A.M., calling us to the noon rally.

I stuck my head out the Taylor Hall door to see what was going on. Yearbook reservations could wait. Sorority girls in mohair sweaters, pins hanging off their bosoms, waved their fists and chanted.

"Guard off campus! Guard off campus!"

This was new. Until now, there had been a deep division between the Greeks and the rest of the student body over the Vietnam War. I smiled, happy that at least for today we could stop bickering among ourselves.

The sorority girls continued their chant. Shocking. The Guard was still patrolling the Commons. I walked over to where the Greek sisters stood. I felt out of place next to them in my home-sewn dress meant to hide my increasing girth. Anti-war chants spewed from their pert little mouths. All it took was the National Guard on campus to unite us.

"One, two, three, four. We don't want your fucking war!" Amazing. They'd always sided with the pro-war faction before.

I turned back toward the Taylor door, but stopped and just for the hell of it, joined in. "One, two, three, four, we don't want your fucking war!" *That felt really good.*

The protesters around me giggled and laughed between chants. It was more of a pep rally than a demonstration. The big schools—Harvard and Berkeley—were used to these wild anti-war upheavals, but not sleepy Kent State.

A jeep packed with guardsmen drove across the Commons toward us, and one of them yelled some garbled words through a bullhorn. It sounded like, "This assembly is illegal."

A confrontation between the National Guard and the protesters was too exciting to miss. I stayed to watch, thrilled to think the Guard might back down. *Would the Guard back down?*

The jeep made a rapid circuit across the Commons and sped away toward the still-smoking ROTC building where they were staked out. Then a contingent of guardsmen moved across the field toward us. A third of the way out, they stopped. One of them fired a small rocket. *Teargas.* It landed at the bottom of Blanket Hill, the incline that led from the Commons to Taylor. It fell short of the crowd that greeted it with jeers and hoots.

A straggly haired guy with faded jeans and a red bandanna around his forehead grabbed it and tossed it back. His toss was lame, and the smoking canister hit the ground far from its target. More hoots and hollers.

As the smoky cloud wafted over us, people retreated uphill to escape. The wind changed and blew the gas all the way up the hill. Soon it reached me, and peppery tears blinded me. I didn't want to miss this confrontation, but I had to be able to see. I rushed into Taylor along with four or five other girls. In the bathroom, I cupped my hands under the faucet and brought pools of water to my eyes trying to wash out the burning sting. It didn't help much.

Outside again, I saw people far away across the Commons but the crowd on Blanket Hill had thinned considerably. *Where had they gone?* I peered around the edge of the building and saw the last of the protesters trail over the crest of the hill.

Hot and sweaty, I wondered if I should go back inside. No, I wanted to be part of the action. Following them won out. *What would happen next?*

From the Commons the noise on the other side of the hill was muffled. By the time I reached the top, the guardsmen had marched onto the practice football field that lay beyond Taylor. They would hit a fence and have to turn around. *They had to be hot in their riot gear and gas masks.*

I paused to watch. Down below, a few protesters in baggy shirts and faded jeans jumped up and down, waved flags and made fools of themselves. Most of the crowd was far from the guardsmen over in the parking lot.

"One, two, three, four, we don't want your fucking war," they yelled. "Pigs off campus!"

I laughed. The whole scene was absurd—like a panty raid but even better. A VW bug decorated with Pop-art flowers was parked in the space closest to Taylor, a premium spot.

I took the walkway past the metal sculpture toward the parking lot at the bottom of the hill. A few weeks earlier, I had been quick footed enough to climb over rocks when we went hiking. But walking here called for caution as the baby weight was throwing me off balance. I had to be careful. I worried more about falling than about the guardsmen.

Losing track of them as I picked my way toward the parking lot, I stopped and turned to look. They had marched back across the field. They were behind me, almost to the top of the hill, going back to the Commons. I resumed my walk, ignoring the few protesters around me who surged forward. I sweated in the hot sun.

As I walked, I heard a pop and then another series—*pop, pop, pop. Firecrackers?* A chill went through me as I looked over my shoulder. Guardsmen were aiming their weapons at us from the top of the hill. Little puffs of smoke burst from the ends of their guns.

People ran and dove to the ground like in a movie shootout. *Aren't they overreacting? They're firing blanks, right?* But what did I know? Maybe blanks could hurt.

I was more worried about getting my dress dirty than whether they might shoot me. Beside the metal sculpture there was debris everywhere. Dirt. Grass. Twigs. No clean place to lie down. Everything in slow motion.

A few feet away the stairs to Taylor looked safe. I walked over and lay down just as the firing stopped. I shook as I lay there on the steps, afraid to raise my head. It seemed like endless minutes passed. *Maybe they aren't blanks.* When I looked up, everyone was still on the ground, but they were stirring. I was confused. There was dead quiet all around. No jeering, no chants. I didn't know whether to be angry or terrified. I stood up.

A boy dressed in dark clothes lay face down in the middle of the parking lot driveway. *Poor guy, he must have tripped.* He was so still. A trickle of blood flowed from his head onto the asphalt. *Wow, he hit the ground hard.* Other people fell too. *How could they be so clumsy?* I saw another one lying just beyond the injured guy. I wavered between disgust for the Guard and fear they might fire again. I didn't know what to do.

I started counting those who were still down. A flag-waver approached the guy in the driveway turning him over on his back. Half his face was gone. *My God, he hit his head hard.*

My brain wasn't working. Each time I tried to count the bodies, I'd get to seven or eight and shake my head. *This can't be right. That's too many.* Then I'd start over.

2

Spring 1965

"Walk right down that hallway. Sister Mary Robert will measure you for your habit." Reverend Mother stood up and ended the interview.

I rose to leave, relieved to be out from under her scrutiny. What did she mean about a habit? No one had mentioned that.

I was only half-serious about wanting to join the convent because I hadn't saved any money for college. This whole fiasco started a few months earlier when my friend Lynn told me she was joining. She said they would pay for college once you joined.

Mom and Dad never talked about money, so it shocked me to learn that they had enough trouble putting food on the table, let alone financing a college education. But I dearly wanted to go.

Since first grade, I'd been at the top of my class. The nuns at St. Joe's wanted me to skip a grade, but Mom and Dad would have none of it.

"Tommy Jeffers skipped ahead last year, and he ran into lots of trouble. Social skills. They said he lacked social skills," Mom lamented.

By sixth grade, I was the uninvited misfit. I lacked social skills without even skipping a grade. Paula Boyle didn't invite me to her slumber party.

"Not enough room," she said.

But I knew better. I was an outcast.

I just wanted to fit in. I spent most of high school scrambling to do so. I hung out on the edge of the 'in' cliques hoping to be noticed. I wisecracked in class, so the cool girls would laugh, but in my junior year, Saint Mary's became an all-girls school. The boys transferred to public schools, or to Hoban, the Catholic boys' school across town. I gave up on finding a boyfriend then.

Other girls could figure out the Y-Teen scene and the Friday night football games, but not me. After a year of floundering, I decided to become a nun.

Now it was happening for real. Reverend Mother was sending me down the hall to be measured for a habit. I didn't think things would get so serious on my first visit.

⌘

As I walked, the long hallway echoed with every step. My stomach churned. There was a small room at the end of the hall. Inside, a nun bent over, finishing my friend Mary's measurements.

"Come in, dear," said the stout young nun, as Mary walked out. "I'm Sister Alice."

The convent had been a lark until now, partly influenced by the romance of Julie Andrews in *The Sound of Music*. Who wouldn't want to be dancing in the Alps? But when Sister began measuring me, things had gone too far. The nuns weren't kidding. For some reason, I thought this visit was to gather information. Now I was scared.

The habit was all black, a below-the-knee dress with a head-scarf that let wisps of hair show through, opaque stockings and grandma-like low-heeled shoes. The only reason anyone would wear this getup was that it led to the postulant's outfit a year later.

Postulants wore an all-white habit. That wasn't too bad. Mary and I joked about the different habits as we sat around and waited for the others to be measured.

"I wouldn't be caught dead in that," I said, indicating the black one.

She laughed.

⌘

On the four-hour drive home back to Akron, we said little in front of Father Snider. The dashing bon vivant parish priest had volunteered to drive us to the motherhouse in Michigan for our interviews in his own T-Bird. Adorable as he was, he might be a pipeline to the nuns. He left us in the school parking lot and walked out of sight toward the rectory.

We burst out talking. "Did they measure you?"

"What did Mother say?" cascaded out in a storm of teenage giggles.

"Reverend Mother said we have to talk to someone else in Cleveland. What does that mean?" No one knew.

On Monday, a note from the office informed me that a Doctor Smith, in downtown Cleveland, would interview me and determine my mental fitness for the convent.

"He's a psychologist," Mary said.

I wasn't sure what a psychologist did, but the nuns at Saint Mary's told us messing with the human mind was a sin. I needed to be careful.

⌘

Doctor Smith's office was dimly lit by a few floor lamps. "Sit," he said, as he motioned me toward an over-sized dark brown leather chair.

"So, you want to enter the convent. What can you tell me about that?" Doctor Smith began.

I started with a little speech I had rehearsed, part fantasy and part puffing. "Well, I've always been religious. I love the Church and the Virgin Mary. I go to Mass almost every day."

Doctor Smith sat quietly at his desk for a few moments. "What can you tell me about your family?"

I fumbled. A sinking feeling flooded my gut, but I stumbled ahead. "I have three brothers and a sister. I help take care of them, especially the two youngest."

He nodded but looked as though he disapproved. "Hmm." He took notes, his head downcast.

"What can you tell me about your parents?"

"I love my parents and we get along well." What a liar. I hope he doesn't have any way of checking. Mentioning that I hated my parents seemed like bad form.

"What about getting married? Don't you want a family?"

"Oh no! I don't want to end up like them," I blurted out. Oops. Too late.

He scribbled furiously in his notepad without looking up. "What do you mean by that?"

Trapped, I hesitated. "Well, they fight a lot. I don't want to end up like my parents."

"Do you mean you don't want to fight, or you don't want to be unhappy?"

"Both." I hadn't thought this through.

He continued, "That's all the questions I have. Now I want you to take the test we give candidates for the convent." He handed me a thick booklet.

A test? I was good at taking tests. The booklet had hundreds of multiple-choice questions. I whipped through it and handed it back to Doctor Smith in about ninety minutes. He nodded in thanks.

"We'll let you know."

I was in! I was sure of it. Why wouldn't they want a person like me? Good grades, smart, very religious.

⌘

The wait was hard. Every day I ran to the mailbox looking for a letter addressed to me. Finally, a month later, toward the end of May, a small square envelope came in the mail. It looked like it contained a postcard. I held it up to the light, then opened it. A small piece of paper folded in two fell out.

"Dear Miss Scott," read the typewritten note. Just a note, not even a letter. "We regret to inform you we are not able to admit you into this year's novice class. We recommend you attend college for a year and then reapply if you are still interested." It was signed by the Reverend Mother.

My jaw dropped.

No explanation, no consolation. Devastated, I tried to hold back tears. One slid down the side of my nose. As I turned, Mom, who was reading over my shoulder, looked at me with a crazy grin but said nothing. I was so mad. Why didn't they want me? Well, I'd fix them. I'd figure out how to pay for college on my own.

3

―――

Summer 1965

The only flaw in my plan to escape from my parents' house was a huge one. I had put all my eggs in one basket, hoping for admission to the convent with its promise of a free college education. So convinced I'd make it, I hadn't even applied to any of the colleges I could afford. The only scholarship I received was one for five hundred dollars to a small Catholic college in Columbus about two hours away. I hadn't applied for any other scholarships or loans either. Now my life was falling apart.

Not one to give up easily, I looked at Mom. "I still want to go to college." I tried to hide my desperation. Mom just grinned. Why did she enjoy this?

The next day my parents sat me down for one of their talks. Mom began.

"If you are too immature to join the convent, then you're too immature to go to college. We want you to work for a year and save up money for tuition."

Immature? Who said anything about being immature?

"Where do you get that?" I parried. "That wasn't what the letter said."

"Oh, but that's what it meant." She looked delighted.

What was going on with them?

I panicked. They kicked me while I was down. I made one last valiant attempt.

―――

10

"But I want to go to college." I almost cried. Pitiful. They gave me no hope. They shook their heads. "You will be working and that's it," my father said. The answer was *no*.

With all the convent drama, graduation was just a footnote. My friends left for college or nursing school while I went on to nothing.

Embarrassed that I had kept my wish to join the convent secret from them, I had hoped it would all happen magically. That somehow in September, I would join the convent and not have to deal with my parents. Now I had to be honest. I still hoped to become a nun but that would have to wait.

I sighed. "Okay, okay. I'll look for a job." Of course, all the better jobs were already filled by girls who studied stenography and typing. That wasn't me. At a loss for places to apply, I had only gone to the five & dime stores like Woolworth's.

Mom heard that Ohio Bell was hiring. Early the next morning I took the bus to downtown Akron to apply.

An imposing Art Deco building on Bowery, the Bell sat about a block off Main. In 1965, downtown Akron still looked prosperous, the result of all the rubber company money spent. I pulled the heavy glass door at the entryway. The guard inside stopped me.

"I'm here to apply for a job."

He directed me to an office across from his desk. "You want Personnel. Over there." He pointed.

This was my first job application ever. The nuns at St. M's assumed we'd be going to college, so they hadn't taught us how to complete one. I shook with nerves as I pushed the Personnel door open.

⌘

Exasperated, Mom yelled from the kitchen, "Did the Bell call?" Her voice sounded angry, just one notch below a scream.

"No." Best to keep this interchange short. I lay in bed, luxuriating in the freedom that came with graduating from high school.

"Did you check with any of the places you applied?"

"No." I didn't tell her I had only applied for one job. I wondered what had gotten into her. The end of June was coming fast.

Maybe that was it. I applied to the phone company right after graduation. *Don't I have to wait for them to call me?*

"I think you'd better call them back, young lady. You need to find a job, so you can start paying rent." Mom was all business. After several days of my stalling, she'd had it. She pulled me out of bed.

I said, "Did you hear about any of those jobs?"

I shook my head.

She stomped out of the room. A minute later the front door slammed. I couldn't imagine where she went, but it couldn't be any place good. She didn't like to let neighbors in on our family problems, so she must be headed somewhere else.

I dressed hurriedly and slammed down a bowl of Cheerios, wondering what took her so long. An hour later, the door opened. I looked up. Mom came into view wearing a maniacal grin on her face, the one that let me know trouble was afoot.

"You have an appointment with Father Jones," she told me gleefully. "Get ready. It's in thirty minutes."

Oh, my God. What's going on? I hadn't committed any sin I could remember. Father Jones, the pastor at St. Joe's, was a sweaty man with a perpetually red face. The rectory, located on Second Street, was about a half-mile away. It would take me fifteen minutes to get there if I didn't walk fast enough to work up a sweat.

Stricken, I tried not to show it as Mom sat back gloating. I had never spoken to the pastor without one of my parents present. He wasn't that scary, but he was old, almost deaf and had a reputation for hating teenagers. She was sending me to the executioner for a crime beyond my control. It wasn't my fault I didn't have a job yet.

I sighed. Mom was making a bigger deal of this than necessary though I kept my complaints to myself. I put on my best dress, a tailored blue-and-white striped shirtwaist with colorful patchwork appliques. I tried for a casual look with white tennis shoes. I tried to fix my hair a little, but it was still bumpy on one side. I walked out the door, hoping I wouldn't meet anyone I knew. Hot and humid, the summer day had barely any breeze. Leaves drooped from the trees. A scent of honeysuckle floated in the air. If I'd gotten the Bell job, I wouldn't be in this predicament.

The rectory, a gray-shingled Craftsman house, sat on the corner across from the church. A long cement walk shaded by a couple of huge maple trees led up to the front door. I hoped my track record as shy, but cooperative would ease me through this appointment.

I rang the bell and Mary, the elderly housekeeper, ushered me into a front parlor, while she retrieved Father Jones. He appeared shortly, still dressed in his black cassock as if he had just come back from saying Mass. His face was florid, but of course, he was about fifty pounds overweight. He was sixty-five and not in the best of shape. He sagged into a chair across from me.

"What brings you in, Patty?"

Mom had been here telling on me less than an hour ago. Maybe he decided to play dumb.

I played along. "Mom sent me. You know, Jane Scott, Paul's wife. She . . . well, I guess both my parents, want me to find a job." I tried to sound super-reasonable, even though I shook.

"Have you been looking?"

"Yes, Father."

"Did you follow up with any of these places yourself?"

"Well, not yet. I just started looking." I was the essence of cool reason. How could he fault me?

"Are you fighting with your mother?"

I tried to look shocked. *Can't he see how crazy she is?* "Well, she is mad at me because I haven't found a job yet." *Can't he see I'm trapped in a family of irrational people?*

"I think she wants you to search harder."

Embarrassed, I could hardly argue with his conclusion.

"Patty, I want you to go home and tell your mother you're sorry. Tell her you'll look harder."

Desperate to leave, I nodded my head in agreement. Anything to get out of there.

"Will you do that?"

I guessed he wanted me to say it out loud.

"Sure." The irony was I had nowhere else to go but home. My friends either had summer jobs or were on vacation. I walked the five blocks back to Meriline Street, hoping Mom had found someone else to harass while I was gone. How did things fall so far so fast? I went from happily awaiting acceptance to the convent to being regarded as an unemployed bum in one month, all while my friends were still recovering from graduation parties.

Mom was in the kitchen cleaning a chicken for dinner. I didn't stop to talk. I went straight to the phone and dialed. Surprisingly, I was transferred to the personnel lady at the Bell.

"We were just going to call you. Can you be here Wednesday at 9:00 A.M.?"

"They want me," I announced triumphantly to Mom. She nodded her head, glad I had an appointment, but she wouldn't be happy until I brought in a paycheck. Wednesday couldn't come soon enough.

⌘

The personnel lady eyed me. "You did great on the test, but I'm worried you won't stay with us. You say you plan to go to college."

She was suspicious of my motives. Time for some quick thinking.

"Oh no, I want to work here." *At least until next fall when I can start school. I need a job so Mom will back off.*

⌘

The Bell was boring. I trained to be an information operator. As far as I could figure out, information operators ranked below long distance because they didn't sit at a real switchboard. We learned how to alphabetize, and how to flip through five or more bulky phone directories speedily.

I dispensed phone numbers and other information to people too lazy or incompetent to look them up in their own phone book. I needed a sharp memory for the location of various esoteric entries like "the municipal building," a moderate amount of speed in flipping through the thick directories piled up in front of me, plus the ability to speak clearly and slowly. All this needed to be done in less than a minute per call because a supervisor monitored the amount of time spent with each caller.

I mastered the speed, but again, like in school, I had trouble fitting in with the cliques of girls who called the phone company their home.

"I almost have enough money to move out," my friend Judy said as we sat in the cafeteria. The company had its own elaborate cafeteria serving breakfast, lunch, and dinner. Judy shifted in her seat to reach the ashtray across the table. She wore a fitted skirt, shiny black stilettos and lots of makeup. She had worked here a year and recently graduated to a daytime schedule with no weekends. Seniority paid.

Her boyfriend, Tom, waited for her after work, idling in front of the building in his brand-new LTD. Judy dreamt of getting her own apartment with a couple of friends and working until she and Tom married in a few years.

Then there was me, taking the bus, working a split shift, ten to two and six to ten, feeling like I ran on a hamster wheel. Most days as my peers got ready for lunch, I waited for the city bus home in front of Polsky's, the big department store on Main Street. I went home to wait until my second shift started. I'd be taking another bus back to work four hours later. I was usually scheduled to work both weekend evenings. Not much time for a social life.

Mom and Dad were proud of me now. They finally had a child who amounted to something.

⌘

"Of course, you'll be paying rent," Mom told me. "Fifty dollars a week."

If I could save enough money to pay for school, I would be happy.

More than one guy called regularly for *Cheap Jack's Slop Shop*, which I later discovered was really "Cheap Jack's *Swap* Shop" or for "Lemon Butts, Sr." At first, I thought these crank calls, but when I found these names listed, I discovered another side of Akron—a wild and sleazy side I was unaware of growing up in Cuyahoga Falls, a lily-white suburb.

Kids called asking for help with their homework and for instructions on how to make brownies. *Where are their parents?* Then bored men called every Saturday night almost as if they were on a date. One guy, a repeat offender, thumped something against the earpiece of his phone. "Operator, guess what this is?" His lascivious tone didn't leave much to the imagination.

I muffled a scream, imagining his dick. I tried to grab my friend Judy's attention, so she could run across the room and listen. The joke for us was that more than one person was hearing this obscenity. Even with the supervisors gone, we weren't permitted to hang up on these guys, no matter how foul the call. The Bell ruled the customer must hang up first. Many times, customers were so rude all I wanted to do was pull the plug.

On the day shift, a supervisor monitored calls from her desk in the front of the office. They timed my calls and counseled me on how to increase my speed and how to put "a smile in my voice." The big boss who resembled Margaret Thatcher, decided I needed extra counseling to improve my tone. Polly, one of the floor supervisors, pulled up a stool behind me, plugged her headset into my station and listened. I almost gagged at the combination of smells emanating from her—coffee, stale cigarettes, and perfume. Not meant to be inhaled by seventeen-year-olds early in the morning.

Being an Information operator required a moderate amount of skill and I had that, but in my mind, it was quite a tumble from my lofty goal of going to college. True, I didn't know what to major in, but I did want to go. Working at the phone company just strengthened that desire.

Short of open rebellion, for which I could be fired, I couldn't think of any other way to protest except by conveying contempt vocally. *Let me out of here!* was my most frequent thought.

I applied to Kent State, ten miles away. I could live at home and commute. I counted the days until I could begin the next fall. More than four hundred! I needed a scholarship. Going away to school now seemed impossible. I was a year behind everybody else and would be paying for everything on my own.

I jumped for joy when a letter came telling me I had been admitted and had won a full scholarship. All I needed to pay for were my books. Mom and Dad were happy for me, but I kept quiet about it at work. I needed to pretend I loved the Bell for a few more months.

A class war raged between the long-distance operators and the information gals. Unsure of its origin, I looked on as the long-distance operators snubbed us in the halls. They ignored us in the cafeteria, in the hallways, and in the elevators. It was high school all over again.

When I worked the late shift, I sat alone in the cafeteria on my break and listened to the jukebox. Most nights someone punched B16 and I listened to Simon and Garfunkel's "The Sound of Silence." *Hello, darkness my old friend.* My life: lonely and bleak.

I counted the hours and minutes until my last day. School began on September twenty-first. I planned to take off two weeks to buy school clothes and supplies and get myself organized. I'd be commuting from home in the seafoam green Mercury Comet Dad found for me.

Finally, my last day arrived. I had managed to last fourteen months, three days, eight hours and seven minutes without punching anyone out or running away.

I turned in my notice to the same personnel lady who hired me. Just over a year ago I swore to her I would be here forever. She shook her head when I told her I quit. I didn't care.

I was so excited I almost skipped out the door. *Kent State, here I come.*

4

Fall 1966

Registration day. My first on campus. The azure sky and the deep green rolling hills vibrated. No more dark gray and dingy black of Akron. Since I started college a year later than most of my friends, I didn't expect to recognize anyone. I found a parking place next to a beat-up rust brown jalopy and walked the short block to the gym where registration took place. I carried a list of freshman classes that counted toward graduation in my shoulder bag.

A steady stream of students passed, joking with each other. "Don't get lost in the locker room," followed by belly laughs and giggles. I didn't know what was so funny but laughed anyway, to fit in.

I wanted to major in Journalism though Mom convinced me I'd need a backup plan that included a teaching certificate. I found the end of a long line leading to the gym, snaking its way up and down staircases. An older, bearded guy stood in front of me. He acted like he'd been through this before. He turned and offered me advice.

"Sweetie, by the time you reach the gym, there won't be much left. You should try for some appreciation classes. Get those out of the way. Then you can worry about your major later."

Looking up from the course catalog, I thanked him. His advice threw me. I wanted to take a reporting course at least. After about a half hour online I made it into the cavernous gym. Waning afternoon light filtered through the dusty air. Hundreds of people milled about, their faces buried in course catalogs. Odors of jock straps and Gold Bond mixed with the haze of sweaty students.

Locating the Journalism table. I stood in line. The girl at the front of the line turned, shoulders sagging and walked away. I tapped the back of the guy in front of me and asked, "What's going on?"

"It's the last day of registration. What do you expect? All the good classes are filled."

My stomach sank. When I reached the front of the line, all the Journalism classes were closed.

I registered for general education requirements, just happy I had enough hours to keep my scholarship. By the time I finished, it was almost dusk. Outside, the Administration Building, which housed the gym, was silhouetted by the setting sun. One of the gray stone turn-of-the-century buildings, it sat on the semicircular driveway that framed the front campus. Black squirrels frolicked in the grass. Couples lay on blankets on the gentle hill that sloped down to Main Street.

I clutched my class schedule like a prize. I'd gotten into English, history, biology and art history. I could go home. But, first, I had to pay. With the scholarship, I only owed fees for labs and parking.

Books were sold separately. I could buy them second-hand off campus. In high school books were free, so the book bill came as a big shock. Almost a hundred dollars. Once the sticker shock from my books wore off, I was thrilled. The first day of classes couldn't come soon enough for me. They wouldn't start until Tuesday. I had a hard time sleeping.

⌘

Kent State burst with activity. Every couple who married after the war in 1946 or '47 now sent their kids off to college. Hundreds of students packed into every introductory class and there weren't enough parking spaces. My assigned parking lot was so far away from campus I had to take a bus.

The commuter bus made a loop around campus before returning to the shopping center where I parked. There was a

stop close to Bowman Hall where I had my first class. My heart
beat fast, but not because of the walk from the bus stop. Elated
not to have to continue at Ohio Bell, I felt like I'd escaped a death
sentence.

English was my first class. The young teacher wasn't much
beyond twenty-four or twenty-five. That must be the reason for
the pipe and his elbow-patched jacket. I had expected a professor
with gray hair and a beard. As I found a seat, Mr. Bremer, an
English grad student told us the class requirements.

I sat next to a guy who smiled and extended his hand. "Hi, I'm
Frank."

I managed to smile back. "Patty," I said. After years of a
male drought, my heart jumped to see the class almost evenly
divided between men and women. Mr. Bremer explained the
requirements, and everyone quieted. Would the work be too hard?
Maybe I couldn't handle the class load. The requirements for this
first semester were a couple of essays and a book to read, *Native
Son*. I relaxed a little.

At the end of class, Frank caught up to me. "Why don't you
give me your phone number?"

I hesitated.

"We can go out some time."

Maybe this was what Reverend Mother had in mind when she
told me to attend college for a year. He was cute with longish
curly brown locks. What could it hurt?

After class, I found my way to the Student Union, which held
The Hub, a dark, crowded lunchroom smelling of hot grease.
They sold hamburgers, fries, Coke and ice cream concoctions.
The jukebox blasted "Summer in the City." I didn't see anyone
I knew. There weren't any free tables, so I went outside and ate
alone, seated on the stone wall in front of the Union. I spent my
lunch hour reading the campus newspaper, the *Daily Kent Stater*
and skimming a book for biology. The *Stater* had a long list of
campus activities. Enthralled with the possibilities, I was eager
to try some.

5

My eyes settled on a blurb promising a tour of the campus television station starting at 6:30 that evening. *Kent has its own radio and TV station. How cool!*

Being a journalism major, I thought *I should check this out.* I wasn't expected home at any particular time, so I could stay late. I'd walk the three blocks over to Music and Speech past Blanket Hill. A warm September day, it would stay light until at least eight.

The leaves swirled in the wind as I ambled across campus past the foot of Blanket Hill toward Music and Speech. I loved fall with its rich yellows and golds. This year was especially beautiful. The Music and Speech building was cool and quiet, almost deserted. The afternoon crowd had left, and the evening students hadn't arrived.

The long hall echoed as I walked along, reading the signs and nameplates on various doors. *Speech Clinic, Theater, Radio and Television* and finally *TV2* off to the right.

The heavy wooden double door blocked out sounds from the hallway. A sign read *Control Room.* Another red and white sign hung above it, *On Air.* This was where I needed to be. I walked in. Five or six other people waited for the tour in the dimly lit room. I took a seat in the second tier of chairs directly behind the control console. Everything was shiny chrome and laminate. It looked like a smaller version of the control rooms I'd seen on TV with banks of monitors. Beneath the monitors, two giant plate-glass windows opened onto a studio.

The director sat in a chair in the middle of the console and spoke into a headset.

"Camera 2, wide shot. Take 2."

He directed the news show being taped in the big studio in front of us. Two other people sat at the consoles with headsets, listened to the director and then followed his commands. As we watched, a cute guy with dimples and a Friar Tuck haircut came into the control room. He glanced towards us.

"I'm Dan. Are you here for the tour?"

We nodded.

"First, I'll show you the studio."

He motioned for us to follow him. We passed through another heavy door and walked forward in a little clump. He took us toward the set, leading us behind the two camera operators focused on the reporters.

As I passed by, the second cameraman, a tall guy with curly black hair and a red plaid shirt leaned over toward me.

"What's your name?" he whispered as he pushed the mouthpiece of his headset aside and smiled.

I smiled. "Patty," I answered *sotto voce* and turned to follow the tour group. How embarrassing. I didn't want to call any attention to myself. I lagged behind already. *Was he interested in me? Be cool.* He was the first person to notice me since I'd been on campus besides Frank from English class. As I followed Dan, Plaid Shirt trailed behind me, at least as far as the cord on his headset would allow.

The tour finished and Dan ushered us into the control room to watch the end of the news. As I stood to leave, Plaid Shirt appeared again, this time with his headset wires dangling. I felt my heart jump. *He is kind of cute.*

"What's your name again?"

I laughed. "Bad memory, huh?" I said sarcastically. "It's Patty."

"I'm Bob, Bob Turner."

He seemed interested. "I'll walk you out." We walked toward the heavy door. "I'm on the radio every evening at eight. What did you say your name was?" he asked again, and I burst into giggles.

"You really do have a bad memory." I tried not to act flustered. Not used to this much attention, as I looked into his eyes again, I felt an electric shock pass between us. A new feeling for me. Thoughts of reapplying to the convent faded away as this wave washed over me.

My heart pounded as I left the building. He was cute, with his black hair and dark brown eyes. I'd check out his show. I hoped I could find it on the radio. Suddenly, the TV and radio stations loomed much larger in my consciousness than any old English or biology class.

I wanted to see Bob again. Kent was a big campus, and I was brand new. *How could I find him?*

The bus ride to the parking lot wasn't so lonely that evening, but how could I find Bob without revisiting the TV station? That would be too obvious. Although I was just mildly interested in broadcasting, I was very interested in Bob. Maybe I could volunteer or I could figure out where he was and manage to run into him.

The next day, I dropped by the radio station. WKSU was on the third floor of the Music and Speech building. I brushed past hundreds of students going downstairs as I climbed up. I pulled open one of the heavy double doors marked WKSU and went in. Hanging from the ceiling ahead of me was a hand-lettered sign reading *Student-Run Radio*. The long, wide hallway was deserted, but voices came from the rooms adjoining it.

Be cool, be cool. I tried to calm my racing heart. I planned on acting surprised if I ran into Bob.

Someone hunted and pecked on a typewriter in the nearest office. A girl close to my age with frosted blond hair sat at a desk, typing. She wore a pullover with a pin on it and a short skirt with nylons and flats. She looked up at me, expectantly. Was she the receptionist or a secretary? She was a sorority girl. Did I need to join a sorority to fit in? No way did I have the money for that.

I gathered my wits and smiled. "Hi, I want to volunteer. Can I talk to someone?"

"Oh, sure. Down the hall on the right. Somebody there can help you."

"Thanks, uh, Shana," I said, reading the nameplate that sat on her desk. I took a chance. "Does Bob Turner work here?"

She laughed. "Oh, yeah, Bob," she said and nodded. "He's usually here in the evenings. Do you want to leave him a note? His mailbox is down the hall."

⌘

The sign on the door read "Continuity." I heard voices inside, so I pushed the door open onto a spacious room where two guys lounged on beat-up leather couches with sagging springs. Mailboxes lined one wall. There were a few desks, a small dorm-sized refrigerator, and a coffee maker. A smaller room off the back wall had a Dutch door that opened in onto a bank of Teletype machines.

A slightly built guy with curly blond hair and big horn-rimmed glasses poured himself some coffee. He glanced over at me while the guys on the couches debated what song would be number one next week.

I smiled and walked toward the horn-rimmed guy.

"Hi, I'm Patty. I'd like to volunteer." I nodded my head toward the other office. "Shana told me to check with someone in here."

"I'm Jack, the music director."

He seemed shy, so I smiled and repeated myself. "I want to volunteer." I didn't tell him my main goal was to find Bob Turner.

"Oh, we have lots for you to do. What are you interested in?"

I had to think fast. I took a stab. "Well, I'm a journalism major. Can I do something news-related?"

He took a breath. "You should talk to Sandy. He's our news director. He'll be in about three o'clock."

I checked my watch. Only a half hour.

"That's Sandy's desk, over there." He pointed. "You can wait for him. I need to go down to the music library and pull records for tonight."

I decided to wait.

⌘

Sandy turned out to be another diminutive guy with wavy reddish-blond hair.

"I've been here since June when the last director graduated," he said.

"The news at the station is mostly AP and UPI wire copy. We rip it from the Teletype machines and paste it into three-minute newscasts. The disk jockeys read it on the hour and the half hour.

"We need people to pull copy for us. Would you like to start with that?"

This was my chance. I would come in two days a week after class to pull and edit copy for a couple of hours. If I dawdled enough, I would eventually run into Bob. I hadn't edited news before, but how hard could it be? You just cut out the boring stuff.

⌘

An easy job, it called for judgment about what news was important enough to read on air, cutting the important news out of the endless stream of stories being sent and then pasting stories together in order. Then a disk jockey read it. What I liked most was watching everyone through the windows of the Teletype room. The staff used the Continuity room for breaks. I used the desk in the larger room to rip and paste things, so I had a natural excuse to hang out.

The atmosphere at the station was different from the rest of campus. There was a cult of personality like in a regular broadcast radio station. I was used to hearing of deejay fan clubs from the Top 40 stations in the area, so this was no surprise.

At WKSU, the deejays with the biggest clout were those with what the other staff referred to as *ten-ton balls*.

"What in the world does that mean?" I asked Shana one day.

"It means they have a really deep voice." She had become my guide to this new world. By that standard, the most important deejay was a quiet guy named Rich. He was hulking at 6'4" and about two hundred pounds. He had the deepest voice.

But there were other ways to dominate. Both the most persistent interviewer and the wittiest person were popular. Bob fell on the witty spectrum. Though I still hadn't run into him, other people told me how funny he was. *Witty* might not have been the best description as they mentioned practical jokes and pranks he pulled like the time he locked the on-air disk jockey out of the control room.

The radio station staff was a party crowd. At nineteen I couldn't legally drink, but I wanted to make up for the lost time. I was invited to parties every weekend—mostly at the music director's house. While the rest of us were commuters or temporary citizens of Kent, living in the dorms or off-campus rooms, Jack was born in Kent and still lived in his mother's split-level house on the outskirts. Perfect for parties.

While I was dying to go, I didn't want to go solo. How would it look if I showed up to a drinking party by myself? I would wait.

6

I showed up every other day to pull news copy from the wire machines, but my plan to meet Bob didn't work out. He hadn't come in early for his 8:00 P.M. shift and I hadn't managed to invent an excuse to stay late. Then fate intervened.

My Lit class met at Bowman Hall three days a week and afterward, I walked two blocks to spend my lunch hour at The Hub. Along the way, I got an education about campus life.

On my way to the Student Union, I passed a motley group. For the past month, they had been marching back and forth in front of the ROTC buildings in a ragtag line with broomsticks over their shoulders. I stopped, trying to figure out what was happening.

A hand-drawn sign propped in front of them read KCEWV and underneath in smaller letters, Kent Committee to End the War in Vietnam. I knew about the war. I'd been reading about it for a couple of years on the front page of the local paper, but why were people were against it? The demonstrators looked like clowns with oversized flannel shirts and baggy jeans. A few frat guys walked by catcalling toward the group.

"Your mother's a Commie!"

"Go change your underwear!"

Well, if their protest made the frat boys this mad, maybe there was something to it. Off to the side, I saw Frank from my Lit class among the onlookers. I nodded to him but continued walking, sure the demonstrators would be here tomorrow.

The Hub, a typical college hangout, was dark enough that it took a minute to adjust to the dim lighting. Booths and tables crowded together. The smell of smoke and hamburger grease floated on the air. It was hard to find a seat after 10:00 A.M.

"Hanky Panky" by the Shondells played on the jukebox as I walked in, my eyes adjusting. I made a beeline for the queue waiting to order at the counter. Best to get my chocolate soda and fries before the 11:00 crowd showed up.

Walking back toward an empty table, I got a surprise. Bob approached the end of the line.

"Bob!" I called as I veered to intercept him. At first, he didn't recognize me. He looked puzzled, but I could see it slowly dawning on him. That *Patty* girl.

He pointed. "I'm sitting over in the corner where they're playing cards. I'll be right back."

I couldn't believe my luck. My day suddenly went from dull and boring to peak excitement. Shaking with happiness, I hurried over to find the table. There were several filled with people playing cards, so I asked, "Is this Bob Turner's table?" at each one. Most people were so engrossed in their games they ignored me. I finally found the right one. A brunette with long hair and lots of makeup nodded and I smiled back at her.

"Hi, I'm Patty. A friend of Bob's," I said as people stared at me quizzically. They were playing Spades.

"I'm Charlotte." She cleared some books off one of the chairs and motioned for me to sit down. Bob returned with a burger and fries. For the next half hour, I sipped my chocolate soda and watched them play, a daily routine Bob told me started during the summer session.

Charlotte introduced me to Denny, sandy-haired with a mop top, and Bob told me Charlotte dated his high school friend.

I casually mentioned I volunteered at the radio station.

"Really?" Bob was impressed. "I'm not usually on the air in the afternoon. I have classes then."

Soon it was time for me to leave if I were to make it to my 12:00 on the other side of campus. I smiled and joked a little as

I stood. My social skills, good enough for an all-girls high school, were going to need some sharpening. Bob walked me out.

We visited for a bit on our way to our next classes. He told me he loved broadcasting and dreamt of owning his own station one day. I reminded him that I volunteered at WKSU.

"Oh, we'll probably run into one another. My show runs Tuesday and Thursday evenings."

I didn't tell him about my plan to bump into him.

I was so happy I had found him. I tried to be in The Hub whenever Bob was.

After a few weeks, Denny failed to show up one day. Charlotte asked me to sit in on the card game. I took her into my confidence since she dated Bob's best friend.

7

Winter 1966

"I like Bob a lot," I said and waited for her reaction.

She took a deep breath. "He's dating someone. Missy Felton. She works at the radio station."

At least she's honest. Missy Felton might be a minor problem. I'd have to work around her. Maybe I should be direct with Bob. How should I start? *How's Missy?* Nah, too brash. How about *Seeing anyone?* It never occurred to me to ask him out on a date. But before I tipped my hand, Bob started talking about her.

We sat in The Hub waiting for Charlotte. The Supremes "I Hear a Symphony" played on the jukebox.

"I love the smell of *Tabu*," Bob said, dreamily.

Why did he bring this up?

He continued, "My girlfriend wears it."

"Oh, who's that?" The height of sophistication, I tried to convey a hint of disinterest.

"Her name is Missy. Missy Felton. She has beautiful emerald eyes, black hair, and the whitest skin."

Yuck. She would be hard to compete against.

"She works at the radio station."

In a perfect world, I'd have known enough to ask, "Why are you telling me this?" But I was the awkward girl who wanted to join the convent. "Oh," was all I could muster.

Bob continued to rhapsodize about Missy.

If I were going to have a chance, I'd need to buy some Tabu. With her green eyes and milky white skin, I didn't have much hope.

I never heard a guy say they loved someone's perfume. The wind was taken out of my sails. Me? I had mousy brown hair and freckles. Skin and bones with no visible bust line, I couldn't compete. All I could do was laugh at his jokes, listen sympathetically and lie in wait.

In his next breath, Bob had a suggestion. "Why don't you meet me at the station after my shift tonight?"

Hmm. What happened to Missy? I guess I'd pretend she didn't exist.

I floated on air. This was a major step forward. I arrived at 8:00 and sat on one of the leather couches someone had drug into the hallway. I waited through the news and the hour of easy listening music that followed for him to sign off. Most of the students who worked at the radio station during the day were gone. His on-air voice was piped through a speaker out into the hall, deep and melodious. I thrilled just hearing him.

Shortly before Bob's hour ended, the nine o'clock deejay, Rich, came in. Big, hulking, huge, he was the guy with the ten-ton balls people joked about. He nodded as he went toward the music library and pulled his records. He grabbed the news copy already pulled off the wire and pasted together, ready for him to read. He piled the news copy on top of his LPs and quietly opened the control room door.

Suddenly, Bob was right in front of me and he was all mine.

"I'm starved," he said, so I drove him over to the Red Barn across the street. He ordered a Barnbuster. We sat and talked for hours about silly things: gossip at the station, who dated who, our classes, our cars, his dorm. He told me his Falcon had broken down. He said he'd fix it when he could afford to.

"Ford stands for 'fix or repair daily.'"

This joke was new to me and I laughed. He had a pretty good sense of humor. The hours slipped by. Finally, I noticed it getting late.

"I'd better get going."

He walked me to my car. We held hands for a moment before he turned and walked toward his dorm. I cruised home dreaming of the time when we would be together.

I maneuvered my schedule so that I ran into Bob every day for at least a few minutes. Days we were both in The Hub it was easy. I had to be creative on other days. I figured out how to run into him accidentally as he walked to class. Infatuated, my stomach leaped when I thought about him. My heart pounded a little faster. He was so good-looking with his black wavy hair and nice clear skin.

I was falling in love, something new for me. True, I didn't know that much about him, but I felt sure Bob was the perfect guy for me. We weren't dating yet, and he did have that girlfriend, Missy, but those were minor considerations. It felt great to daydream about the life ahead of us.

I wanted to get together with Bob over winter break and gave him my phone number. In my imagination, I was picking out the kitchen curtains but I tried to be cool. I wished him a Merry Christmas when I bumped into him on the last day of classes.

Winter break dragged. At home with the family, I did Christmassy things, but all I could think about was going back to school. I cut back on gifts, trying to stretch the money I'd saved from the Bell so I could live on campus. Life would be perfect if I lived in a dorm. Then Bob and I could spend lots of time together. Every time the phone rang, I jumped to answer it, but no Bob.

⌘

Back in school after winter break, I continued plotting how to move into a dorm for the spring quarter. Again, I figured out when Bob had breaks between classes, so I could run into him. He was still dating Missy. *Bummer.* I commuted in the snow and slogged to class wearing clunky boots. Nineteen sixty-seven was the first year Kent coeds could wear slacks. At least the wind wouldn't blow up my skirt anymore.

⌘

The Association, my favorite group, would be playing for the Winter Ball in February. Their song, "Cherish," hit number one on the charts. So romantic. I didn't have a date, as all my energy focused on getting Bob's attention. On good days I ran into him in the Hub. On bad days I didn't bump into him at all. He always smiled and acted glad to see me. For my part, I concentrated on being as witty as possible. I couldn't compete in looks with Missy Felton, the green-eyed beauty, but I could be fun to be with.

February came and I began drawing a Valentine's Day card for Bob, a take-off on a *Peanuts* comic strip, a cartoon where Lucy, noticeably pregnant, shook her fist and said, "Damn you, Charlie Brown!" On the inside, it read simply, "Happy Valentine's Day." Hilarious. On Valentine's Day I spotted Bob sitting at the usual table with Charlotte and Denny. I smiled, but not too much. trying to be cool. I didn't want him rejecting me if I'd misread things between us. I pulled the card out of my book and casually handed it to him as I sat down.

Bob opened it and laughed, showing his dimples. He passed the card around to Charlotte and Denny, who laughed too. He excused himself, stood and left the table. I didn't know what I had done wrong. I tried to make small talk with Charlotte and Denny, but I was so upset I wanted to cry.

Soon, Bob returned with a small bag that held a greeting card. I opened it slowly, savoring the moment. It was a Valentine's Day card all right, but the front of the card read, "To Grandma," in flowery handwriting. I burst into gales of laughter as Denny and Charlotte looked on skeptically. They didn't get the joke, so I passed the card to them.

"That was the only card they had left," Bob announced, apologetically. He laughed himself, unable to hold it in any longer.

We settled down and the conversation turned to the upcoming Association concert. Of course, he would take Missy. I tried to hide my disappointment. I wouldn't see Bob again before the concert. It never dawned on me to ask someone else or go alone.

That Saturday afternoon, I was home ironing when the telephone rang. "Patty!" my sister Jenny yelled from downstairs.

I flew to the phone. It was Bob.

"Would you like to go to the concert tonight?"

Would I? "Sure," I said, trying not to sound too desperate.

"I have two tickets, but my car broke down again. Can you drive up here and meet me?"

"What happened to Missy?"

"I still need to call her. I'm going to break up with her."

I was so eager to go I overlooked this breach in dating etiquette. Since the concert started in four hours, I'd have to hurry. I didn't know what people wore to these things. I picked my best Kelly-green dress and black heels. I was in my Comet by seven, backing out of the driveway. Plenty of time to pick him up for the concert at eight. When I pulled up in front of his dorm, he ran out.

⌘

We sat on the bleachers as The Association sang "Cherish." So romantic. He took my hand and I turned all buttery inside. My dream was coming true. I was Bob's date. He dumped another girl for me. I was so happy.

We walked hand and hand back to my car. The snow, which looked so dirty earlier in the week, now glistened in the moonlight. He bent over and gave me a kiss right on the lips. We were meant to be. I couldn't hold back against his tongue, pressing my lips open. Deep inside, a thrill rose along with a lot of heat. Any thoughts of the convent, which had been fading for a while, vanished.

"I'll call you," he said, and he did. We talked about our lives and our plans. I told him I saved enough money to spend the spring quarter on campus.

"I'll be right across the quad from you in Allyn Hall."

"Great. We can spend more time together."

He called me a couple of times a week, even though it meant standing in line waiting for the dorm pay phone. We had one more date before the end of winter quarter. We spent it driving around Kent late one Friday night. Pulling into the university's airport parking lot, we parked for a little while. He drew me close, then kissed me deeply. This was what I'd been dreaming of. I could hardly wait for us to be together full time.

Three weeks later Bob phoned. "I have some bad news."

"Oh, no. What happened?"

"I flunked out of school. My grades were too low."

I almost burst into tears but managed to hold back. My lip quivered. I had been planning to move on campus to be with him and now he was gone.

"What will you do? Will you be drafted?

Bob played it cool. "I'm going to work for one of the companies my dad does business with. I can deliver parts for them."

No matter how brave he acted, I guessed his parents were angry and working was the only choice he had if he wanted to stay at home rent-free.

Devastated, my hopes for us to be together were dashed. I started to cry. Just when everything was going perfectly this had to happen!

"What does this mean?" I asked him. I was breathing too hard and my stomach was doing flips.

Bob was fatalistic. "Well," he explained, "my GPA is too low. They told me I should work for a quarter and then I could reapply for admission to Summer School"

When people flunked out they usually didn't come back.

"What about the draft?" With the war blazing away if Bob wasn't enrolled in college, there was a good chance he'd lose his student deferment and be drafted.

"I'll have to take my chances," he said cavalierly. He sounded relieved to be done with school.

"When will I see you? You know I'm moving into Allyn Hall."

"Oh, don't worry. I'll come to visit you on the weekends."

8

Spring 1967

Spring break dragged until the phone rang one day. It was Frank from my first quarter Lit class.

"How would you like to go out? My brother and his girlfriend are going to see *Thoroughly Modern Millie*. We could double with them."

"Sure." I didn't have anything else to do.

"We'll pick you up Saturday at 7:00 P.M."

I'd forgotten I gave him my number. That was long ago before the Association and Bob's kisses. Well, Bob might be out of the picture now.

Saturday came and I pulled out my Kelly-green dress again. A double date? I didn't know what to expect. Turned out Frank's brother Jim was older. He joked with Frank in a way that took the pressure of a first date off me. After the movie, we went for pizza.

"Just act normal, Seminary Boy," Jim said and his girlfriend, Linda laughed. Frank blushed red.

Seminary? This was news to me, but it wasn't the right time to ask about it. I smiled as if I was in on the joke but then Jim explained.

"Frank was in the seminary until August. It didn't agree with him." Jim laughed again.

"Frank, I thought I saw you at one of those demonstrations by the Student Union," I said.

"Right." Frank was quick with a comeback. "Are you still a journalism major? An observer?" he sneered. "Those demonstrators made some good points."

He had an edge to his voice, needling me. *No one had ever attacked my major before. Weird.*

Jim intervened. "Our other brother just joined the Army. We're all worried about him. C'mon Frank, eat up."

The night ended uneventfully. I wasn't interested in Frank, but he got me thinking about those demonstrators and why I was on the sidelines rather than up there among them.

⌘

I couldn't wait to move out of the cramped upstairs bedroom I shared with Jenny. Mom and Dad were skeptical, but I ignored them and their looks. One of the best things about moving out was that I would escape their constant questions.

"How are you getting up to Kent?" Mom watched me pack some clothes in my blue graduation suitcase.

"In the Comet," I said, but I could tell she didn't like my answer. Dad had me finance the car to establish credit and now it was paid off, but something was afoot.

"You are not taking your car with you."

In a second, I was boiling. I paid for that car. *What were they up to now?*

"I need it at school." I tried to act reasonably though I was ready to explode. They couldn't take it away.

Outwardly, I was the picture of tranquility. She wouldn't ruffle me this time.

Mom persisted. "No. You do not need it. We can take you. Dad doesn't want you driving around that big campus when you should be studying."

Jesus Christ. I was probably the most boring girl at Kent State. The nunnery rejected me. My boyfriend flunked out. What could I do except study?

"That's my car. I bought it. I'm nineteen years old. I bet Dad wants me to leave it at home, so you can use it," I yelled. So much for staying calm.

Mom shook her head. "Oh, no. We don't want to drive your car. We don't think you're mature enough to keep a car at school."

There she goes with that maturity stuff again. I was hot. "What do you want from me? My grade point average is 3.7! Don't you think I'm studying my ass off?"

"Watch your language, young lady! Let's wait until your father gets home. You two can settle it."

I had defied my parents in the past, but only in small ways: teenage angst. Now I was mad. It was mine. I didn't know why I needed it, but I wasn't putting up with any more of their limits on me. Yet I understood Dad's stance too. He helped me find this car. Now he wanted Mom to use my car while he was at work.

My brain worked overtime, as I tried to follow the letter of Dad's law while keeping Mom from driving it.

I came up with a plan. I could remove the license plates and park it in the backyard. This way, I left the car at home, but nobody else could drive it.

My brother Mark came upon me as I knelt behind the Comet unscrewing the plate.

He chuckled. "What are you doing?"

"I'm hiding the plates."

Mark shook his head.

Triumphant, I locked them in the trunk. "Will you help me move my stuff up to Kent?"

Mark, who was a senior in high school, agreed to help. He was silent when I explained the car drama.

He helped me unload and carry things into the dorm. In a rush to be finished loading the car, I had stopped packing the suitcases and thrown the rest of my clothes into the trunk still on hangers. He didn't mind and carried them up the three flights of stairs to my new room.

9

I was still mad about my parents' handling of the car, but I settled down enough to meet my roommates. Mardi was a slightly built Japanese girl with long black hair. Gloria was tall, thin, mousy with brown hair, horn-rimmed glasses, and a pageboy.

"Welcome, roomie," shouted Mardi above the din of the record player as I stuck my head in the door. Gloria, who was reading, looked up from her bed and smiled. They shared the same room for two quarters and had lost their third roommate to poor grades. Since last year, three students had been crammed into dorm rooms built for two.

I'd have my work cut out trying to fit in.

"You get the top bunk," Mardi told me and showed me where the communal bathroom and the pay phone were down the hall.

The room was small, much smaller than anywhere I lived before, including bunks at Girl Scout camp, but it was heaven to me. With three bodies it was cramped.

Mardi and Gloria were cool. They knew the best times to go to the cafeteria, advised me about which resident assistants to avoid and where to hang out in the Commons to meet men. The dorms were single-sex, but the newer ones shared a dining room with three other residences. Men weren't allowed above the first floor of the women's dorms.

My roommates were heavily involved in campus organizations. Mardi with Angel Flight, the women's auxiliary to Air Force ROTC, and Gloria with the Future Teachers of America.

Disappointed my master plan for Bob and me to live on campus hadn't worked out, I still hoped I would see him on weekends. The pay phone at the end of the hallway was usually occupied. I guessed I'd wait for him to call me. Waiting for boyfriends' calls was one of the main pastimes in my dorm.

I could call him collect, but then I would run the risk of one of his parents answering. They didn't know me. I needed to wait for him.

My roommates listened raptly when I told them about Bob. He finally called midweek.

"Spring Fling is coming in April. Would you like to go with me?"

Coached by Gloria, I invited him to the Saturday events.

"That's cool," he said.

"The parade starts at 3:00 P.M."

"I'll be there."

He told me about his job delivering electronic parts to various businesses on the east side of Cleveland. Sounded boring.

"It's my punishment for flunking out," he said. "I flunked out twice and don't have much negotiating room with my parents."

No kidding. They had paid his tuition. Since Bob wouldn't be around day to day, I signed up for a heavy load of classes with lots of reading. I could sit on my top bunk and study. Mardi and Gloria's campus activities kept them out of the room most afternoons and evenings.

I settled into a rhythm of going to class and volunteering at the radio station. I even dropped by the school newspaper, *The Daily Kent Stater,* and landed a job as a copyreader. I missed Bob but life on campus was exciting.

The *Stater* newsroom differed from my other haunts. While I corrected typos and grammatical mistakes, the air around me sizzled with a different sensibility than other parts of campus. One of the first articles to cross my desk told of a "Peace Train" traveling from Cleveland to New York for a rally to protest the bombing underway in Vietnam. While my roommates were worrying about what clothes to wear and the deejays at WKSU were debating the Top 40, the talk at the *Stater* centered on the Vietnam War.

How could they write objectively and personally want to end the war? It puzzled me. Could Frank be right? Was being a journalist wrong?

10

It had been a few weeks since Bob phoned. He agreed to go to Spring Fling, which was soon. I found a funny card at the bookstore and wrote him a long letter describing my days at school and how much I missed him. True, we'd only had two dates, but I hoped there would be more.

Bob called me right after he received my letter.

"How's it going?

"Fine. I miss you a lot," I said, forgetting my plan to be cool. "Are you coming for Spring Fling?" I crossed my fingers.

"Sure. What time should I be there?"

"The parade starts at 3:00 P.M. and the carnival is afterward on the front lawn of the campus. There's a concert that night."

"I'll pick you up at the dorm."

Beyond excited, I was glad Mardi and Gloria would finally meet this boyfriend I talked about so much.

I counted the days until Spring Fling. I could send Bob another card, but maybe I'd look too desperate. I'd wait until he called back. Music blasted from transistor radios. No one studied. As I walked back to my room, I heard "Cherish" playing on someone's radio. Our song! I longed to feel Bob's lips on mine and have him hold me again.

⌘

Spring Fling Saturday finally came. I woke up early, ate breakfast in the cafeteria and then studied. Bob wouldn't be here until 3:00 P.M. I could only concentrate for so long before I fidgeted. I could hardly wait to see him again. About 1:00 I started to get ready and took an extra-long time with my hair. We hadn't seen each other for weeks and I wanted to look especially nice.

I pulled a flower-print skirt out of the closet and topped it with a pink blouse. My roommates had already gone. Mardi would be marching with Angel Flight. Their uniforms were blue serge tailored suits with white epaulets, piping, and short navy-blue skirts. Very smart. Gloria was volunteering at the Future Teachers booth at the carnival.

At 2:30 P.M. I stared out the window, but there was little chance Bob would find a place to park out in front. I couldn't pace because the floor space was too small. The minutes dragged by ever so slowly.

By 3:00, I looked at my watch every few seconds. I read some more psychology but couldn't focus. I argued with myself. Call him or not? Traffic might be bad. There could be thousands of cars making their way down the narrow two-lane Rt. 43 to Kent. No matter how much I tried to settle down, I kept looking for Bob, jumping at each sound and listening for the house phone at the end of the hallway to announce his arrival.

At 3:30 I couldn't help myself any longer. I walked down the long, deserted hallway to the pay phone. I dropped my dimes and dialed Bob's number. A woman answered. His mom.

I mustered my courage. This would be the first time I'd called him at home. "Is Bob there?" I hoped the answer was "No" and he was on his way.

"I'll go find him."

A few minutes later Bob picked up the phone. "Hi." He breathed heavily like he'd been working.

"Hi," I said and then stopped, unsure how to proceed. But when he stayed silent, I plunged ahead. "You said you'd come at 3:00." I blurted out.

"Oh, yeah. I'm not allowed to leave until I finish mowing the lawn."

"The lawn?" I was almost speechless. *His parents were still punishing him for his bad grades.*

"I'm not done cutting the grass yet."

I wanted to yell, *The lawn? Why didn't you finish it yesterday?* I took a deep breath.

We obviously didn't agree on what we were going to do today. "When can you be here?" I tried not to let desperation creep into my voice.

"I need to finish the grass and take a shower. Maybe around 5:30 or 6:00."

Frantic, I tried to calm down. *All right. It will still be light out.* At least I'd have half a date. We could still make it to the carnival.

"I'll be waiting for you."

The halls were deserted. Nobody witnessed this humiliating conversation. I slunk back to my room. It was too early to go to the cafeteria for dinner, so I took my skirt off, hung it up neatly, then climbed back up on the bunk bed to study. Some Spring Fling.

Bob arrived at 6:00, all apologies.

"Dad wouldn't let me leave until I finished," he told me again.

I wondered why he didn't cut the grass earlier in the week, but I was so glad he made it I said nothing.

My anger dissolved as he mimicked his father, all huffy and authoritarian, exerting his will over my hapless boyfriend. He regaled me with stories about his boss at the electronics parts company and about his mom, who went back to work after staying home with his younger sister.

I was so happy we were together, I forgave him.

11

Summer 1967

June came and my first year of classes ended. Without Bob to distract me, I earned a 4.0 GPA.

I needed to find a job for the summer. No way would I return to Ohio Bell, not that they'd take me back. I hated that place so much. I wanted to work in Kent, so I would be near Bob. He said he would re-enroll for the summer session.

Mark worked at a Pancake House five minutes from home. He said there were openings at the Kent restaurant. I applied, and they hired me. It was only a 10-mile drive and with Bob living on campus maybe we could spend more time together. The job was part-time and low-paying at sixty-five cents an hour, but I figured with tips I would save enough to pay for books in the fall.

Waitressing? How hard could it be? I bought a six-dollar black sheath uniform at a supply store and showed up early the first day. Though not in school, I was happy. I found a job in Kent and Bob would start summer school soon. I hoped my weekly take would be at least a hundred dollars. I soon found out in a college town tips were scarce.

Celia, an older lady with years of waitressing under her belt, showed me the ropes. Even skinnier than me and tall, she sported an old-style kinky perm. Her face was lined and her teeth yellow from smoking.

"Avoid Johnny, the cook. He's in a permanently vile mood," she said. Johnny had tattoos. A cigarette dangled from his lip. He sneered when I walked up to the pickup counter and smiled at him.

My first few customers were easy. Pancakes with syrup, coffee, and orange juice. Not bad. I handled my three tables well. Then Sunday came with the church crowd. People lined up at the door pushing. Celia was off, and I had to cover six tables instead of three. I rushed from one table to the next and made my first mistake.

A man sitting in the window seat of a booth held up his coffee cup for a refill. I leaned over to reach it. With the stretch, my hand began to shake.

"Goddamn it," he yelped as the hot coffee spilled over the side of his cup, down his arm and into his crotch.

"I'm so sorry," I blurted out, practically falling over in my lunge to blot him with napkins. His boothmates giggled, but he was mad. I needed to settle down. I still had another five tables to wait on. In the Sunday morning commotion, no one else noticed, and I went unpunished for the accident, except for the measly tip.

Johnny was not only the cook but also the manager. At the end of the evening, he told me to collect the unused coffee creamers and pour the leftovers back into a large pitcher sitting in the cooler.

The glass pitcher had a narrow opening at the top. The little creamers were ceramic. It turned out only one knock of a creamer against its glass lip produced a chip. I didn't notice the chips falling into the pitcher. The next morning, Johnny called to me as soon as I walked in the door. Trouble.

"Come here, Patty. What's this?" he asked threateningly, holding up the pitcher. Little chips outlined by the white cream floated near the bottom.

"I don't know." Better to play dumb like at a traffic stop.

"Glass!" he yelled. "Now you throw that whole pitcher of cream out. It'll come out of your pay."

I couldn't let my hatred for Johnny show or I'd lose my job.

Being a waitress at the Pancake House was akin to being a miner in a company town. Too many mistakes could result in owing money at the end of the week rather than taking home a paycheck.

⌘

I still didn't see much of Bob even though he returned to school. We spoke by phone.

"I've been busy with the radio and TV stations."

"I sure miss you," was all I said.

In July, the number of customers patronizing the restaurant plummeted. A rubber factory strike started in Akron and people stopped going out to eat.

The professors who ate out every day stopped tipping. Bad for me. After a few nights of no customers after 7:00 P.M., Johnny started closing the restaurant early. I could only work half my shift. I wasn't desperate for money yet, but close.

Another week passed, and I still wondered where Bob was. He hadn't phoned, and he wasn't on the air at night. When I called the station, they told me he hadn't come in. Then the phone rang.

"I'm in the infirmary," Bob said, chagrin in his voice.

Stunned, I imagined him swathed in bandages.

"They say I have an infection. My gums are bleeding. I bet it's from those dirty forks in the cafeteria. Can you come visit me? You'll have to sneak in. They don't allow visitors." He said this in a rush. Was he afraid someone would overhear?

Gee, it's the infirmary, not the Tower of London. Why all the secrecy?

"You're kidding. Where *is* the infirmary?"

"No. I'm not kidding. It's on Pill Hill. The hill near the water tower on front campus. I'm stuck here. They won't let me leave."

Bizarre. "I'll come by tomorrow, after work."

"Come between 3:00 and 4:00 when the nurses change shifts."

I wasn't sure why I had to sneak in. I'd never heard of a hospital that didn't allow visitors.

The next afternoon I drove up and down Lincoln Street looking for a road that led to the water tower. Finally, I saw it and turned into a little alley, tree-lined and shady. I drove up the hill in my Comet. A small yellow brick building sat at the top. It was ivy-covered and old enough to be one of the original campus buildings. Giant classroom buildings dwarfed the infirmary.

I saw only one way in. I parked and approached the front of the building and walked toward a white door wreathed in ivy. I pushed it open. Inside, the hallway looked deserted, dark and cool. Bob said he was on the second floor, so I went up the first flight of stairs midway down the hall, treading quietly in case someone was around. The second floor was empty too. I walked along the hallway peering into each room, tiptoeing so I didn't alert the staff. The rooms were small and mostly white, like hospital rooms in the old Doctor Kildare movies. Standing screens closed off parts of the rooms, providing privacy. This floor looked like a regular clinic. Of course, it was summer. With only a few thousand people on campus, there couldn't be that many sick at one time?

I acted like I belonged there and walked on purposefully, listening for Bob's voice. I didn't have to go far. I found him sitting in bed on the far side of a room staring out the window.

I scurried in quickly. "What's going on?" I didn't want to kiss him or hold his hand if he were contagious.

"I got sick on Sunday. I had a fever and nausea. I came to the infirmary to find out what was wrong, and they kept me." He sounded indignant and helpless at the same time with both arms crossed against his chest.

"Why can't you just walk out?"

"They won't let me. They say I might be contagious."

"Well, what's wrong with you?"

"I don't know, and they won't tell me."

I sat down in the chair beside the bed. He looked pitiful.

"Why didn't you go to the doctor sooner?"

"I hate doctors," he snapped. "My parents are coming to visit tomorrow. Maybe then I'll find something out."

A nurse came into the room. "You'll have to leave, Miss," she said, without skipping a beat.

Guess they were used to having people sneak in. I handed Bob the box of cookies I brought.

Puzzled, I tried to make sense of this *I hate doctors* line. I couldn't figure out why he waited so long to get help. I might get more answers if I talked to his parents.

⌘

The next Sunday at the Pancake House the morning rush was done and there were a few empty tables. I only had forty-five more minutes left to work.

I stood in the back filling a coffee pot when Celia came up behind me. She pointed toward the door. "There's a couple out front asking for you."

I peeked around the corner and spied a casually dressed duo in their mid-fifties craning their heads, looking around. Must be the Turners. I put on a smile. As I smoothed my apron, I felt syrup that had spilled down the front.

"Hi, I'm Mary and this is Jim. We're Bob's parents." She held out her hand.

Both were tall like Bob but heavyset. Mary's hair was short and graying, cut in a Buster Brown do. Jim was balding. Both wore glasses and sported Bermuda shorts. They looked like they were on their way to a picnic.

"Well, hi," I said, hoping Johnny wouldn't notice I had stopped working. "How is Bob?" I acted as casual as possible. "What's wrong with him?"

"He's fine. They don't know what he had, but he's getting better now. They're going to release him tomorrow. We just wanted to stop in to meet you. You're busy." Mr. Turner nodded his head.

"No, we're at the end of the rush. I can leave soon. I tried to visit Bob yesterday, but they kicked me out."

His mom and dad were nice. Not ogres, as Bob had led me to believe. I waved good-bye as they turned and walked out the door. I couldn't imagine what he was complaining about.

12

My hours at the Pancake House worsened as the Akron rubber strike continued. My income of sixty-five cents an hour plus tips dwindled to almost nothing, so I looked for another job.

A photo processing plant opened just blocks away from home. They were hiring people for their midnight to 8:00 A.M. shift and I applied. Turned out the job was not working with photos or film at all, but rather doing the billing for each individual packet of pictures. The plant was in an old grocery store on State Road, the main drag in the Falls. The processing equipment took up less than half the floor space. The rest of it was a cavernous, echo-ridden and empty shell.

My coworker, Jan, and I reported each evening at midnight. An older and way-more-experienced woman supervised us. She called herself Lovey, a childhood nickname. Slightly built with dark gypsy-like skin and flowing reddish brown hair, each night she appeared with a new pattern of hickeys on her neck. Purple and spreading, they proved to us how experienced she was. She was married and, according to her, her husband was a wild man. My eyes grew bigger as I listened to her tales of their sexual escapades.

Bob and I had hardly gotten to second base that summer. Impressed, I made mental notes as Lovey talked. Mom had never given me any sexual advice. Too embarrassed to ask anyone else, I tried to imagine how things worked on my own.

One night as we waited for the first set of prints to appear on the billing counter, we heard gales of laughter from the girls working on the photo processing line, followed by long silences and then more laughter. I couldn't stand the suspense.

"What's going on?" I asked Lovey.

"Oh, somebody probably sent in porno pictures."

"Porno pictures?"

"Customers take pictures of their privates or their wife on the bed and send them in to be developed," Lovey explained patiently. "We make extra prints and pass them around. It's against the law for us to return them to the customer, but we always print them so everyone can take a peek."

I ran to the spot where I'd last heard the laughter. The prints were disappointing, poorly lit, but from then on, I knew what the laughter meant.

While we toiled through the night concentrating in the air-conditioned quiet, all hell broke loose outside. The riots that plagued LA and Chicago for the past few summers had finally arrived. For a two-week stretch in mid-July, there was a curfew every night as National Guard tanks rumbled down State Road into Akron. The floor shook each time one rolled by. The news showed shots of bloodied people being arrested. The riots were scary, but I continued working, unaffected.

⌘

My days and nights were turned around working the graveyard shift. I slept in the third-floor attic, the quietest part of the house during the day. The rest of the house stayed cool in the summer, but the attic sweltered. By 2:00 P.M. it could reach ninety degrees. The air hung in oppressive sheets, clearly not conducive to sleep, so, I was awake and available for whatever Bob wanted to do by early afternoon.

Both of us were broke. We took long drives in the country on his days off. Bob landed a part-time job at the local AM radio station, WKNT, a big accomplishment, given the competition. As the evening disk jockey, he developed a playlist for his program, pulled copy off the ticker and pasted it together for an hourly newscast. In his spare time, he wrote and recorded spots for local advertisers. He emptied the wastebaskets and swept up at the end of his shift too. Bob loved it.

"I always wanted to be a deejay. I even bought a professional turntable and pretended I was broadcasting from my bedroom."

I laughed at the image of him spinning disks to an imaginary audience but thought about how lonely he must have been. We spent our free time together now getting to know each other.

"I like your family," he told me as we drove along. "I only have one sister, Kitty, but she's retarded. I didn't have anyone to play with when I was a kid."

I asked him more about Kitty, but Bob was reluctant to talk.

"What is wrong with her?"

"They never figured it out. She's not Mongoloid. They did all kinds of tests. My parents dragged her from doctor to doctor. I had to sit in the waiting room while the doctors examined her. She can't talk and has trouble with her balance."

I was stunned.

"She wasn't allowed to go to regular school, so my mom opened a small school for Kitty and kids like her in the basement of a church. I get mad when people joke about being retarded. They don't understand. That's why I won't go to doctors. I spent so much time sitting in waiting rooms I hate doctors now. My parents put her in Apple Creek a couple of years ago. I can't forgive them for that."

"What's Apple Creek?"

"A state hospital down south by Wooster. I won't visit her. I can't stand to think of her caged up. My parents go once a month. I get into fights with people who use the word retarded. It makes me mad. I almost got into a fight with Jaycee."

Jaycee worked at WKNT.

"He called someone retarded. I didn't fight him even though I wanted to. I told him I had a retarded sister and he stopped."

I felt sorry for both Bob and his parents and secretly resolved not to call anyone retarded ever again. I hugged him and held him close when we parked by the railroad trestle on the road to Brady Lake. Bob had been through so much. He suffered. I was especially tender when I kissed him goodnight as he dropped me off at work.

13

"Let's go visit my parents." Bob was all smiles when he picked me up. A sunny Sunday afternoon, neither of us had to work.

Bob's parents grew up beside each other in identical houses a block from Lake Erie. When Jim's parents died, the Turners moved into their house.

This was my first time visiting. Mary showed me around. The interior was gloomy with twenties-era wallpaper and a maroon living room suite. The kitchen wallpaper had little line drawings of pink teapots and flowers.

The Turners were like giants in a fairytale, towering over the furniture and appliances. Mary returned to fixing Sunday dinner. We chatted for a while and she invited us to stay.

"We'll use the dining room table. Bob, you set it up."

I was still uncomfortable around Bob's parents. Our only other meeting had been when they dropped by the Pancake House when Bob was in the infirmary. They were nice enough then. Jim wore a plaid flannel shirt and Sansabelt slacks. His right eye stared straight ahead, from glaucoma Bob explained to me. Mary wore a stylish red-and-pink flowered top and a skirt with hose and flats. An apron dangled around her neck.

Bob retrieved an extra leaf for the table from the basement while I offered to help Mary.

She stirred the gravy. "Oh, no. I'm almost done. We'll have a beef roast, potatoes, and salad. For dessert, there's ice cream."

"Sounds good to me." I tried to be enthusiastic. I carried things to the table.

With everyone seated, Jim said grace, then passed the food. While we ate, the conversation turned to a visitor they had a few weeks earlier.

"Your cousin Ronnie is a lieutenant now," Mary told Bob. "He's in Vietnam," she said proudly.

We hadn't talked about it much, but I was pretty sure Bob didn't have any military ambitions.

"I hope he gets fragged," Bob said defiantly.

Both his parents reacted to this gibe. "Oh, how can you say that?" Mary pleaded. Jim gave him a threatening look.

"He has always been a jerk to me."

Jim reached for a roll. "We had him and his family over for dinner before he shipped out."

We ate in silence for a few minutes. At a loss for small talk, I asked about their daughter.

"How's Kitty doing?"

Bob kicked me under the table. Guess I shouldn't have brought her up. They looked at me with surprise.

Bob passed the potatoes. "I told her about Kitty."

Mary continued eating, looking down. "She's fine."

"Maybe we could visit her someday," I ventured.

"Oh no, that's not a good idea," Mary said. Jim shook his head. "She's settled now, and we don't want to upset her. We go to visit her every other weekend. She knows us and behaves for us now. Someone new might upset her."

My look must have told them I didn't understand, as Mary added, "She can't talk. She just grunts," and gave a quick imitation of chimpanzee noises. "We bring toys for her to play with then we take her out for a picnic."

Could I manage a child like that? Words failed me. I couldn't think fast enough to change the subject. We ate the rest of the dinner in silence until Mary asked if we'd like ice cream.

I helped Mary clear the dishes while Jim and Bob watched the end of the Browns game.

"I don't mean to scare you, Patty. Kitty outgrew me in the past year. I couldn't care for her anymore. I was afraid she might hurt me. Like I said, she can't talk, so what she wants to say comes out as shoves or pushes. Bob refuses to visit her. I don't think he'll ever forgive us for putting her in that place, but he doesn't understand how hard it was for me."

I could feel Mary's sadness as she continued.

"It breaks my heart that Bob refuses to visit his own sister." Mary sucked in a breath and changed subjects. "Did Bob tell you I'm buying a new car? A Buick convertible. I always buy Buicks."

I was impressed she had the money to buy a new car. It would be hers alone, not Jim's. Not like in my family where cars were community property and you used the last one parked in the driveway.

"The most fun is driving a convertible in the summer with the top down and the air conditioning blasting. Bob and I love to ride around like that."

I nodded and smiled at her. *Running the air with the top down? Too much for me.*

We finished the dishes and went into the living room. The conversation turned to Bob's grades.

"I'm doing great. All I have is broadcasting classes right now."

Later on the drive home, Bob asked, "What were you and Mom talking about in the kitchen?"

"Oh, nothing. Just girl talk." I left it at that. I wanted to find out more about his cousin the lieutenant and Bob's feelings about the war. "I don't think your mom liked that smart remark you made about Ronnie."

"It wasn't 'smart.' He always bullied me."

"But what about going to Vietnam? Would you?"

"Nope. I'd go to Canada first."

At Bob's house, we'd held hands innocently, only once. He didn't want his parents prying into our relationship I guessed. But afterward, the night ended like most others. As we neared the Falls, Bob found a deserted park and glided to a stop in a secluded parking lot. He'd had his arm around me since we left Euclid. As soon as he cut the engine, we fell together and kissed deeply. The twinges in my lower regions made it hard to resist him. I didn't notice the passage of time or that another car had pulled into the lot. Our car windows were steamed up.

Soon there was a sharp rap on the window next to my head. We both jumped as one of the local policemen shone a flashlight on us.

"Hey, move it along," he yelled through the window. We dressed hurriedly and drove off.

14

Fall 1967

Bob and I became a couple. He shared his passion for radio with me. He invited me to help him write silly vignettes we recorded with his friend Gary and his girlfriend, Jane.

"Why don't you drop by the radio station tonight? We're taping another one of our soaps."

Their favorite was a soap opera they named Jamaican Place, a take-off on *Peyton Place*. In their soap, a hapless broadcasting duo buys a radio station in Jamaica, which turned out to be underwater. We spent hours writing and recording predicaments involving the Jamaican station. Bob aired these skits during his eight-o'clock show.

"I'm a great sound effects man. Crashing chairs is my specialty," he told me. "You won't believe the jokes I play on people. One time I locked Rich Bennard out of the studio right before his shift started. He got so mad he yelled at me." Bob laughed.

Dating Bob, I developed a social life. There were parties every weekend, mostly at John Henning's house. These parties amounted to little more than drinking and make-out sessions, but I belonged someplace, just because I was Bob's girlfriend.

I hung out at the station. I made friends with John, the music director, and on-air personalities. Rick was a dark-haired Easterner a year ahead of us in school. He had a huge audience for his radio show. Then there was Jaycee, the guy Bob almost fought when he called someone retarded, who worked another shift.

I spent more time at the *Stater* editing feature stories from fledgling writers. The talk there was about the war and how to cover the escalating number of protests taking place on campus.

Broke after spending the summer at menial jobs, I was commuting again. The colder it got, the closer in I tried to park. One day I noticed an almost empty lot next to the old gym. Hilly, rutted and muddy when it rained, it was close enough that I could walk to most of my classes. After dark, it sure beat having to take the long bus ride out to the shopping center, only to climb into my car and drive home.

Bob and Gary spent their free time together while Jane and I were in class. One shivery, rainy November night, I trudged toward my car in the rutted gym parking lot, wind whipping around me, only to find someone had removed my tires and left it resting on concrete blocks. I panicked. At first, I thought someone stole my tires, but that didn't make sense. My beat-up Comet wasn't worth much. Slowly, I began to suspect I had fallen prey to one of their pranks. I couldn't see either of them. The closer I came to the car, the angrier I became. I couldn't imagine how I was going to put the tires back on the car myself in the dark forty-degree weather.

"Damn!" I muttered under my breath. I was insanely angry. How could they do this to me? Wasn't I immune to their tomfoolery? As I got closer to the car, muffled laughter came from behind a nearby Volvo. My visions of calling the campus police melted as Gary and Bob popped up. They laughed crazily, proud of what they'd done.

"Goddamn it! How could you do this to me?"

"Relax. It's a joke," Bob called out. The look on Gary's face told me this was Bob's idea. They quickly put the tires back on.

"Never do this again," I yelled at them, surprised I was so angry. Bob laughed harder. I was so mad I wouldn't kiss him. I drove home.

Why did he do this? I was furious. I vowed I would never speak to him again. On the radio, Buffalo Springfield's "For What It's

Worth" played. They were right. Something was happening here. I wondered about my commitment to Bob. Was it worth it?

It was late when I walked in the door. I missed supper. Bob had already called. The phone rang again.

Mom shot me a scowl. "What the hell's going on?"

Bob was on the phone.

"Are you okay?"

With my parents sitting two feet away I couldn't yell at him.

"I'm fine," I said and started to hang up.

As the telephone moved closer to its cradle, I heard Bob say, "I'm sorry."

I made a meal with leftovers from dinner and went to my room to study. At 11:00 I fell into bed, exhausted. As I lay in bed thinking about the tire incident, I heard a soft clunk on the street-side window. Maybe a branch brushed against the house. Then I heard it again. I moved the blind slightly. Below in a pool of light from the street lamp, Bob pitched pebbles toward the window.

I'd better go downstairs before he wakes everyone up. I motioned for him to come in. My parents wouldn't stand for having a boy in the house at night after they've gone to bed. I shushed him.

"I'm sorry. I don't know why you're so mad. We thought it would be funny," he whispered.

He looked pitiful. I felt a surge of remorse for yelling at him earlier.

"It's all right." I had to get rid of him before he woke Dad. He gave me a kiss on the cheek, turned to leave and waved good-bye. I guessed we were back together again.

At school the next day, Bob acted like the tire escapade never happened. He put his arms around me when we met in The Hub. I melted. He was sorry.

"I can't believe you threw rocks at my window."

Secretly, I was flattered he went to such lengths. He hugged me again and everything was back to normal. All morning I flipped back and forth between anger at what he had done and worry that I overreacted. Bob never mentioned the tires again.

⌘

We still hung out in the Hub. We watched the parade of people on their way to the lunch line. A cute girl with reddish-brown hair styled in a pixie cut and freckles stopped by the table. She was a female Howdy Doody.

"Hi, Bob," she said, too enthusiastically, flirting with him. They talked for a second before she moved on.

"Who is that?"

"Oh, she's just a girl from my bowling class. Carole."

"Oh," was all I could manage.

Bob went on, volunteering too much. "She's a commuter. She lives in Stow. She's funny. She's on my bowling team."

Carole was competition for me. My mind raced a mile a minute as I thought about their interaction. I'd have to ride this out. I wondered if he wanted to make me jealous. Maybe he was retaliating for my saying I was breaking up over the tire incident.

Weeks went by and his talk of Carole waned, then stopped. Only when we had bumps in our relationship did Carole's name crop up again. *Was this his way of getting my goat?*

Bob laughed when I told him he was my first boyfriend. I didn't count my prom date, who was so shy he wouldn't even hold my hand. Bob had more dating experience than I. Almost anyone with a pulse would. I was a wallflower from an all-girls Catholic school who wanted to be a nun.

"I've dated some wild women," Bob said. There was Cathy, his prom date at Euclid High. He talked about her like she was Barbarella. Then there was Aura. She was the stuff of legends. Bob told me she had been in the convent. No way would I confess I'd tried to join the convent too.

"When she left the nuns, she was hot to trot." He said she had raven black hair and blue eyes. "She loved to neck in the backseat of my Falcon."

He convinced me she was the make-out queen of the Western World. Gary sniggered when Aura's name came up. Bob told me he dated her during summer school, right after he started Kent.

"If she is so cool, why aren't you still with her?" I asked each time he mentioned her. His story usually degenerated into a bunch of mumbles. She was looking for a more mature man.

60

That point was lost on Bob. He thought he could go back to her anytime he wanted.

I told myself to ignore Bob's bragging. I didn't know why I was attracted to him. He was handsome and funny, and I liked the sex, even though we were still at third base. If we broke up, I would need all new friends. I wouldn't worry about these other women.

15

Bob lived in Johnson Hall. I hoped I'd get a room in Lake, a dorm just across the commons. These dorms shared the same cafeteria, so Bob and I could eat a few meals together. I plotted and saved and by Christmas break I had enough money to move back on campus. Student Housing assigned me to Lake Hall. Ecstatic, I called Bob to tell him the news.

"We're going to be neighbors!"

Bob hesitated. "Oh, good."

Did he flunk out again? His response was underwhelming.

"What's wrong?"

"I'm moving off campus. I can't afford the dorm anymore."

I panicked. I didn't tell him about the plotting and scheming. I'd wait to see what this new development brought. I tried to be casual.

"What about your food?" It would be so easy for me to pop into the Lake cafeteria for a quick meal.

"I hate cafeteria food. I'll eat at Burger Chef."

Bob found a room on North Mantua Street about five minutes from campus. Off-campus was tremendously liberating. It was cheaper and there wasn't a curfew.

His landlords, the Heatons, lived on the first floor. Quiet and middle-aged, they always smiled.

"They never come upstairs," he said when I stopped to see his new digs.

His room in the front of the house extended across its width. Furnished with a double bed, chest, and dresser, it had a big closet. He had set up his portable TV, his oversized turntable he bought from a now-defunct radio station and his speakers. Box after box of LPs and 45s lined the edges of the room. Bob got free record samples at all his jobs. The best parts of the rental were the backyard parking lot and a private side entrance to the upstairs. Though the house looked small from the street, there were four separate rooms upstairs. Three were rented to students and one to a math professor.

⌘

At first, Bob was wary about letting me stay, but soon caution fell by the wayside and I was in. I began spending most of my free time with him in his room. Since there weren't any chairs, most of the time we sat on the bed.

Things quickly escalated from sitting on the side of the bed kissing to full-on petting under the covers. We whiled away our afternoons exploring each other as the winter sunlight filtered in through the curtains.

I was reluctant to go any farther. I loved him, but did he love me? He hadn't said so.

⌘

Bob shared the upstairs with neighbors close enough to notice his every coming and going. Jimmy was a red-headed, slightly built junior with glasses who wanted to join the Marines. Rich, a tall, dark-complected guy with hearing aids and a speech defect, lived in the room next to Jimmy. He was a theater major. The math professor came home late and shut his door, avoiding the undergrads.

Bob found a soul mate in Jimmy, someone who liked to pull pranks as much as he did. Rich became their target. Bob laughed when he told me about their latest escapade.

"You won't believe what we did to Rich last night. We piled boxes against his door, then knocked real loud. He opened the door, and the boxes fell in on him."

Unimpressed, I let him know it. "I don't think that's funny."

"Oh, where's your sense of humor? What's wrong with you? Don't be a spoilsport."

"You complain about other people teasing you. Can't you imagine what Rich feels like when you tease him?"

He didn't see the connection.

⌘

Spring quarter began quietly. I finally took a reporting course. It had taken me almost two years, but now I was really starting on the road toward becoming a journalist. Bob was busy with the campus radio station. Bob was safe from the draft while he in school but we still worried about the war. After President Johnson announced he would not seek reelection, candidates began making Kent a regular stop on their campaign tours. Protests and rallies were common on campus. The Vietnam War was the hottest election topic, especially since General Westmoreland, the U.S. Commander, was requesting an additional two hundred thousand troops by year's end.

⌘

Late one night while studying, I got a phone call. Bob was on the line. "Have you heard the news? Martin Luther King has been shot."

Stunned, I stood there for a moment. "When? Where?" was all I could ask. Bob was at WKSU for his night shift.

"I have to go. The record's ending."

Shaking my head, I walked back to my room trying to make sense of what Bob said. A segregationist, George Wallace, was running for president and the primaries had gotten wild after Johnson withdrew. Had his rhetoric provoked this terrible deed?

In the morning the *Stater* headline blazed "Martin Luther King Killed by Assassin" and the campus went into mourning. Students marched in memory of Doctor King but afterward, things returned to normal.

Late in the quarter, Bob's time slot at the local off-campus radio station, WKNT, expanded. He had started out as a weekend sub and now it paid off.

"This is my dream," he said. "I hoped I'd get more hours."

He joined a group of three other DJs who had started at WKSU and now worked at WKNT. Jim, Rick, and Jaycee were the star

DJs. These guys, along with their wives and girlfriends, became our new social group.

Bob's new responsibilities included selling advertising. He spent more hours at the station and didn't register for summer classes.

In the meantime, the quarter ended. I looked for a job to pay for next year's books and rent. Bob still lived in his room on Mantua Street. But one night as we sat on the edge of the bed one evening watching the television news, a bulletin scrolled across the top of the screen. Bobby Kennedy had been shot. He was near death in a Los Angeles hospital.

"This can't be happening again. He was the Democrats' only hope," I yelled and started to cry. The world was spiraling out of control. Bob took me in his arms and we held each other as we watched the news unfold. Spring 1968 was the end of innocence for us.

16

Summer 1968

A new shopping mall opened just minutes away from my house in the Falls. I applied for work and Penney's hired me. I wanted to save every cent I made, so I could continue to live in Kent.

Though we both worked, we spent more time together. Bob's job didn't pay much money, and he asked me to lend him some.

"For gas," he said. Since he drove me around, it wouldn't hurt me to contribute.

His birthday approached. He'd be twenty on July sixteenth. With both of us working, I wouldn't see him until the seventeenth. I bought a couple of things he needed, a belt and a wallet. I left these presents inside the private entrance at his house as a surprise.

I didn't hear from Bob until the next day. When he called, I was shocked at what he said.

Indignant, he yelled. "I don't consider these presents."

"What?" was all I could muster. Stunned, my stomach sank. *A belt? A wallet?* "Why not?"

"The things you gave me, you can take them back. A present is something you want, not something you need."

Crazy. He's rejecting my gifts? What can he be thinking? Never in my life had a person told me they didn't want a present I gave them.

"You can just come by and pick them up!" Bob growled into the phone and hung up.

My mind reeled like I'd been struck. Our relationship was over. I cried. He was being absurd, but I was torn. I wanted him to have a happy birthday. Obviously, I made a mistake.

No matter how I tried to understand his perspective, I couldn't convince myself I'd done anything wrong. Too embarrassed to talk to anyone about this weird development, I felt alone. I had no one to talk to with all my friends gone for the summer.

I obsessed about his reaction. Was I thoughtless to buy him such mundane gifts? I tried to continue with my life as if nothing happened, but Mom asked about Bob.

"He hasn't been around much lately. Is everything all right?"

"Oh, sure. He's just busy at WKNT." I hoped to quell her curiosity. I was sure she sensed something as the phone wasn't ringing for me anymore.

"He's busy," was an excuse that worked for a few days and afterward, I told her, "We're taking a break." That satisfied her. No way in hell could I imagine telling her how I bought him birthday presents he didn't like or how he'd yelled at me.

Two weeks later Bob called again, all happy talk like nothing ever happened. Cautious at first, I was surprised by his mood. But after a couple of days, I gave in and we were back at it as though we'd never been apart. He never mentioned that birthday or the gifts again.

I couldn't understand him. If he was so insulted by my presents, how could he be so friendly now?

⌘

A few weeks later the Democratic National Convention began in Chicago. The rumor was that protesters would disrupt it. *Stater* photographers and reporters planned to go to Chicago to document the huge war protest about to take place. Neither of us could afford such a trip. We needed to work.

I couldn't help but stare longingly at the TV each night as scenes from the convention played out. With Johnson not running for a second term and Bobby Kennedy dead, Vice-President Humphrey accepted the nomination. Outside the riot police beat on war protesters. Scary, but I wanted to be there. The demonstrators helped to solidify anti-war sentiment. Humphrey promised to end the war if elected. Even Nixon, the Republican nominee, said he had a plan to end the war.

⌘

Summer waned, and Bob and I squeezed in a couple of outings before school started again. We spent a glorious day at Cedar Point, riding the roller coasters and eating cotton candy. We visited Bob's parents at their new condo for a cookout. When my birthday came in August, Bob went with me to my parents' camper in the countryside near the Falls where we swam and hiked. I loved being with him, he was so much fun.

"You could save so much more money living off campus," Bob said when I complained about my bills. I believed him and looked for rentals. Rooms without meals cost half as much as the dorms. He was right. I could save money. There wasn't any reason to live on campus now that Bob had moved.

I wouldn't tell my parents about living off campus yet, not wanting to upset them. School started, and soon I was going to radio station parties and working as a copy editor on the *Stater*. Living off campus would be much easier than commuting. I needed to gather up money, so I could afford a rental.

⌘

There was a listing for a shared bedroom on Allerton, a tree-lined residential street about a mile from campus. The white Cape Cod had a double-wide driveway with plenty of parking. Mrs. Butler, the owner, was a blue-haired woman in her seventies. She rented rooms to women only.

"I have one bed available," she said and ushered me toward the finished attic. Upstairs were two paneled rooms, one larger than the other. "You girls share the bathroom up here. The basement has a kitchen you can use."

The vacancy was in the larger bedroom. It had pecan paneling and a dresser, a chest of drawers, and two desks, along with two single beds with drab olive-green bedspreads. This was a big improvement over the dorms where two sets of bunk beds were crammed into a tiny twelve by twelve space.

"This bed belonged to a girl who moved out last spring," Mrs. Butler said. "The other beds are already rented."

At $100 a quarter, it was about half the price of a dorm room, much bigger and with one less person in it. I wanted it.

"I'll take it," I said and wrote her a check and she gave me a key. That Penney's job was coming in handy. I still needed to tell Mom and Dad, but I was an adult, right? I'd be twenty-one soon, so what could they say?

"You can move in tomorrow."

Good. Classes began in two days. Things were coming together. We were both living off campus and back in school. Although Bob had started a quarter before me, his two flunk-outs put him even with me in credit hours. We were both juniors.

At home, my parents took my move in stride. Maybe they were tired of fighting.

⌘

Early the next morning, I packed the Comet and headed for Kent. I pulled into the Allerton Street driveway where two cars were already parked. I pushed the front door open, balancing my graduation suitcase and a handful of clothes. A couple was coming down the stairs. They said hasty hellos as they passed.

Upstairs, I saw they had piled things on one of the beds in my new room. *My new roommate.* I set my things down on the other bed.

"Danny's my boyfriend," the girl said when they returned. "He rents a room down the street."

Danny was medium height and build with a pencil-thin mustache. Mimi wore a loose-fitting dress and flats, a little formal for school.

I introduced myself and asked about the beds. She shrugged.

"You take the empty one. This is my third quarter here, and this one is mine," she said pointing to the one on the left. "I didn't like the dorms."

"This is my first time off campus, so show me the ropes," I said. I felt like an adult, out on my own, not subject to petty dorm rules anymore. "You must like it here since you're coming back."

"I do. Mrs. Butler leaves us alone. I'm in Music Education and so is Danny. Piano and organ are my areas. I want to teach."

A sophomore, she'd been off campus for two quarters. I was impressed. The rule was that only juniors and seniors could live off campus. How had she managed it?

"Most of my classes are in the afternoon or evening. I'm not an early riser," she added.

I finished carrying my things in and told her I needed to go buy cereal for the morning. I left them to finish unpacking.

As I drove, I sang along with the radio. Elated, I was out from under my parents' scrutiny and free of the financial burden of the dorms. Life could only get better.

⌘

Allerton was a good place to live. The girls were friendly, and the rent was cheap. The other upstairs residents were Trudie, a sorority girl with long blonde hair and a mousy-looking girl with shorter dark hair and glasses, Sherry.

I had learned how to cook well enough from Mom that I could eat cheaply too. I bought a roast at the discount grocery on Saturday, cooked it on Sunday, and had enough for Bob and me to eat throughout the rest of the week.

The basement kitchen was damp and dusty. Spiders lurked in the corners. There were a sink and a '50s-style dinette table, but no garbage disposal, which led to endless disputes about who should take out the garbage.

Even with four women sharing the house, our schedules were different enough that we weren't in each other's way in the kitchen. The bathroom was a different story. It took some planning. I got up early to shower and fix my hair before class. I still worked nights and weekends at Penney's to cover my expenses.

I loved living off campus. The petty irritations of the dorm were gone. I liked being able to make my own decisions about everyday life.

17

Winter 1969

Mrs. Butler's house had peculiarities. I came back from class one rainy afternoon to find the windows and doors flung open. A strong breeze coursed through the living room. The first floor was deserted. The farther into the house I got, the worse it stunk. Acrid. I inhaled and started to cough and gag. Peeking into the kitchen to investigate, I found an open pot boiling on the stove. It smelled like vinegar.

I shrugged and went upstairs where Mimi sat on her bed studying.

"What's going on?" I asked, bewildered and smirking at the weirdness. "What's with the vinegar?"

"Oh, that's Mrs. Butler's cold remedy," Mimi laughed. "She boils it because she thinks it helps clear out her sinuses."

I shook my head in disbelief.

She laughed again. "I know it doesn't make sense."

Another night, as I sat upstairs reading, shrieks and giggles came from the usually quiet downstairs. Next, doors slammed, and bare feet pattered across the floor below. It didn't sound like Betty, the grad student, and her boyfriend, who visited occasionally. Mimi came home.

"What's going on? Sounds like somebody is having a party."

Mimi listened for a minute. "That's Mrs. Butler and her gentleman caller."

Incredulous, I hovered between disgust and admiration. "She's old enough to be my grandmother."

"So, what? She's a widow. She's only seventy. She's not dead."

Those peals of laughter became a regular thing.

⌘

Bob was still working his nightly shift at WKNT and filling in at the campus radio station.

"I have a lot of listeners. People call in to talk to me while I'm on the air."

I admired his determination, working long hours late into the evening.

"I build model planes and describe them as I go along. I have one listener, Auntie Maude, who calls in every night."

I still worked at the *Stater* as a copy editor. In true old-time newspaper style, the campus newspaper had a horseshoe-shaped copy desk. The editor sat in the inner ring while copy readers sat along the outer edge editing stories. This setup made sense on a real newspaper with real deadlines where editors made final changes before a press run. Here, things weren't so urgent, but I loved this job, even if it was volunteer. I was getting experience. I found my home on campus and it wasn't at the radio station as Bob wanted.

"I don't understand why you hang around with all those old print fogeys," he teased. "Why don't you work at WKSU?"

He didn't realize the more he pressured me the more I dug in.

The *Stater* office was open from 6:00 A.M. to midnight. I could drop in anytime to edit copy or help write fillers. The seniors who ran the paper were distant and preoccupied, but I became friends with the underclassmen who hung out there. It was good to have a refuge from the campus throngs. The office was centrally located at the top of Blanket Hill on the edge of the Commons.

I didn't have to figure out how to make friends anymore. Mom was wrong. I talked about myself and people were interested. I had a boyfriend, which seemed impossible to me a couple of years ago—the girl who wanted to join the convent.

I went to parties. I belonged. The more involved I became with the newspaper social life, the more Bob talked about Carole. We needed a break from each other. He could have her. I didn't confront him or tell him about the break, I just stopped answering his phone calls.

⌘

The Beatles released the *White Album* in November, but in Kent we were just getting around to celebrating. There was to be a *Stater* party at Walt Polinski's house Friday night. Normally, I'd ask what Bob planned for the weekend before making any plans, but this was a statement of my independence. I wasn't his possession anymore. I was a free woman. I would go.

Parties began late and ran later. I was glad I didn't have a curfew. Walt was a wild guy. He had a beautiful girlfriend who wore Twiggy-style mini-dresses with white Go-Go boots. She stood out on a campus where women had just won the right to wear slacks. I planned to stay as long as possible, listen to the album and make Bob jealous.

I went with my friend Meredith, a senior noted for her wit and sarcasm. She had long, curly red hair and was a guy magnet. We were both between boyfriends. Walt's house was small with minimal furniture. Meredith and I checked the kitchen for drinks and grabbed some 3.2 beer. I couldn't buy hard liquor for another four months.

In the living room, Walt spun the first record, starting with "Back in the USSR." The buzz was about a cut we waited for called "Revolution 9" on Side 4, so we both plopped to the floor and settled in for a long wait. Our friend Don sat closest to the turntable.

"If you play 'Revolution 9' backward you can hear the Beatles saying something."

We listened but couldn't make out what they said. There weren't any liner notes to explain this album. We'd all heard snippets of it on the radio. You had to listen to the music in sequence to get the full effect the Beatles intended. Rumor had it that they'd planted a message: "Paul is dead."

Playing the song backward involved stopping the record as it revolved and gently forcing it to turn in the opposite direction. We sat cross-legged, bent over the speakers, trying as hard as we could to make sense of the words as the platter slowly turned back upon itself. We'd drunk so much that we kept falling over in gales of laughter. None of us could make out anything beyond a muffled, "Number nine, number nine." That couldn't be the message the Beatles intended.

Bert Hiller, a senior, showed up at the party after his youth group meeting at the United Methodist Church. Chunky, with an Irish face, short-cropped reddish hair, and freckles, he sat across from me at the *Stater* where he was the Sports Editor.

"Where's Bob?" he said as he bent down. Bert was engaged.

"I don't know," I told him. "I'm here by myself."

"Hmm. Trouble in paradise?"

I shrugged my shoulders. Best not to go into the details of our drama.

"Is he treating you right?" Bert asked.

I nodded. "Sure." I got some secret satisfaction from being out without Bob.

"Well, you should be careful."

I wasn't sure what to make of his offhand remark.

18

Spring 1969

I didn't hear from Bob the whole weekend, but my thoughts still revolved around him. What was he doing? Where was he?

I landed a part-time job, a few hours a week, at the town newspaper, the *Record-Courier*, writing copy for the society pages. With hundreds of journalism students searching for work, these jobs were hard to come by.

Betty, the Society editor, was a heavyset elderly woman with gray hair. She'd had her job since the printing press was invented.

"Sure. I'll get back to you soon, Hon," she said as she got rid of one caller and picked up another ringing line.

"Let me tell you," she said when the phone calls died down, "I know everybody who's anybody around here. Town. University. You name it."

Turned out she was right. She had great contacts in Kent, at the University and in Ravenna, the county seat. Betty's fingers were on the pulse of local society. She was invited everywhere, and she understood what to run in her column to get the attention of the community's heavy hitters. She needed someone to write up the little stories, the weddings, and engagements, showers and graduations. That was where I came in.

She wanted me to work a couple of days a week, fitted around my classes. It would be better for her if I worked mornings, so Tuesday and Thursday found me at a desk in the Kent Bureau at

8:00 A.M. I wrote until Betty ran out of assignments, writing the stories she didn't want to cover.

Only a few people were there in the morning—Betty, a local news editor, and one reporter. The difference between me and the reporter was that he went out to talk to people at the police station and the courthouse. Everything I wrote was from notes Betty compiled during phone interviews or from handwritten items sent in by readers.

"Mary wore an off-white peau de soie gown, lined with teardrop pearls." You get the drift.

By the second week, I ran out of different ways to say *beautiful wedding gown*. I earned a pauper's wage, less than two dollars an hour. Though the spring quarter was only ten weeks, I began to fantasize escaping what seemed like a dead-end job. Maybe Frank was right. The war was raging, and I was sitting in a safe office writing engagement stories. But how could I objectively report the news and become part of it as a demonstrator?

⌘

Though I missed him, I was secretly glad for the break from Bob. I came and went as I pleased, but mainly only to classes, the *Stater* for my copy editor's job, and the *Record-Courier* to write those society stories. The active social life with lots of dates I fantasized about hadn't materialized.

Then one night as I was working late, Bob showed up. The roomful of reporters and editors went silent. Heads turned to stare at him standing in the doorway. Boyfriends didn't often show up at the newspaper office. I was surprised he came by. I stood and walked into the hallway with him. He tapped his foot impatiently.

"Let's go eat," he said curtly. "I'll buy."

Gloating, I smiled inwardly. I'd finally gotten to him. I wondered what he'd say.

I finished up my last page and followed him out the door. We ended up at the Red Barn. Bob ordered a Barnbuster and for me, a hamburger with fries. Relieved he'd shown up, I wondered why he decided to come back after almost a two-week absence.

I let him talk first. I sat there with what I hoped was a look of innocence.

"I know what you're doing," Bob said.

This was new. I wasn't sure how he knew what I'd been doing. I hadn't been anywhere unusual except to the party at Walt's. I wanted to date someone else but hadn't found anyone yet. I stifled an impulse to defend myself.

"I saw you coming in late. After 3:00."

He meant 3:00 A.M. Was he hiding in the bushes? And it wasn't 3:00 A.M. I wanted to argue. It was only 1:00. *Stay cool.*

I couldn't stop myself. "You're spying on me?" I asked accusingly. He gave me a smirk.

He'd been lurking about. A chill went down my spine. It felt good to be important to him, but also weird to discover he was watching me. He must have parked his minibus somewhere on Allerton and waited for me to come home.

Maybe a counterattack was best. "I thought we broke up," I said innocently. "I haven't heard from you in weeks."

That was true, and Bob became defensive. "I've been busy. I'm looking for a better job. I'm working the midnight shift at WKNT."

He wasn't ignoring me, just busy. I forgot all about taking a break. I guess we weren't broken up after all. His lips looked so inviting and I wanted to feel his arms around me.

"Are you saying you want to get back together?" I tortured him.

Bob nodded and grabbed my hand. We were together again, and I breathed a happy sigh of relief.

He found us a deserted place to park and celebrate.

19

Bob carried a clipboard with notes on it.

"What's that?"

"I'm writing a book."

"A book?" I was astonished. He'd never been one to study, let alone write anything.

"On electronics."

I misjudged him.

Bob's father was a HAM radio operator. When we went to the Turners for dinner a few weeks earlier, Jim made a point of telling me he had his HAM license.

"I still want to sit for my license," Bob interjected as he reached for another roll.

Jim kept on, "Oh, no. I don't think you're ready for that."

Did Jim think he wasn't smart enough to sit for the licensing exam? Maybe he thought Bob was too irresponsible.

Bob looked hurt. He dropped the subject.

Looking at the hen scratches on the clipboard, I realized this was his way of convincing his father he had what it took to pass the test.

⌘

Antiwar activists began calling for a general strike in October if Nixon had not withdrawn our troops from Vietnam. Kent State went from being a sleepy backwater college to one that was being noticed for its antiwar protests. The Kent Committee to End the War in Vietnam changed its name. Now the Students for a

Democratic Society (SDS), it was the same group of people who'd marched with broomsticks in front of the ROTC building, but they'd become more vocal and more organized.

They led a sit-in at the Administration Building protesting the Liquid Crystals Institute, a campus laboratory SDS claimed aided the war effort. Crystals were used in the manufacture of Napalm. It stuck to the skin. Photos started appearing of Vietnamese children who had been horribly burned during bombing runs.

Four SDS leaders were arrested at the sit-in and jailed at the county seat, Ravenna. They were released. The university was holding a hearing on their suspension later in the day at the Music and Speech Building. I wasn't a reporter anymore. I'd graduated to editor status, but I had classes at Music and Speech. Rumors flew that SDS would to try to disrupt the hearings. Since I was headed there for class, Mary, the *Stater* editor, told me to investigate. I felt important having an assignment that might bring news about the protests to our readers. I shoved that conflict about whether to report or observe down inside me. My heart leaped that I had a legitimate reason to go to the demonstration.

A couple of blocks from the newspaper office, the building was within walking distance. As I approached carrying my books, I saw a disturbance up ahead. Soon I was close to the action.

Hundreds of onlookers appeared out of nowhere. I stood on my tiptoes and watched two guys slug each other in the center of a mob. A long-haired hippie traded punches with a Greek right in front of the entrance. Thrilled, I was glad to be so close.

Coeds jeered and egged them on from the sidelines. "ROTC off campus!" was met with counter chants of "USA! USA!" It wasn't hard to tell the opponents apart as the fraternity brother wore his letter sweater. Neither was winning. Nobody stepped in to stop the fight. I needed to get into the building to find out about the hearings.

Where were the police? The crowd blocked the entrance, but I eased around it. I pulled on the nearest handle. The door didn't budge. Locked. *Now, how am I supposed to make it to class?*

I followed some people to a side door. The heavy tempered glass in the bottom panel was shattered. People crawled in through it, avoiding the jagged edges.

Classes were probably canceled. If I made it to the third floor, I could call an account of what happened back to Mary at the *Stater.*

I got in line to crawl through the jagged opening and climbed inside. Unsure of what to do next, I followed the crowd of students snaking its way upstairs. The hearings were down the hall from the radio station.

Soon, I was upstairs. Protestors occupied the hallway. They were jammed in so tight there wasn't a path to walk. They waited for the hearing to end.

I started to interview some of them, but just as I bent down to talk to a blue-jeaned girl sitting against the wall, the elevator doors swooshed open. Troopers in tactical gear, with face shields and billy clubs, stepped out. They looked like aliens, but everyone took their sudden appearance in stride. These were seasoned protestors.

The first trooper announced sternly, "This is an illegal assembly. You must disperse."

A hush fell over the crowd, everyone's attention riveted on the troopers. Though ordered to leave, nobody moved. They acted like they'd been through this before. Protesters blocked the exit. The hallway was getting hotter by the minute. Sweat ran down my neck. I worried about what would happen next but told myself to stay cool. Nobody budged.

I wanted to remain, no matter how long it took. I could write a good story. Copy deadline wasn't until 10:00 P.M.

People shifted uncomfortably on the terrazzo floor as more troopers came up in the elevator. At the far end of the hallway, a guy in a jacket with leather elbow patches talked with the head trooper. The trooper turned around.

"Anybody who wants to leave has five minutes to do so. Anyone left will be arrested and taken to jail."

People stood up and edged their way toward the doors. I followed. I could file a story from the pay phone downstairs. I'd never done this, but I'd been in the office when other reporters called in. As we descended from the third floor, I was preoccupied, composing my article in my head. I reached for the emergency dime in my purse.

At the bottom of the stairwell, we piled up in front of the same side door with the jagged glass, waiting as people climbed through single file. The opening was so narrow it slowed everyone down. Finally, my turn came. I bent and worked my way through unscathed, balancing my books. The phone was just ahead. The fistfight had ended, and the crowd dispersed. My heart beat fast as I thought of how romantic it was to call in a story as it was happening, like in an old Spencer Tracy movie.

I lifted the receiver and heard a dial tone. Lucky. At the other end of the line, Len Dillon, one of the sports writers answered. I was all business, even as he joked around with me.

"I'm at Music and Speech," I said. "There's a riot here. I want to file a report." He yelled for Mary. She picked up the phone. She typed, taking down my story as I dictated. The next day it ran on the front page along with a photo showing the Greek punching the hippie. I was thrilled.

20

Something held Bob back from getting his HAM operator's license, but I didn't know what.

"You're a knucklehead," Jim told him each time we visited. I couldn't figure out what the Turners knew about him that I didn't. Bob was one of the smartest people I had ever met. Sure, he got himself into scrapes at school. He didn't study as hard as he should or apply himself, but what twenty-year-old did? Maybe it had to do with this Officer Easter episode he referred to, or maybe it was the telephone affair.

"Officer Easter" was code for a police incident that involved Bob. His high school friend, Willie, mentioned it chuckling, but neither he nor Bob explained it.

Finally, I knew him well enough to ask.

He was nonchalant. "We were joyriding on Euclid Avenue, Willie and me, one Friday night. I was driving my Falcon. A squad car pulled up behind us and turned on its lights. After a minute, I realized they wanted me to pull over, so I did. I had run-ins with Officer Easter before." He spit his name out with a hint of disgust. "He told me to get out. I did, but as I tried to stand something heavy struck me on the top of the head. I started to fall but then I grabbed hold of the door handle.

"When I focused again, Easter held a flashlight. That was what hit me. He lectured me about reckless driving and sent me on my way. It was late when I got home, but my parents waited up for me. I told them what happened. The next day they filed a complaint, but nothing came of it."

The telephone affair was a darker secret that Bob wouldn't explain. His high school friends teased him about it whenever we visited. Mary fell silent when I asked them. Jim shook his head in disgust. I couldn't imagine what was so bad about a telephone.

"Bob brought this on himself," was all Jim said when I asked.

I didn't understand how that interfered with his getting a HAM operator's license, but I didn't know the whole story. Bob had his third-class radio license—all he needed to work at a station. But he wanted to own one someday.

"That's why I won't use drugs. You can't have any felonies on your record or the FCC won't let you own a station."

Nobody said anything about felonies. I wondered what he was talking about. We didn't even have an opportunity to buy drugs, much less use them. He must have meant marijuana since it was the only drug anyone we knew sold.

I couldn't stand the secrets anymore. I asked him again. We were driving out to Brady Lake for a hike on one of those chilly Saturday afternoons in late April. The sun was out, but the wind blew hard enough that we both wore jackets. Bob didn't begin his radio shift for a few hours. I would be brave and ask him.

"What is this about the telephones?" I asked as we rounded the curve approaching the lake. The trees were blossoming. Perfect for an afternoon hike.

"Telephones?" he said innocently, looking sideways at me.

"Yes. What everyone jokes about. What does it mean?"

"Oh, it's nothing. Did you meet Willie?"

Of course, I'd met him a couple of times at parties and when he dropped by Bob's house in Euclid.

"Willie's sister, Shana, worked for the phone company. She was older. She used to carry telephones and wires in the trunk of her car. You know how I love old gadgets."

I must have looked concerned because as he continued, he grabbed my hand to calm me.

"Shana gave us some of those phones. In fact, the phone I have in my room is one of them." He paused for a minute, censoring his story. "The police found out. They came after us."

"The police?" I couldn't believe what I heard.

"They went to see Shana first and after they left, she called Willie. He dumped most of them in a swamp in Mentor. They only found a couple of phones and rolls of wire he had in the house. He implicated me."

My mind reeled. This sounded like theft or receiving stolen goods.

"What happened?" was all I could ask.

"Oh, nothing. We went court, but it's over," he said dismissively.

So that was the telephone affair. No big deal. I breathed a sigh of relief.

⌘

Bob was his own boss at WKNT. He picked which records to play and what news to read. His new time slot was from midnight to 5:00 A.M., so there weren't many listeners. He still took phone calls and aired them. He still assembled model airplanes piece by piece and described them between tunes. On Saturdays, he worked a daytime shift, broadcasting from fairs and festivals. For a four-hour gig, he arrived an hour early and put up a small booth, broadcast on location while interviewing passersby. Then he took down the booth and returned the equipment to the radio station. Bob loved his work, but I was still looking for something meaningful to do.

Spring quarter was ending. I needed to find an internship before graduation. The good ones were at newspapers, but the seniors usually grabbed those. I either had to look for one farther away and pay for my own lodging or find something less desirable closer to home.

A posting came in for a copywriting internship in Ashtabula, a couple of hours northeast of Kent. I thought it was with the local newspaper, the *Star Beacon*, so I applied. Turned out Bert Hiller, who was a year ahead of me and about to graduate, already landed that internship. This new listing was for a newsletter editor at Ashtabula General Hospital. The job was more public relations than news. PR didn't interest me, so I ignored it at first. But when no more listings came through, I reconsidered it. If I completed my internship during the summer I could graduate on time next June. I decided a summer on Lake Erie could be mighty good for me.

21

I applied for the public relations opening at the hospital. I needed to interview with the CEO, a Mr. Dubcheck. Ashtabula was a two-and-a-half-hour drive, northeast on Route 90, just short of Erie, Pennsylvania.

Bill Fisher, the professor in charge of internships, was a blowhard from the good-old-boy school. I'd have to take some teasing from him before he'd give me the CEO's phone number. Bob, who took journalism courses in conjunction with his radio-TV major, loved to ridicule him.

"Bill Fisher died today," he announced, lounging in The Hub. All eyes turned toward him. "Yep, you know those three strands of hair he has combed over his skull? Well, he sneezed and whipped himself to death." Laughs all around.

With Bill Fisher jokes rattling about in the back of my head, I had to keep myself from giggling while I talked to him about the internship. I got the phone number out of him easily. He must have been preoccupied.

"Can I use your phone?"

He nodded. Mr. Dubcheck's secretary answered the phone.

"He's out of the office." She offered me an appointment for Tuesday at 1:00 in the afternoon. I wrote down directions. As I hung up, I realized I needed to put a clipping notebook together.

The beauty of newspapers was that my work was published every day, providing an endless supply of clippings to show prospective employers. I saved a pile of them from both the *Stater* and the *Record-Courier*. I could dazzle Mr. Dubcheck with my SDS story, or if he appeared too conservative, I could pull out my wedding write-ups.

On Tuesday I left early and drove up Route 271 toward 90 East and Ashtabula. I found a place to park and walked across the gravel parking lot to the hospital entrance. Built in the 1930s, it was yellow brick and covered in ivy. An elderly volunteer dressed in a pink candy-striper uniform sat at a small desk.

"I'm here to see Mr. Dubcheck," I spoke with what I hoped was confidence. "I'm here for a job interview."

"Take a seat."

The Naugahyde felt cool against my thighs. I perched at the edge of the chair and waited as the ancient candy striper called to tell him I was here.

"Someone will be right out," she said.

A few minutes passed and a tiny redheaded woman of about sixty in a lime green sweater set and three-inch heels sashayed down the hall. Her perfume preceded her.

"I'm Mr. Dubcheck's secretary." She ushered me into a small office.

Mr. Dubcheck rose and extended his hand. An older man with oily, slicked-back black hair, he had a feral air about him. I sat and clutched my notebook to my breast. Butterflies flipped around in my guts. It was my first professional interview. I took in a breath, hoping to settle myself down.

"Did you have any trouble finding us?" He chuckled as if it was a private joke.

"No, your directions were fine."

He regaled me with tales of my predecessor's skills. Nan, a PR major from Kent, did a "wonderful job." In fact, after graduation, she landed a position at a hospital closer to Cleveland. They were still friends. *Great.*

"We're very fond of her."

"You can stay in the nurses' dorm if you decide to take this job. It's connected to the hospital by a long tunnel."

This closed the deal for me. I needed a place to stay and if I could stay free, all the better. I got into my car and began the trip back to Kent.

This didn't seem like the best internship, but I was desperate to graduate before I ran out of money. Mr. Dubcheck offered me the job.

22

Summer 1969

In June, I packed my things, said my good-byes to Betty at the *Record-Courier* and Bob, who still worked at both radio stations. Even though we had gotten back together, I was nervous, especially when I thought about him lurking outside the Allerton house waiting for me to come home. So, I was surprised when he took me in his arms and kissed me deeply. Shocked at my own response, I practically swooned and held him tight against me. Guess I didn't want him to forget me over the summer.

"Write me," I told Bob.

Writing wasn't his style. "I'll call you if I can."

⌘

The nurses' residence was dark by the time I arrived. Spooky. Mr. Dubcheck had sent me the keys. I fumbled, trying to unlock the front door with its heavy-paned glass. It opened on a long narrow hallway that echoed as I walked in.

A second key was for Room 205. I couldn't find an elevator, so I took the stairs. I packed clothing for the first week, a small TV and a fan. I expected to find nurses or other hospital employees walking the halls, but the place was deserted. It smelled like no one had aired it out for days.

The second-floor hallway was even darker than the first. I searched for the room number. Setting my suitcase down, I reached for the old skeleton key that opened the door. My room was dormitory-sized. I locked the door behind me as I fought off the chills running down my spine. I hoped I wasn't the only soul in the big echo chamber of a building.

Sparsely furnished with a single bed, a small dresser, a desk, and a chair, the room reminded me of a convent. I put my clothes away and set the rabbit-eared TV on top of the dresser. With no TV stations close by, I hoped to be able to tune into Erie or Cleveland, depending on the atmosphere.

I'd work on the TV problem tomorrow. I washed my face, brushed my teeth and lay down on the bed to read. About nine o'clock, something rustled out in the hallway. It was the nurse anesthetist Mr. Dubcheck told me lived across the hall. I peeked out through the keyhole and saw a shadowy figure unlocking the door.

Since I had to report for work early in the morning, I turned down the covers and got into bed. I fell asleep fast.

Monday morning, I dressed and walked through the tunnel to the hospital cafeteria where they served bacon and eggs. So far, the job was great. Free room and cheap eats. I sat alone at a small table while lots of people in uniforms filed by getting their morning coffee. A young woman with sandy blonde hair smiled at me as she walked by with a tray.

"Mind if I sit with you? I'm Karen," she said, "the new dietician."

"What's with Mr. Dubcheck's secretary?" I asked as we finished our coffee.

"Oh," she said, laughing. "That's his wife. She has a lot of power around here, so don't cross her."

After breakfast, I walked over to Mr. Dubcheck's office.

"We want you to write and edit a monthly newsletter for the staff and handle any publicity or news-related questions from the press," he said.

Not exactly the *New York Times* but it sounded simple enough.

Mrs. Dubcheck intercepted me as I left. "Let me show you to your office."

It was almost bare, with only a desk, a chair, and a short bookshelf. "Where's the typewriter?" I asked, innocently. A pile of manuals and magazines lay on the desk, but there were no writing materials.

"Oh, we don't have a typewriter for you yet. That'll come next week. You can read those brochures while you wait.

No typewriter? How could a hospital with hundreds of staff members not have an extra typewriter? I didn't want to get into a discussion about my equipment, so I thanked her and sat down.

Where was Bill Fisher when I needed him? I had to figure out the next move on my own.

⌘

Late in the afternoon, Mr. Dubcheck poked his head into my office. "How's it going?"

Trying to be diplomatic, I raised the typewriter question again.

"Well, we don't have one for you yet. Can't you write your stories longhand?"

Speechless, I just nodded. I was used to taking notes in a reporter's notebook then typing my stories out directly. Welcome to the boondocks!

⌘

I never ran into Bert Hiller, but I became friends with Karen and met my dorm neighbor, a much-older, wrinkled woman with dyed blonde hair, the nurse anesthetist. When we talked, I noticed a slight odor of alcohol wafting my way. I realized her after-hours interests didn't involve talking to young college interns.

Finally, I got a typewriter, a manual Smith Corona and was set to go. Since there weren't any major news stories coming out of Ashtabula General to take up my time, I finished the first newsletter in a week.

⌘

The most interesting thing happening that summer wasn't in Ashtabula, but more than 238,000 miles away. The astronauts walked on the moon. Determined to watch, I thought I could catch the broadcast on the rabbit-eared TV. Of course, I hadn't been able to see any other TV images so far. The reception was terrible. Ashtabula was isolated from the big local stations.

On July 20, I rushed back to the dorm in time to tune in to the moonwalk. I stared at the tiny 10-inch screen.

"That's one small step for man . . ."

I couldn't see anything but shadows on the screen, but my spirit soared as I watched.

23

I missed Bob. My attempts to get together with him failed. When I was home, he was in Cleveland. When I was in Ashtabula he was in Kent, too far away to come for a visit in his beat-up Falcon. I would call him while he worked at the radio station. He'd answer the phone hoping it was a listener he could put on the air. I crept out into the deserted, darkened hall at the nurses' dorm each night and clunked my coins into the ancient pay phone. He didn't have much time to talk unless he'd cued up a long record. *Light My Fire* was a good one.

I sent him letters, upbeat and cheery because we were still recovering from our spring quarter breakup.

One weekend, I had the bright idea to stop by his parents' new condo on my drive back to Ashtabula. He planned to visit them on Sunday. It would be a nice surprise.

I wore one of my best shorts outfits, picked out especially for this visit—a white top, yellow and white flower-print sailcloth shorts with cute sandals. Bouncing up the sidewalk in the warm evening air, I tried to dodge a swarm of tiny flying bugs. Bob called them Canadian soldiers. They flit about crashing into my face every few seconds. Excited to see Bob, I knocked on the screen door. He and his dad sat at the dinner table. He came to the door, looking surprised.

"What are you doing here?" He sounded confused. He shook his head and invited me in. "We're just about to have dessert."

I was so happy to see him, I gave him a big hug. Jim nodded hello to me.

"Hi," Mary called from the kitchen where she dished up shortcake.

"I thought I'd stop by on my way back to Ashtabula."

Bob hugged me back. Jim saved the day, asking about my weekend and the drive ahead of me.

"I've been visiting my family. I needed a break from the long drive."

"Would you like dessert? We're having strawberry shortcake," Mary offered. We sat around the dining room table as she served it. "You know, I went to college, too."

I was surprised. Bob never told me.

"I had to drop out when my dad died."

"Oh, when?" I asked, innocently. Bob skipped this part of the family story.

Mary had a strange look. "He was killed in a train wreck in Lake County, out near Mentor during my freshman year at Ursuline."

"Oh, I'm sorry," I said, dumbly. "I didn't know about it."

"He was with his secretary. I had to drop out of college and find a job. It was during the war. I landed one in downtown Cleveland at the gas company. Jim was already gone to the Army. He was drafted right after Pearl Harbor."

Jim nodded quietly as he polished off his shortcake.

There was more to this story, but judging from Mary's down-cast demeanor, I dared not ask. Something about it bothered me, but I couldn't put my finger on it.

We finished our dessert and after a few more minutes of visiting, I stood. "I need to be on my way. Ashtabula is a long drive."

Bob had been strangely quiet since I arrived. *What was wrong?* He didn't seem pleased to see me.

He stood too. "I'll walk you out."

We held hands. I was happy I had followed my impulse to stop. He said he'd be going back to Kent tomorrow morning.

"Let's go for a walk," he said. We passed the patio in the middle of the courtyard. He guided me toward the sidewalk that circled the inner perimeter of the complex.

There had been recent rain and the patio was covered with standing water. As we strolled, Bob held my hand tighter. Then he swung me around playfully, slowly then faster and faster. At first, it was exciting, and we both laughed as his arcs sent me closer and closer to the standing water. He spun me harder, and I screamed in delight. Suddenly he let go of my hand and I went flying.

The momentum carried me to the edge of the patio where the deeper water slowed my feet. I toppled over face first, but I stopped my tumble before I fell flat. Stunned, I stayed there, balanced on my hands and knees for a few seconds before I managed to stand. My knees and palms were scraped in the fall.

Startled, I stared at the damage. "Look what you did," I said, almost in tears. My hands and knees dripped with blood.

Bob laughed nervously. We both stood silent, me staring at the seeping blood.

Bob shook his head. "Can't you take a joke? It was an accident."

Confused, I tried to regain my composure. Too embarrassed to let his parents see me like this, I brushed myself off as best I could with tissue from my pocket.

Then I turned and walked, almost ran, toward my car. He followed and tried to give me a quick kiss as I reached for the door handle.

"You're taking this too seriously," he said.

I still had another hour and fifteen-minute drive ahead of me. I gunned it and backed out of the parking space as Bob waved good-bye.

I drove off toward I-90, a long stretch of road with few cars and fewer exits. I couldn't figure it out. Still shaking. I cried a little, then bit my cheek to make the tears stop. I was so upset, I could barely see through my tears. My hands and knees hurt. I needed to pull myself together.

What turned a romantic walk to my car into a freak accident? I couldn't understand Bob. I resolved to stay away from him.

On the long drive back to Ashtabula my mind drifted. What kept me from breaking up with Bob? Was it something in my past?

⌘

It was the day before eighth-grade graduation. The other kids watched me argue with Mom and Dad. Jenny played with Penny, our dachshund, and Roy was only a baby. Tim and Mark sat quietly watching.

"I don't want to go to St. Mary's. None of my friends are going there. Mine are going to St. V," I pleaded.

This same argument about what school I would attend went on for weeks. There was the cool school—St. Vincent, where all the football stars and cutest girls went or the dorky one, St. Mary. My parents pushed for St. Mary.

Finances were tight. Dad worked two jobs and was gone from early morning until late at night. St. V's tuition might be too much for them.

In the past with Dad gone, Mom had done some odd things, like the time she choked three-year-old Tim for not being able to swallow a vitamin pill. Tim was the sickly one and Dad thought vitamins would help him. It was Mom's job to make sure he swallowed them.

"Tim, what's wrong?" She glanced over her shoulder as she washed the dishes. Tim's face was turning red.

"Swallow that pill!"

Mark and I played nearby on the kitchen floor. We were used to hearing him gag and struggle to get that monster pill down. Suddenly Mom was on him. She grabbed him by the neck, choking him.

"Swallow," she threatened under her breath, her mouth contorted in a grimace.

A chill went through me. She's closing off his windpipe. She choked him until he turned purple. At six, I knew that wasn't how to get him to swallow. At last, she let go, and I breathed a sigh of relief. Tim gagged again and threw up the pill along with his breakfast. Mom wiped his face, hugged him and let him down from the highchair. She went back to washing the dishes as he toddled away. Mark and I stared at each other, wide-eyed.

To avoid Mom's craziness, I tried to be extremely good.

Now, as Mom and Dad sat across from me at the dining room table, I wondered whether their insistence on my going to St. Mary's was some sort of punishment? I hadn't done anything wrong lately, had I?

"Don't you want me to graduate from your alma mater?" I put up a valiant argument. Everyone else in my family, my uncles, my aunts, my cousins had gone there. My grandfather even hauled the giant limestone blocks up out of the valley to build St. Vincent's church. I felt tears welling up. My voice broke.

Mom shrugged. "What's gotten into you? St. Mary's will be free with your scholarship. What's wrong with you?" She shook her head. "How can you be so ugly?"

I didn't understand that no matter how good I was, it wouldn't change her mind about me.

24

I finished my internship in good stead with Mr. Dubcheck and he gave me a decent evaluation. Not up to Nan standards, but I took it. Eager to begin my senior year, I wanted to graduate in the spring. For a few weeks after the patio incident, I stopped taking Bob's calls, but then he sent me cards and dedicated songs to me on his radio show. I weakened.

I slept in the front bedroom on the second floor, sharing with Jenny. One night after I went to bed, I heard tapping on the window. Was it Bob again? To my surprise, he stood in the driveway below, tossing pebbles, like when we first met. He'd parked his Falcon across the street. I guessed he didn't want to risk my hanging up on him if he called. I raced downstairs to stop him before he woke anybody else.

I opened the cellar door and let him in.

"I've got to see you," he said in a loud whisper.

He looked pitiful. We'd gone through this before, but he tugged at my heart and my feelings for him came rushing back.

"I miss you," he said.

"I miss you, too!"

We embraced passionately. We had been apart too long, but I needed to shoo him away before anyone heard us. As I grabbed the door to push him out, he kissed me again.

"Please forgive me. I love you."

We were soon hanging out on the weekends, mostly at the radio station or in his room on Mantua Street. Lying in bed we watched the news one August evening. There was a massive music festival underway in upstate New York. We gazed at each other pitifully. Bob knew I wanted to go. We didn't have the money. Woodstock featured some of my favorite bands, The Who and Jefferson Airplane. In my fantasies, my friends who'd made it to the Democratic National Convention in Chicago last year were on their way to New York.

⌘

My knees were still scabbed over, but Bob never mentioned them. Mom asked about the scabs and I told her I tripped carrying things out of the nurses' residence. One day I stopped at Burger Chef and saw Bert Hiller standing in line ahead of me.

"How goes it? Are you done with your internship?" he asked.

We sat at one of the tables catching up.

"What happened to your knees?"

The scabs showed. Blushing, I tried the same lie again. "I fell carrying boxes." I hoped this sounded convincing.

He paused and then gave me a laser-like stare. He leaned in and whispered intensely. "If Bob is hurting you, you need to get away from him."

Shocked he'd guessed my secret, I shook my head.

"He's not," I lied with emphasis and conviction. "But I'll remember what you said."

"How's Janet?" I changed the subject.

He dropped his pursuit of Bob and we finished our lunch with small talk about his fiancée and their upcoming wedding.

⌘

Despite Bert's warning, Bob and I were deeply involved again. Sure, we had rough patches. I hoped I could change him, but I provoked him sometimes.

Even though I was cautious around him, I loved him. He must have sensed my hesitation because he redoubled his efforts to woo me. He spent more time with me now. We could hardly keep our hands off each other. Bob's touch thrilled me. Amazed at how my body responded to him, I fell into his deep brown eyes. I ran my fingers through his curly black hair. Love was intoxicating.

His parents were going camping over the Labor Day weekend. He had a key to their condo and suggested we stop on our way up to Fairport Harbor to help Bill Donaldson with his boat.

Bill, one of his high school buddies, had bought an old fishing boat that was sunken and abandoned. He salvaged it and towed it east of Cleveland to his parents' dock. It still needed work. I didn't like tagging along to the boat, but I was intrigued by an empty condo.

Never one to rise early, Bob arrived about one. I grabbed a light jacket to throw over my shorts and halter top and jumped into the car. As we drove the hour to his parents' condo, he held my hand. My heart surged with happiness now that he was so attentive. He did seem sorry for my scraped knees.

Bob opened the door and ushered me in. The condo was deserted. Bob had changed. He was solicitous and charming. He stuck his head into the bedroom hallway and called, "Hello?" Nobody answered.

We had experimented sexually for some time in his rented room, but now we would be together without an audience listening in. He kissed me, and we held each other close, melting into each other.

"I missed you so much!" he whispered. He took my hand, led me down the hallway to the spare bedroom. Piles of neatly folded laundry lay on both the beds. He laughed. No way could we use one of these without his mother noticing. He looked into his parents' bedroom next. We fell on the twin bed closest to the bathroom, Mary's bed.

"We can't do this here," I whispered.

He ignored me. "Come on, let's try it."

He meant to go all the way.

I was ready. I loved him.

"What if I get pregnant?"

"You won't," he assured me. "I'll pull out before I come."

This sounded like a good idea. St. Mary's had offered no Sex Ed classes.

"I'll get a towel in case there's blood." At least I knew that much.

I was a virgin. That didn't surprise him.

I grabbed a hand towel from the bathroom. He had stripped naked by the time I came back. He undressed me slowly then laid me gently on the bed. We kissed for a moment but couldn't wait any longer.

"Hurry," I whispered in his ear.

Bob moved against me urgently, pressing his hardness into me. I reached down and guided him. He pushed and poked until I sensed a slight give. I grabbed his back.

"That's it. Keep going." We joined together, transported by the excitement of these new sensations. He thrust a few times and then fell over on his side. Was he done? I was so intent on making sure he deflowered me I thought I might have missed the main event.

"I almost came inside you," he gasped. "That was great."

Too embarrassed to tell him I hadn't felt much, I raised up on one elbow and took his hand. "That was wonderful! We'll have to practice a lot."

He took me in his arms. "I love you," he said. We lay together, our arms entwined.

"I love you, too." We both sighed.

The next time would be better. I'd know what to expect.

I untangled my arm and reached down to check for blood. My hand was damp and a little bloody. *Good.* I lay back and luxuriated in the warmth of his embrace.

After a few minutes, he sat up and dressed. We straightened the bed, locked the door, and drove off toward the sunken boat.

⌘

Bob and I were closer than ever. We held hands, truly united. But I had doubts about his pull-out method. Still the staunch Catholic, I wasn't sure what my options were. Only married women could get birth control pills. I'd never seen a gynecologist. Mom said if you weren't having sex, you didn't need one. I decided not to tell her things had changed.

I would talk to Bob about the risks we were taking. One night over dinner, I posed the question. "What will we do if I get pregnant?"

He gazed into my eyes. "We'll get married." He nodded decisively.

I sighed with relief. He really loved me.

25

Fall 1969

We knew girls who dropped out of school when they got pregnant. Abortion was illegal, and I wouldn't know how to get one, anyway. Everyone had heard stories of back-alley doctors and of cousins who'd been sent away to have their babies in secret. Who wanted to go through that?

Thoughts of joining the convent and dedicating my life to God dissolved in hot lust. Who cared about becoming the best damn nun? My high school friends were already married and lots of my college acquaintances engaged. I loved Bob and he said he loved me.

Years ago, Mom cautioned me not to talk about myself. Now I'd found someone happy to listen to me ramble about mundane things. Mom called me ugly and now I found a guy who thought I was beautiful. How could she be so wrong? I started to doubt everything she'd taught me.

The second time we made love was amazing. In Bob's room, we slowed down. I felt so protected in his arms. The world disappeared as we kissed and caressed. He entered me slowly, and I guided him to a rhythm that worked for me. Afterward, he held me, and we talked for hours about our plans. He still wanted to buy a radio station. I imagined myself working alongside him, writing news copy and pulling albums for his show. By mid-September when school started, we spent almost every day together.

⌘

I was still rooming at Mrs. Butler's house. Now Mimi was different too. She had broken up with Danny and had a new boyfriend, Chip—very worldly. He had a blue Camaro with a personalized license plate. A Vietnam vet, he was out of the Army and working. An older man! Mimi told me she loved him, and though she never admitted it, Bob and I bet they were sleeping together too.

Sex at my house was taboo even when Mimi was gone. I couldn't bear to let Bob come upstairs for a visit with the across-the-hall roommates listening.

Most often, I met him at the radio station and then followed him back to his room on Mantua Street. Since we were penniless, his room became our love nest.

⌘

The fall of 1969 brought other changes too. After the debacle of the Democratic National Convention a year ago, things had grown more political at Kent. Last spring antiwar activists around the country had called for a moratorium if U.S. troops were not withdrawn from Vietnam by October. But in October the fighting was still going strong. Those against the War prepared for a one-day strike on the fifteenth. They planned to hold teach-ins to educate people about the War. In Ohio, several universities shut down, but not KSU. The Kent Moratorium committee would hold a teach-in and a march. About thirty-five hundred people— students, townspeople and antiwar activists turned out for the march.

They sang as they marched through downtown. They chanted: "Bring the troops home now!" and "Get out of Vietnam." Parents held their toddlers' hands, guiding them along. Old folks walked alongside their college-aged sons and daughters, laughing and singing.

I watched from the Main Street sidelines, torn between reporting and joining in. Beside me stood some clerks from a nearby store. "I don't think they're going about this in the proper manner," said one.

All over the country, people marched peacefully. Then in November, a march on Washington was scheduled for the fifteenth. My *Stater* colleagues planned to go.

"I want to go too," I told Bob. I would have anonymity amid the hundreds of thousands of protestors. My conflict between observing and participating might vanish.

"I don't think we can afford it, but we'll figure something out," Bob said.

I was the *Stater* news director now, plus the copyeditor for the yearbook. Combined, these jobs paid $500 in a lump sum at the end of the quarter. Bob lived on the little money he made at WKNT. Finally, we decided we couldn't pay for the trip to Washington. I sank into a gloomy malaise. The weekend of the march we moped around Kent, making love more than once in the depths of Bob's room, trying to comfort ourselves.

Late Sunday afternoon, I went to the newspaper office, hoping one of the Washington marchers would return to write a story about it. Shortly after 5:00 P.M. a photographer, Tim, showed up. He was a little crazy and usually short-tempered, so I avoided him. He quickly disappeared into the darkroom to develop his film.

Next, Sam walked in dressed in fatigues and combat boots. We'd joked around in the past few months and I liked him a lot. He was the *Stater* editor and involved me in day-to-day decisions about the paper.

"Hey, you're back," I called across the room, nonchalantly. "How did it go?"

"Fine. I talked with lots of protesters and have some leads on stories. I'm hungry. Let's go eat and I'll tell you about it."

We drove the mile to Chicken Manor, a source of mass-produced dinners, cheap and fast. We sat, and he told me about the march.

"There must have been a million people. We marched down Pennsylvania Avenue to the White House. Pete Seeger sang 'Give Peace a Chance'."

I was dying from envy and thrilled at what he'd witnessed.

As we talked, he absently dipped his napkin into his water glass, then cleaned his glasses. He grabbed another napkin and washed his face. I pretended not to notice.

Sam ate until he was full, paid the bill and dropped me off at the *Stater* office to retrieve my car.

⌘

With the new draft lottery about to start, emotions ran high. Earlier in the year, Nixon had ordered nineteen-year-olds drafted, changing the selection sequence from oldest to youngest first. Then he instituted the lottery system where all eighteen to twenty-six-year-olds were equally eligible. Both changes increased the opposition to the war.

Bob had a philosophical attitude. "If I get a low number, I'll go to Canada."

I hoped he was joking. Gallows humor prevailed as December 1, lottery day approached. Even guys who would be unfit for service, 4-F, worried they'd draw a low number and be ordered to report for a physical. Everyone gathered around the television to watch the drawing and find out when their birthdate would come up. Shouts of glee and cries of dismay echoed as the lottery progressed. Bob drew number 120, a low one. He'd almost certainly have to report for duty by the end of 1970.

His attitude changed from philosophical to angry. "I mean it. I'll leave the country."

⌘

That fall I began having stomach trouble. My physician, Doctor Mader, didn't find anything wrong when he examined me. "We're going to put you in the hospital for a couple of days to do tests," he said as he concluded the appointment.

"I can't do that. I'm in school at Kent."

"We'll do it over winter break.

The quarter ended, and Mom took me to St. Thomas and I waited for the doctor to order tests. Christmas was my favorite time of year. I didn't want to spend it in bed.

My parents came to visit, but Bob was a no-show.

26

We talked on the phone. "I'm busy with all the extra work at the station. The other DJs left for the holidays," Bob justified his absence.

I was disappointed he didn't come to see me, but when he told me he bought me a present, my hope soared.

Maybe this was the engagement ring I hoped for. We'd been together for three years and intimate for months. I spent my days in the hospital listening for his footsteps in the hallway.

"You know I don't like doctors or hospitals." He'd explained this many times before. It was about his sister.

"My parents dragged me from doctor to doctor when I was a kid. I had to sit in the waiting room while they examined Kitty. Nobody figured out what was wrong with her. I hated sitting there with all those sick people while Mom and Dad talked to the doctors. No one could help her."

Okay, so he didn't like doctors or hospitals, but I missed him.

On Friday, two days before Christmas, I still didn't have a diagnosis. As I lay in bed waiting for my evening meal to arrive, Bob burst into the room holding a big oblong gift box. It didn't look like a ring, but he'd fooled me before.

"I bought you something." He pushed it toward me. "For Christmas."

I prepared myself in case this wasn't an engagement ring. I sat up to unwrap the huge box. Something slid around inside. Bob leaned in impatiently as I tore the Christmas wrapping.

"I wonder what it is."

He smiled. He helped me pull the lid off the box. Inside, wrapped in layers of tissue paper, lay a large gray coat with silver buttons, a military-style coat. I held it up and stood to admire its length. It was a maxi coat, a trendy design popular in reaction to Twiggy and her miniskirts.

I smiled at him though I was dying inside. I was so disappointed. I tried to stop myself from crying. It was beautiful and looked warm. I stopped myself from hinting about a ring.

The hospital discharged me, and we spent Christmas together—the early morning at my house watching the kids open their presents and then dinner at his parents'. His mother fixed ham, mashed potatoes, and other Turner family delicacies.

Things were good. I wore the maxi coat everywhere. It was perfect for the cold winter. We held hands as much as we dared in front of his parents.

27

Winter quarter started early. Still sick, I threw up every morning. Doctor Mader called and said the hospital tests had found nothing. I felt so bad I finally went to the new Health Center on the far side of campus from the old Pill Hill. It looked like a real clinic, with shiny stainless steel, white linens, and clean hallways.

The triage nurse asked about my problem.

"I can't stop throwing up."

She laughed. "You do look green around the gills. You're not pregnant, are you?"

"Oh, no. I couldn't be." I tried to sound confident.

"We'll give you an IV. You're probably dehydrated." She motioned for me to follow her.

"Lie down on the bed." She took my blood pressure and inserted an IV.

"The doctor will see you later." I lay quietly watching the IV drip into my arm. Within a couple of hours, it drained. Dramatically better, I sat up and got ready to leave. The nausea was gone. As I put on my jacket, the doctor walked in.

"Could you be pregnant?" she asked.

"Oh, no," I said, surprised. That couldn't be.

But now a tiny seed had been planted in my brain. *What if I was pregnant*? I shivered at the thought.

I would have to leave school. Even though Bob and I had an understanding we'd marry, we were in no position to do so. Neither of us had any money saved, nor any job prospects. I wouldn't be able to work very long before I started to show. No employer would want me around customers.

The next day I returned to the Health Center. "I do think I could be pregnant," I told them. "I'd like a test."

The receptionist handed me a container. "Gather your first-morning urine. Pee in this and bring it back."

Early the next morning I collected my urine and took it to the Health Center again.

"Call in a week for the results," said the receptionist as she took the bottle.

Anxious and ill-tempered while I waited, the suspense killed me. I was still throwing up right after I woke up. I couldn't make it to my early morning classes. My grades plummeted.

Finally, I could call for the test results. I made myself wait until after 10:00 and then picked up the phone. The same receptionist answered. I gave her my name and date of birth. After a short pause, she came back on the line.

"It's negative. You're not pregnant."

I sighed. "Thank you," I said and hung up. Relief flooded through me. Now I could stop worrying.

The specter of a shotgun wedding dissolved. Life brightened. I renewed my resolve to finish the quarter, but I still threw up. Not only did I feel sick in the morning when I woke, but if I didn't eat soda crackers soon enough, I was sick all day and missed classes. I spent my days lying on the bathroom floor.

By this time, I'd missed my period for several months. I'd been irregular in the past, so that wasn't unusual, but the two symptoms together along with Doctor Mader finding nothing wrong, made me think I should find an obstetrician.

Maybe the Health Center pregnancy test was defective. I didn't want to ask any of my housemates who they saw. I was ashamed to admit I was sexually active. Good girls were virgins. I wouldn't ask my mother. That would lead to a mini-Inquisition. Too humiliating.

I ran my finger down the column of obstetricians in the Yellow Pages and found a doctor in Stow, fifteen minutes away. I called.

"What's the reason for the appointment?" When the reception- ist heard I might be pregnant, she suggested I bring in a first- morning urine sample for the rabbit test. Rumor had it if you were pregnant, the rabbit died. I didn't know how this worked, whether someone made the poor rabbit drink the urine, or in- jected them or what.

"How do you want to pay for the visit?" she asked.

My parents still carried me on their health insurance, but I told her I would pay myself. Best to keep them out of this.

Early the next morning I peed into a cup and transferred it to a bottle. Straight away I took it to the office. The crowded wait- ing room was filled with young women, eight and nine months pregnant. *My God. What have I gotten myself into?*

"Call us in a week. The results will be back by then."

Lulled into a false sense of security by the Health Center test, I forgot to call on the appointed day. Late that afternoon while I studied for an Art Appreciation midterm, the upstairs phone rang.

"For you, Patty," yelled Trudie, my across-the-hall neighbor. I leaped to answer it.

"It's Doctor Stein's office. Your results are back. You *are* pregnant," she announced this with glee. Who wouldn't be happy at such blessed news?

"What?" I couldn't believe it. "What did you say?"

She repeated herself.

Stunned, I argued with her. "The last test was negative," I told her.

"Well, honey, our rabbits don't lie. Somebody is pregnant." She added, "You need a follow-up appointment. Call back when you're ready to come in."

I sank to the bed in disbelief. What was I going to do now? Bob and I were getting together after his last class. I would tell him then. I was glad we had discussed our plan if his "pull-out" method failed.

Bob picked me up and though I was bursting to tell him, I waited until we got to Burger Chef. As we sat in the molded orange chairs, I was silent, trying to figure out how to break it to him.

"The doctor called today," I said, with as deadpan an expression as I could muster. I would have to catch Bob up with what had gone on since my hospitalization during winter break. I hadn't told him about my latest bout of sickness. I was so nervous I raced on with my news. "I'm pregnant."

He sat there for a minute, stunned. "What do you mean?" He looked shocked. Both of us were surprised.

"I had one pregnancy test done at the Health Center. It was negative, but I still had symptoms. So, I had a second test at an obstetrician's office. Their test results came back this morning. I'm pregnant." I dropped the information like a bomb. A tear of relief ran down my cheek.

After a long pause, he gulped and said, "We'll just get married." He was calm and focused. "That's what we'll do."

We sat quietly for a few minutes with no idea of what to do next.

Finally, I took a breath, "We need rings. We should get engaged." He grabbed my hand and squeezed it. It was too much to deal with while students milled around us in the middle of Burger Chef. We needed to take one step at a time. We finished our meal in silence and barely talked on the ride home.

Bob dropped me off at Allerton. "Call me tomorrow," he said and gave me a quick kiss.

28

Away from Bob, alone in my room, I sobbed. We loved each other, but we weren't prepared for a baby.

One minute I was elated because my dream of getting married was coming true, the next frozen with fear because we had to tell our parents. Mine would be bad enough, but Bob's? I fell into a deep sleep exhausted from the emotion.

Early the next morning, I drove to my appointment with Doctor Stein, trying not to puke, too numb to sort out what to do. I hoped the doctor would tell me my due date, so we could plan.

Again, the waiting room was packed. The girl next to me asked when I was due.

"I don't know yet. I hope to find out today."

Doctor Stein was a no-nonsense kind of guy. After examining me he said, "You're about eight weeks along. Everything looks normal. This is a group practice. I'll try to be there for your delivery, but it might be one of my partners who'll be on call. Stop at the front desk to arrange for payments."

At least they didn't want the full amount in advance. I could live with that. I balled up my gown and threw it into the corner.

"Over here, honey," the girl at the checkout window called. "You'll come in every month for now. The doctor will tell you when he wants to see you more often." She handed me an appointment card and motioned toward a door down the hall. Go there next," she said, pointing.

Down the hall was the billing clerk. "Sit. Give me your insurance card."

"I don't have insurance. I'll pay for this myself."

"Okay, Miss Scott," she continued without missing a beat, "that will be ten dollars for today. I'll set up a payment plan for you. Doctor Stein's bill including your labor and delivery will be seven hundred dollars. The hospital bill is separate."

Not bad. Seven hundred dollars over nine months? We could handle the cost between us. If we split it that would be fifty dollars a month each. We would get jobs after we graduated. At least Bob would. I might have more trouble.

I sighed with relief as I left the office. I couldn't call Bob until later. It was only 9:30, so I tried to make it to my 11:00 class, one I'd been missing regularly. I stopped at the drug store to buy the prenatal vitamins. Could I keep my condition a secret from my housemates? I planned on hiding the vitamins, but most of them had seen me lying in bed sick. It wasn't much of a secret.

I reached Bob right before he went on the air. We would meet after his shift.

"Come out to the station."

Standing in the wide-open *Stater* office using one of their phones, I didn't want to go into any of the details of my visit. "Okay. Later."

⌘

That afternoon I drove to WKNT and turned into the long driveway winding through the alfalfa fields and past the driving range. I pulled up to the cement block building that housed the station. Inside there were two rooms plus the studio and a small office with a desk and chair. The Teletype machine sat in the hallway, to muffle any clacking sounds from the airwaves. At first, the radio station had impressed me, but that wore off quickly as I spent hours sitting there studying while waiting for Bob to finish his shift. I timed it, so I arrived as Bob signed off and Jim signed on. Bob met me at the door.

"Hi," he said tenderly and took me in his arms. I must have looked bereft, as he added, "We'll get through this."

I loved him so much. He would protect me.

We crossed the highway to Chicken Manor. Even though the restaurant was usually packed with Kent students and their parents, I saw no one I recognized, so we could talk freely.

"What should we do next?" Bob asked.

We had enough pregnant friends to know the drill.

"Well, we'll buy the rings like we said and then tell our parents." I hoped if I didn't piss them off too much they might pay for the wedding.

Bob wasn't hot on telling any of the parents. He gave me a wary look and shook his head. "I'm going to wait to tell mine."

They had been nasty to him in the past. I acquiesced to his plan to wait.

"There's a place in Akron where we can get rings." Bob worked another part-time job as a salesman at Olson's, an electronics store in downtown Akron. There was a jeweler across the street.

Not a good time for comparison shopping. We agreed to go on Saturday.

"What about the wedding?"

"I'm not sure. I might need Mom's help."

Bob groaned. I thought he liked my parents, but my mother teased him about his rattletrap car making him uncomfortable.

"Okay. We'll tell them together."

So, we had our plan. First the rings, then the parents. I was so happy. We were finally getting married.

I woke up early Saturday and got ready to go. Of course, Bob didn't show until 11:00.

"I had a report to finish, and I had to buy gas."

Our drive to downtown Akron was short—only half an hour on the icy back roads from Kent. We parked on a steep side street in front of the jewelers. I wore my best green dress and heels, not wanting the salesman thinking of us as deadbeats. Bob had on his usual short-sleeved red shirt and socks, his trademark.

As we entered the store, a salesman came from behind the counter to greet us. He was sweating.

"What are we looking for today?"

I didn't know what I wanted. I'd seen plenty of engagement rings lately. This was my senior year and most of my friends sported them. I wanted something different.

"We," Bob said, mocking him, "are looking for an engagement ring."

The salesman glowed. "I'm Jack. I'll help you today. What type of ring do you want?"

We looked at each other. Bob smirked. We didn't know anything about diamonds. I pulled myself together, trying not to laugh. "Nothing too fancy," I said. With small hands, I didn't want to flaunt a gaudy rock.

"Come right this way." For the next hour, he pulled out tray after tray of rings. Small ones, big ones, baguettes, ovals, solitaires. I didn't see many I liked. Desperate, he brought out "one last tray."

My eyes latched onto a ring set that was very different from the others.

"That one." I pointed to a small ring with one square stone in a simple setting. The band itself was beautiful, with a layer of gold encircled by a smaller ring of silver.

"That's brushed platinum," he announced with a reverence that made it even more desirable. "There's a matching wedding band and we have a man's ring to go with it. This one is $200."

I couldn't believe we found something so elegant. We could almost afford it.

"This is it," I said with conviction, looking at Bob. "Do you like it?"

Bob never wore jewelry, and I only had a few cheap necklaces for dress-up occasions. He nodded, a little uncertain.

"How would you like to pay?" Jack asked and we both just stared at him. "The options are cash or credit. We offer a monthly payment plan if you need it."

We nodded in unison. Monthly, for sure. Jack pulled out his sales pad and went to work. Something so momentous had taken us only ninety minutes. Most of my friends had spent months looking, but we didn't have the luxury of dragging this out.

"You can pick them up early next week after they've been sized."

My heart leaped. Things would be fine. On the way back to Kent, we talked about the next step—when to tell my parents.

"Let's do it after we pick up the rings," I said.

So, we decided. We would tell them we were engaged. Sleet fell as the wipers swished. We hurried back to Kent before the roads got worse.

We ate dinner at our old hangout, Burger Chef, then went back to Bob's and made love. I was closer to him now. We held each other, and I thought about what we'd been through. We were graduating, had a baby on the way and would land real, full-time jobs soon. All was well.

29

Jack, the ring guy, called Bob the following Wednesday morning.

"The ring is ready."

"We'll pick it up tonight after class and then go tell your parents."

I was so excited. My dream was coming true. No matter, I was pregnant. Things would work out. Soon we sat in front of Jack trying on the ring. It fit perfectly. I held out my hand. Sparkling and elegant, it was understated. Just what I wanted.

"I love it!"

Bob and Jack smiled.

⌘

It was dark when we pulled into my parents' driveway. By the time I stomped the snow off my shoes, the door at the top of the stairs opened. Mom wiped her hands on her apron as she looked down at us. She didn't turn on the light.

"You!"

Sarcasm. I hadn't been around her much since winter quarter started. She tried to make me feel guilty for not visiting.

Bob came in right behind me. "Hi," he called out cheerfully as if he could bluff his way past her.

"Guess what." Excited, I thrust my ring hand upward toward Mom. The words, "we're engaged," formed on my lips but never made it out of my mouth.

"You're pregnant?" Mom laughed.

How dare she? I was so stunned I gasped. *How could she know?* My wits failed me. All I said was, "Yes."

The whole tenor of the visit changed with that one utterance. My old anger at her flooded back in an instant. This would be harder than I thought.

To me, the ring was meaningless now. I must figure out a whole new way of announcing our news. I rehearsed it in my head as I hung up my coat. *We're engaged. We are getting married. Sure, I was having a baby, but not yet.* I had hoped to keep that secret, but it was out now. My cover was blown. Devastated, I tried to salvage the moment, but I wanted to scream and cry in humiliation. How could the rest of the country be going through a sexual revolution while here in my own house I was a sinner?

I climbed the stairs. The weight of our actions bowed my shoulders. What began as an innocent plan to announce our engagement might deteriorate into an accusation-filled interrogation. Ashamed, my face flushed.

"So, you're pregnant?" Mom asked again.

I dived right in. Maybe a positive approach might be better. "Yes, I'm pregnant," I started. "About five weeks along, the doctor said." I gulped. I was already lying.

"You saw a doctor?" She paused to take this in. "You're sure?" Mom was hoping I had made a mistake. Thankfully, she spared me the full inquisition about my periods and my symptoms with Bob and Dad in the room. She wouldn't ask about birth control, which was not available to a single Catholic girl in 1970.

Bravely, Bob ventured, "We will get married. We're engaged. We came to show you the ring."

This wasn't helping, but I didn't want to stop him.

"We'll get married in June after we graduate."

This spurred Mom to action. "No, you can't wait that long," she told him. She turned to me. "When are you due?"

I knew the answer to this one. "The first part of September."

"Then we need to start planning soon. How about spring break?" She smiled. She meant we should rush things and marry in March.

Spring break began on March 19, a week-long interruption between quarters.

Mom's slight smile told me she was getting a little too much enjoyment out of our predicament. Dad sat there, looking dumbfounded.

"So, you're not a virgin anymore," Dad said. Virginity was still a highly prized commodity in our house.

"No. She's not," my mother growled.

I changed the subject. "Don't you want to see my ring?" I asked, holding out my hand. "It's beautiful!"

She wouldn't be distracted from setting a date. "Where should the wedding be?" We hadn't talked about it, but both of us spoke at once. We echoed each other. "The Newman Center," where we went for Sunday mass.

"We'll set a date. We could have the reception in their hall, right?"

Things were happening faster than I planned, but it was good to be getting married.

Mom was rolling now. "We'll need a dress and flowers, and cake and punch. Oh, and you'll need invitations. We'll have a small wedding."

Jenny, a high school sophomore, would be sixteen in April. With such a condensed timeline, I couldn't imagine asking a friend or two to shop for bridesmaid dresses and be in the wedding. She would do fine as a bridesmaid. She'd be honored. A year before, I was in Mark's wedding. His mother-in-law had sewn dresses for all the bridesmaids. Maybe she could make one for Jenny.

Mom was thinking along the same lines. "I'll ask Rita if she can make Jenny's dress."

Mom didn't know I still wasn't making it through the day without throwing up. I'd missed so many classes since this started. Bob didn't know either. I hoped my morning sickness would be gone before the wedding.

My best strategy for surviving the wedding preparation might be to agree with whatever Mom wanted. I hoped things would go smoothly. Not that I objected to her suggestions. I was thankful she shifted from blaming into planning mode.

Bob wasn't used to my parents. My high school years had taught me how to withstand their ploys. I said *they,* but really meant Mom. Trying to build up as much goodwill as possible, I thanked them for listening, then gave Bob a conspiratorial look and inched toward the door.

"We'd better get going. It's getting late." Our best defense was to remove ourselves from Mom's line of fire.

We went down the stairs to the cellar landing. As we did, Mom leaned in for one final gibe only I heard.

"I know you've done it more than once," she snarled into my ear.

Stunned and humiliated, I froze and didn't respond.

We put our coats on. I sighed. "I'll call you tomorrow and let you know about the Newman Center."

Bob backed out onto the street. "Well, that went better than I expected."

I just rolled my eyes. "She's pretty mad." I couldn't believe she was so nasty, especially in front of Bob.

Later, we agreed Bob would call his parents and tell them our news. He did and said it went well. Skeptical, I wished I could have seen their faces when they heard the news.

30

I hoped I would feel well enough to handle my classes and wedding plans. If it lasted all day, why was it called *morning sickness?*

If things worked out right, we would be married in eight weeks. The copy-editing work I'd been doing for the yearbook would be finished by then when the final draft went to the printer. Since the start of the winter quarter, I had taken a demotion at the *Stater,* and now just edited the inside pages. Same pay for less work.

Early the next morning, I called the Newman Center. We lucked out. The Friday of spring break week was open. Planning could proceed. I called Mom to tell her and pulled myself together to go to class. No sense letting my grades get totally out of control.

⌘

Mom came with me to shop for my dress. Our trips to Polsky's and O'Neil's, the big downtown department stores, were a bust. The dresses either didn't fit right or cost too much. Someone told us about a woman who sold dresses out of her living room.

The next Saturday afternoon, we piled into the car and took off for Brown Street, at the edge of the ghetto, near downtown Akron. I drove and Mom watched the house numbers.

"920, 922."

We found the address and pulled into the driveway of a gray-shingled house. Two steps led up to a large enclosed front porch. I knocked and after a minute a middle-aged black lady in a house-dress came to the door.

"Are you Mrs. Easton?"

"I sure am, honey." She smiled and held the door for us.

"I'm shopping for a wedding dress. Do you have any?"

"I do." She waved her arm toward racks of dresses on the porch—elegant floor-length prom dresses, fancy date night numbers and long satin wedding gowns.

Mom looked relieved. We searched the racks.

"When you're done here, come see the ones in the living room."

Perfect. We picked some for me to try.

As we made our way along the aisles, Mrs. Easton brought a couple of dresses over.

"You are such a tiny thing. I had these set aside, but one of them might fit you." She held some gowns out.

"Can I try them?"

"Oh, sure, honey. Use the bedroom." She pointed down the hall.

The gowns were beautiful, so I gathered up a few more, one encrusted with pearls and another with rhinestones. Mom led the way into the darkened bedroom. She turned on the light and a tabby cat sleeping on the bed stirred. She lifted the first dress over my head.

None of these dresses had price tags on them, so I could judge them by their beauty and how they fit rather than worrying about the cost.

After five or six dresses that didn't fit, I reached for the two Mrs. Easton had offered. The first one I tried was perfect. Pure white, it had an empire waist to hide my growing stomach and a bodice with teardrop pearls scattered across. The short train would be easy to manage.

This was the dress for me. It didn't swallow me up or make me look like I was playing dress up.

"There's a mirror out in front. Come here," Mom beckoned, and I followed her.

Thrilled at the long satin gown, I nodded. "This is the one."

"We like this one," I said.

"Oh, honey. Glad you like it," said Mrs. Easton from her perch in the dining room.

"How much?"

"That one is on sale. It's ninety-nine dollars."

"Ninety-nine dollars?" I couldn't believe my ears. Mom nodded. "We'll take it."

Still ashamed of my pregnancy, I wanted to put the least dent in my parents' savings possible. They hadn't given me a budget, but I tried to keep things simple with a cake and punch reception. My brother Tim's band could play for free. Bob only needed to rent tuxes for himself and his best man. The Turners could pay for the rehearsal dinner.

Bob wanted to keep his parents clueless for as long as possible. They didn't like me much. I occupied Bob's time on weekends, keeping him from visiting.

"We need to tell your parents about the baby," I said one night as he drove me home from class.

Bob looked aghast. "That's not a good idea. I'll tell them later."

Against reason, this became a challenge for me. "They won't be so happy if they find out after the wedding. When do you plan on telling them?"

He was adamant. "We should wait until after the wedding."

I reacted like he'd lost his mind and his moral compass. "It's not right to lie to them. Won't they be angry if they spend money on this wedding and then discover you tricked them?"

"No." Bob was emphatic. "You don't know them. You don't know what they're capable of."

I knew they'd disowned him in the past, but he wouldn't tell me about his offense. He probably borrowed money from them and didn't pay it back.

No matter how strong his argument, I refused to listen. I didn't want to be accused of tricking them out of their money. "Let's call them."

"They're still getting used to the idea of us getting married. Let's give them a few weeks."

I let it rest. We had other things to worry about.

⌘

"Finding a dress was the hard part," Mom assured me. "The rest of it will be easy."

I wanted to believe her. I hadn't thought about how many weddings she'd planned besides her own. She was right. Choosing a gown set a lot of other things in motion. We ordered the invitations, sampled cake and punch flavors and selected the flowers.

"March twentieth is the first day of spring, Patty, why don't you carry spring flowers in your bouquet?" Mom was a fountain of ideas.

⌘

I shared these developments with Mimi each night until one evening in early February when she gave me a strange look.

"What's wrong?" I asked.

"Oh, nothing." Then her face reddened, and she laughed. "I'm pregnant too."

"What?" I thought I didn't hear her right, but her face said it all. We both laughed so hard we almost fell off the beds. If anyone had seen us, they would have thought we were both nuts. I laughed until I cried. Mimi and Chip would be getting married a few weeks after us. Here I was keeping my secret from her while she went through the same drama.

I finally had someone I could talk to about my predicament. "Do you have to take those awful vitamins?" The prenatal ones were like horse pills and got stuck going down.

"You mean the ones in the aqua bottle? Yes. I can't swallow them."

"Have you told your parents yet?" Mimi's mom and dad had always been more forgiving than mine.

She thought about her answer. "We told them we are getting married. Chip asked my Dad's permission. They don't know I'm pregnant. We won't tell them until after the wedding."

I considered this for a minute. They were doing what Bob had wanted. "Won't they be upset when they find out?"

"Yeah," she said like I was a dummy, "but I figure they'll recover."

An only child, Mimi's would be the only wedding her parents got to throw. They were going all out. It would be a blast.

I was astounded there could be two such different realities. Getting over it wasn't something my parents did.

I was glad I had someone to talk to though these weren't optimal conditions. Neither one of us lived with the father of our child. But that would soon change.

⌘

Bob and I still cooked our meals in the basement. One day, I opened a cupboard and in the corner was another aqua-blue pill bottle. Hmm. Mimi left her pills in the basement.

Next time I saw her, I asked.

"They aren't mine. Somebody else must be pregnant," Mimi said. We burst into giggles. What a den of iniquity! Laughing felt good after weeks of tension and uncertainty.

"Let's go see whose they are."

We sneaked downstairs into the gloom of the basement. It was deserted, so I reached for the bottle and read the label aloud.

"Trudie Anthony."

They were Trudie's! Three of us girls were now pregnant. Trudie hadn't said a word to us. Her boyfriend, John, graduated and moved down south for work. Again, we broke into giggles.

⌘

Bob and I needed to find an apartment. Since neither of us had a full-time job, it had to be as cheap as possible. We added the expense of the doctor's bill to our meager budget. Insurance didn't cover prenatal care for babies conceived out-of-wedlock. We figured together we could pay no more than two hundred a month for rent and groceries. Bob paid for a phone and we both had cars to keep up even though Bob's broke down regularly. His Falcon had broken down so often he junked it and now drove an ancient VW mini-bus that someone repainted lime green and white with obvious brush marks. It didn't run any better than the Falcon. Bob had to push it to get it started, but VWs were all the rage now.

We found a couple of big houses in Kent, the kind with wide front porches and huge backyards. I fell in love with one, a white three-story on Main Street. My dream home. It would probably cost at least four hundred a month to heat. We kept looking.

Bob called early one evening. "I found something in Tallmadge. It's only one twenty-five." Tallmadge was a small town twenty minutes from campus toward Akron.

We went to see it the next morning. Northeast Avenue was on the route to Kent. Not bad, I thought, even if it wasn't in the heart of Kent like I wanted. The landlord was a sixty-something lady, short and fat. Her greasy gray hair was tied back in a ponytail. She barreled into the driveway in an old white Ford station wagon and parked next to us.

"I'm Mrs. Miller. You called about the rental?"

We walked in together. The building held four small one-bedroom units with a hall down the middle. She guided us past a month's worth of trash spilling out of garbage cans in the back hallway. She opened the door and let us in.

The apartment had just two rooms. The larger one had living and dining room areas and a tiny linoleumed kitchen. The ancient refrigerator hung over into the living room. The bedroom was small, with an even smaller bathroom off it. The entire unit was carpeted with a buckling gray rug that showed every piece of lint and debris. We hesitated, so Mrs. Miller jumped in.

"I'll let you have the furnishings for only $25 a month extra."

I gave Bob a pained look. "Let me think," I said.

My grandmother had the same couch in her old house in downtown Akron. "The Chesterfield," she called it. Besides the couch, which was maroon with doilies on the back and arms, there was a dinette set, two dressers, and a double bed. At least we wouldn't have to borrow furniture.

Bob was in a negotiating mode. "We'll call you."

"Don't wait too long. These units go fast."

As we pulled away, I let out a long sigh.

Bob gave me a sideways grin. "How about that ponytail?"

We burst out laughing. We couldn't help ourselves. Nothing else seemed funny lately.

"Listen," he reasoned with me. "We haven't seen anything cheaper." He was sold.

I didn't like living so far from campus, but the drive only took about twenty minutes. It could take longer than that to navigate Kent during rush hour.

"Let me think about it," I said again, but in my heart, I knew this would be our first home.

⌘

When I got back to Allerton, Mimi told me to call home. Mom wanted to talk to me. I called and got a surprise.

"We'd like to take you to dinner," Mom said. "Tomorrow at the Brown Derby. The one in Kent."

"Sure," I said. I was ready for a good meal, now that my morning sickness had lessened.

"Just you. Not Bob," she said.

31

On Tuesday evening I hurried to the Brown Derby after my last class. There weren't many waiting for tables. Mom and Dad stood in the lobby. They both smiled. Strained, but smiles nonetheless. We weren't a hugging family, but Mom reached out to put her arm around me, then stopped herself. Dad avoided eye contact. Something was up.

They seated us quickly. I already knew what I wanted. I had ordered the same meal here since I turned thirteen.

"Steak, baked potato, and salad." I could hold down more food lately, especially at night. This would be a feast. I began telling them about the apartment, but Mom cut me off.

"We've been thinking about you a lot, Patty," she began. "We have an idea."

Oh, no. It was never good when she called me by name. The *we* was a bad sign too. It usually meant *her* with Dad as an unwitting accomplice. What was going on?

"If you want to," she continued, sounding as enticing as possible, "you can go to Germany."

I was confused. Mark was stationed in Germany near Munich. Did they want me to drop out of school and move in with Mark and his young wife, Anna? I was a quarter away from graduating. Why would I do that?

While my mother spun this idea, Dad sat nodding. The waiter brought our food, and it sat there growing cold.

I was disgusted by her suggestion. "You want me to leave the baby in Germany?" I asked incredulously.

"Yes, you could put it up for adoption," Dad added in his most reassuring voice.

Am I the only one who thinks this is a crazy idea? I was so mad. I tried to hold back the tears.

"No," I said emphatically. I wouldn't dignify their proposal by arguing with them. *How do they come up with these things?* Suddenly the baby which had been a theoretical concept until now became real. My baby? No way am I giving it up!

Mom continued calmly. "You and Bob have had some rough times. We want to give you another option."

Okay, that was reasonable, but I was furious. "We're fine. Everything will work out. We can handle this."

The rest of the dinner passed in silence. I glared at my parents. *How dare they try to split us up?* Glad I hadn't told Bob about this dinner, at least now I wouldn't need to explain their idea to him.

"We love each other. It will be fine."

Mom and Dad struggled to make small talk about the family. I was so angry, it was all I could do to sit there without screaming or crying. I choked down my steak, determined not to let this one good meal go to waste. We said good-bye in the parking lot. I could barely look them in the eyes.

⌘

Back at Allerton, Mimi was still awake. "What did they want?" she asked, one step ahead of me.

"You won't believe this," I said angrily. "They want me to give the baby away."

"What do you mean?" She attempted to calm me down, her voice steady. At least she kept her head.

"They want me to have the baby in Germany and put it up for adoption."

She stared at me in disbelief then burst out laughing. "Well, are you going to?"

The absurdity of the whole situation hit me. I laughed through my tears. I couldn't tell if I was more hurt or angry.

"Of course not. We're getting married." Any doubts about Bob and our relationship faded away. Money problems, unpredictability, and intermittent squabbling aside, I was totally committed. Marriage it would be.

⌘

There was one thing left to do before the wedding. Bob's parents still didn't know about the pregnancy. We were being dishonest if we didn't tell them. I urged Bob to call, but he ignored me.

One night while we studied upstairs in Taylor Hall, I decided I couldn't stand the suspense anymore. "Let's call your parents tonight. We can use that phone," I said, pointing to the pay phone down the hallway, pleased I'd come up with a plan.

"That's not a good idea." Bob hesitated. "You don't know them the way I do. They won't understand." By understand I guess he meant they wouldn't accept the news that I was pregnant.

Heedless, I continued. "We're lying to them, tricking them." I gave him a look of guilty misery.

Bob looked at me in dismay. "Dishonesty is good sometimes."

He wasn't joking, but I saw his fear of them as a character flaw. In my world, honesty was best, even if it meant trouble. I would not stop until I got my way.

He sighed with resignation. "I'll call them. We'll need to call collect. I don't have any money on me."

Maybe he thought the no money remark would stop me.

He dialed the number. I stood by his side, so I could listen in. Jim answered.

"Can you put Mom on?"

After a minute, Mary picked up the extension. "Hi, Bob, what's up?" Now they were both on the line.

"Well, the wedding plans are coming along fine, but we want to tell you one other thing."

Silence.

"Patty's pregnant." He gulped. "That's why we're getting married as soon as we can."

More silence.

"We wanted to tell you before the wedding."

We stood in the hallway, waiting for some response, some acknowledgment. It never came.

"Well, okay," Bob stammered. "Good-bye." He hung up.

A chill went through me. I shook my head.

He drove me back to Allerton in silence. Yelling would be better than this. Bob was right about his parents all along. Honesty wasn't the best policy with them.

I hugged and kissed him before jumping out of the van, but these little gestures couldn't make up for their silent treatment. We'd need to give them time to cool off.

⌘

A few days passed, and we still hadn't heard from Bob's parents.

"They're like that," Bob said. "They'll cut me off."

I wanted to call them again, but Bob cautioned against it. He said we should just wait.

They had disowned him in the past. The way he told it, he did something perfectly normal for a teenager and they got so angry they cut him off.

I didn't know what "disowning" meant in their world. They didn't seem to have any money or property except for the house—nothing for him to inherit. Bob's explanations didn't help. I couldn't stop worrying about them.

"They're funny about things. Give them time."

I tried to ignore them. Bob did too.

"How can you stand this kind of treatment?" I asked one night as we ate supper in the basement.

He shrugged. "What else can I do? Besides, it's a relief when they don't speak to me."

Bob and his parents usually began talking again after a crisis. I hoped he didn't have to manufacture another one to get back in their good graces.

⌘

Bob told me about a conversation he had with Sandy, news director at WKSU. Sandy and his girlfriend, Cindy, married a year ago and now had a baby girl. Sandy had a real job on weekends. During the week, he was still finishing his classes.

"Sandy is having second thoughts about his marriage."

"What do you mean?"

"He told me Cindy and the baby are holding him back. He had a job offer in Virginia, but he couldn't take it because it didn't pay enough to support a family."

I shivered. Did Bob have second thoughts too? I ignored these bad feelings. We would manage somehow. We were in love, right?

⌘

The Catholic Church required Pre-Cana conferences as part of marriage preparation. They were held for groups of couples who'd be marrying soon, but since ours was the only wedding booked at the Newman Center, we had Father White to ourselves. The newly ordained chaplain of the campus ministry, he was young and baby-faced. We kept my pregnancy a secret. Every time the subject turned to marital relations we both giggled, more out of embarrassment than naughtiness. What could he know about sex?

I held my breath to keep from laughing as he rambled on. Our life wasn't much different now from that promoted by the Church: celibacy before marriage. We had stopped having sex when I discovered I was pregnant, mostly because my morning sickness lasted all day. Now, we kissed and held hands. Neither of us was afraid of sex, but morning sickness was incompatible with lovemaking.

Both of us were working and finishing school so we didn't spend a lot of time together. One evening we met for dinner. Worried about our finances, I asked Bob to drop out of school and find a full-time job. I'd suggested this to him before, but he always resisted.

After dinner, Bob drove me back to Mrs. Butler's. While we sat in his van in the driveway, I tried one last time to talk to him about getting a job.

"I'm not getting another job." He said adamantly. "I already have two jobs. I'm not dropping out of school. I'm graduating."

Frustrated, I played my trump card. "I'm not sure I can marry you if we won't have enough money for the baby."

That was all it took. Bob looked at me with wild-eyed anger.

"We *are* getting married," he growled threateningly, in my face. I saw a flash of metal out of the corner of my eye. Bob waved a jackknife at me.

What the hell? I'd never seen him with a knife before. I was scared. *Where did he get it?* I shrank back against the door.

"I'll . . . I'll cut up your coat!" he stammered and stabbed his knife at my maxi coat.

Even if he tried, he couldn't make much of a dent in it with such a puny knife. The idea that he thought he could intimidate me stirred up the rebel in me. My plot for him to quit school backfired.

I breathed in deeply before saying anything. In the instant that breath took, I saw how desperate he was. I shook. I was worried that he'd escalated so fast, from calm conversation to threat. This was crazy. If Bob could do this, what else might he try?

I retreated from my manipulation and tried to calm him down.

"I'm sorry. Never mind what I said. Of course, we're getting married," I said as I reached behind, fumbling for the door handle.

Casually, I opened the door, said good-bye and edged out of the van. I was shaking. I wasn't scared of the knife, but I'd accidentally gotten a laser-like glimpse into the workings of Bob's psyche and what our marriage might be like.

He was a scared little boy. But not the kind of boy I could push around. I had to be very careful around him. I needed to marry him to keep me and the baby safe. Bob let me leave. He didn't know how much he'd upset me.

I couldn't get inside fast enough. Mimi looked concerned when she saw my face. "How are things?"

She couldn't read my mind, but she sensed something.

"Fine," I said with a wry smile. I tossed and turned that night wondering how he could be so meek with his parents and so aggressive with me. I hoped going ahead with the marriage would calm him and that married life would melt his insecurities. His behavior frightened me. There had been his stakeout watching my every move late at night. Now the threat with the knife. I conveniently forgot about the other things he had done.

133

I prayed the next few weeks would pass quickly with no more drama. I kept my doubts to myself and tried not to do anything else that might provoke him.

32

On Sunday, I lay on my bed studying English Lit. I did badly on the midterm. The class started at 8:00 A.M. and I still fought morning sickness. I had cut a lot of Lit classes, but I wanted to pass this class.

Bob came to pick me up at 2:00. We were having dinner with our friends, Pauly and Caroline. I wasn't sure why we were getting together so early. Maybe we would play Hearts before we ate. Bob dropped me off at the entrance to their building then stayed behind fooling with the car. I shrugged, rode the elevator up and knocked.

"Hi! Come on in." Caroline smiled.

"Surprise!"

Friends and relatives packed the tiny living room. Gasping, I tried to hold back tears as I sagged onto the entryway bench to catch my breath. A bridal shower!

Bob, who came in behind me, laughed at my reaction. He and Pauly left. Caroline grabbed my hand and showed me to a chair in the center of the room. At least ten people were there: Mom, Jenny, Aunt Gert, Mimi, and two of our housemates. Mary and the disk jockeys' girlfriends were there too.

I was so happy these women cared enough to come and support me. No one guessed I was pregnant. *Showers were a normal thing, right?* We could be a normal couple. Even Mary was cordial. I settled down a little.

⌘

Winter quarter ended the week before the wedding. I turned in my papers and sat for my final exams. Bob did too. Friday night I moved out of Mrs. Butler's and back home. The twentieth, our wedding day, was next Friday. We would honeymoon then move to the apartment in Tallmadge.

Back home, everyone was on their best behavior. We had a week for dress fittings and last-minute wedding preparations. I loved my dress. It was floor-length and pure white with an empire waist, perfect for hiding my little pooch of a stomach. Jenny's dress was long too and pale pink, with a layer of see-through organza on top. Bob and his best man would wear tuxes. Jenny would be my maid of honor and Jerry, Bob's high-school friend, his best man.

⌘

After the rehearsal, Jim and Mary hosted dinner at the Kentwood, a hip restaurant a mile up the road from the Newman Center.

This would be the first time I saw or talked to Bob's dad since that disastrous phone call six weeks ago. The Turners looked at us like we stunk. They hadn't forgiven us. Bob ignored them. He was his smiling genial self, cracking jokes.

Jerry proposed a toast, "To the best friend a guy could ever have—and his woman."

Afterward, Jim and Mary kept their distance.

"See you tomorrow night," Mary said.

Bob and I kissed good-bye before we left. Glowing with happiness, I breathed a sigh of relief as I turned on to the road home.

"I'm just glad we're done," I said to Jenny, my passenger. She wasn't privy to any of the drama going on and I kept it from her.

⌘

Friday, March twentieth, dawned icy and cold, more like January than the first day of spring. Mom was an optimist picking this date. The wedding didn't start until 8:00 P.M. giving out-of-town guests time to arrive. We had the whole day to kill. Everyone went about their normal lives while I fussed over the wedding details. I fixed my hair and makeup, packed a small overnight bag for the honeymoon and put my going-away outfit, a powder blue pantsuit, in the back of the car. I'd wait until later to hang my dress, draped with a bedsheet in the back of the car.

"Eat a snack," Mom ordered before we left for the Newman Center. Guess she worried about the baby. Jenny and I would change into our gowns there.

⌘

The parking lot was slippery, filled with hacked up ice. Navigating it without falling was a trick since I left my boots at home. We had plenty of time after we changed to stand around and act nervous. Bob came on his own.

Mom and Jenny helped me dress. My gown looked beautiful, long and flowing. Mom made the veil as we couldn't find one that looked good on me. She arranged it around my face. The dress hid much of my belly. Jenny still didn't know I was expecting, and Mom held her tongue.

We dressed in the restroom then walked to the vestibule. The flower lady waited there. The church was modern with a stylized blond wooden cross hanging behind the altar. There were a few wooden statues, the Blessed Mother, Jesus, and Joseph. Bob and I wanted the Beatles "Let It Be" for my trip to Mary's altar, but Mimi, our organist, didn't think Father White would approve.

In honor of the first day of spring, our bouquets cascaded wildflowers, pink and purple freesias, delicate yellow roses and lots of baby's breath. The florist handed them to us and primped my hair one last time. We stood in the back, waiting.

We'd only invited about twenty of our friends. Paul, Bill, and Doreen sat in the pews. The rest of the church was filled with family and my parents' friends. Few of the Turners' friends showed up.

Mimi craned her head around the divider that hid the organ, waiting for a signal to start. At 7:55 P.M. "Nessun Dorma" wafted through the air. Jerry peeked out of the sacristy. Mom rearranged the flowers. My brother, Tim, and Bill Donaldson, our ushers, stood in the back awaiting further direction.

Bob's parents were coming from Euclid on icy roads. Eight o'clock. They were late. The flower lady waved her hand to settle us.

"We'll wait a few more minutes," she said.

At 8:10 P.M. the Turners strolled in. They looked surprised to find us waiting for them. I remembered Mary's story about her mother-in-law showing up at their wedding in a long black funeral dress in silent protest. I feared she might do the same. Not to worry. She was dressed in robin's egg blue. No mourning black for her. Mary had made a big deal about my brother Tim's bushy Karl Marx beard. She said she wouldn't let Tim walk her down the aisle. He shaved it yesterday and even trimmed his shoulder-length hair.

In the rush to seat them, Bill Donaldson cut in front of Tim and took Mary's arm to walk her down the aisle. He sported giant mutton chops, which stretched to his chin. *Will she balk?* She rolled her eyes, gave me a *Lord help us!* look and grabbed his arm. Tim seated Mom, and we were ready to go.

Jenny was radiant in her pink gown, her long reddish hair swept back. She looked more sophisticated than her sixteen years.

My dress was made of satin and organza. I was lucky I could still fit into it. Dad walked me down the aisle, his black tux complimenting his pale complexion and his deep black hair.

I clutched the bouquet hard enough to snap it in two. I tried to hold back the tears brimming from my eyes. It was a long service—mass, then the wedding ceremony. I was glad there wouldn't be any incense to make me throw up.

Bob met me at the altar and as we joined hands my heart swelled with joy. We turned together and knelt on the prie-dieu. He was dashing in his tuxedo. We tried to keep things simple and that helped things go smoother now. Jenny and Jerry knelt on either side of us as the mass began. Jenny touched my back once when I giggled nervously. The whole service was a charade because I was pregnant, but there was no sense destroying the mood for my parents and the rest of the guests.

We said our vows, and I made the trip to Mary's altar to lay a single white rose at her feet. *What an impostor I was.* That rose signified purity. How far I'd fallen since my days at St. Mary's when I wanted to join the convent. I slowly walked back to the center of the altar. Then Father White turned and intoned in a solemn voice, "I now present Mr. and Mrs. Robert Turner."

Organ music soared. I might burst with happiness. We walked down the aisle, smiling. As we approached the vestibule, my Uncle Dick crept out with his movie camera lights glaring up at us.

"If your uncle doesn't get out of our way," Bob whispered in my ear, "I'll kick him in the teeth!"

A joke, I hoped.

The reception was simple too with cake, punch, Jordan almonds and mints. Tim's combo played swing music. The night blurred with good wishes and dances with relatives. Jenny caught my bouquet.

For his going-away outfit, I'd helped Bob pick out a new Carnaby Street-inspired brown suit with a yellow shirt and a brown-and-yellow striped tie. I took off my dress, which now had several footprints on the hem and donned a powder blue pantsuit with a modern art scarf of orange and blue. We said our good-byes. I was happy it was over. We could relax. We ran out the front door in a hail of rice. Shouts of hooray mixed with catcalls from Bob's friends.

I searched for Bob's beat-up VW van, our getaway car, in the parking lot. I didn't see it anywhere. Instead, in the first parking space sat a red Volkswagen convertible.

Bob pointed. "It's ours. A present from your parents."

33

Washington was our honeymoon destination, but it was too late to make it there. We drove as far as Youngstown before fatigue took over. My lids drooped. Bob was tired too.

"Let's stop here tonight. There must be ten hotels." We'd drive to D.C. tomorrow.

At the motel, I played a joke. In the bathroom, I put on long underwear that covered me completely. I flung the door open dramatically and made my entrance into the bedroom. Bob wasn't amused. He stared. *Oops.* I quickly shed the underwear. We fell into each other's arms and made love for the first time as man and wife. He was tender and gentle. Soon our rhythms synchronized, and we were both satisfied.

Though March was still wintry back in Ohio, Washington burst with daffodils and tulips. We visited the White House, the Smithsonian.

We stayed at a motel right off the beltway in Virginia, across from the Iwo Jima Memorial. Ironically, it was named the Iwo Jima Motor Hotel. The room, though not sexy, was patriotic. The shower curtain sported a print of the Memorial, soldiers raising the flag on Iwo Jima. This provoked endless jokes from Bob.

"Would you like to see me raise my flag?"

On our last night in D.C., we ate at a Chinese restaurant across the street from the motel. "Try sweet and sour pork," Bob said.

Delicious. At the end of the meal, the waitress brought us dishes of orange sherbet and fortune cookies. My fortune read *She will have a girl.* I showed it to Bob and we both nodded.

⌘

On our drive home, we figured out our finances. Altogether, we had about a thousand dollars in wedding gifts, enough for a few months of rent and utilities.

"Maybe you could land a part-time job," Bob suggested.

We tried to imagine where I might work, but I was beginning to show. Nobody would hire me while I was visibly pregnant. Not much I could do to earn any money except work at the *Stater* and *Burr* jobs I already had. The few hundred dollars I made there wouldn't help much. My unemployability made me worry more than usual. I vowed to be as thrifty as possible with grocery shopping. I hoped we could put off any big expenditures until after the baby came in September.

⌘

Spring quarter began that Monday. Both of us would graduate. We arrived home late Sunday to a chilly, dark apartment. The weather hadn't broken. I wanted our first night together in our new digs to be romantic, but when I walked into the tiny kitchen, I saw that someone had dumped Jell-O into the sink. The room was so cold, it had set. I laughed.

"What's so funny?" Bob called from the hallway where he was bringing in the suitcases.

"Someone pranked us," I said, pointing to the sink.

In the bathroom, I noticed baby corn stalks growing from the shower drain. Funny, but it was late, and we were tired.

We settled into married life. We drove to class in our clunky VW. Our schedules meshed so neither of us waited too long for the other. Bob still worked at the radio station, so he'd drive us home, eat a quick dinner and then go back to WKNT for his late shift.

I dropped by the yearbook office after class one day. I'd finished my editing job, but the office felt like home. The red light above the darkroom door shone and someone told me Jimmy, Bob's old housemate, was inside processing film. I knocked on the door and yelled *hello*.

Jimmy called back, "Who's that?"

After a few minutes, he opened the door and pulled me in. He put his arms around me. I pushed him away. He'd never done this before.

"I'm married now," I said, reminding him of the obvious.

"I know, but I can say hello, can't I?" he said sweetly. He grabbed my waist and lifted me up to the counter. The whole place smelled of Dektol.

"What are you doing?" I protested.

"I want to look at you," he said.

"I'm pregnant."

"Bob told me." He pulled the front of my slacks away from my belly. "I just want to look."

Flustered, I tried to push his hand away. I didn't show that much, anyway. He kissed my stomach, then put me down gently. It was erotic but strange.

"Got to go." I gulped as I rushed out the door.

Bob and I were happy. I didn't need any interference from an old housemate. The pressure of the wedding eased, and we could relax.

⌘

One Saturday morning I got up early to shower. The hot water felt good as I washed my hair. Suddenly, ice water poured down on me from above. *Strange. Someone must be using a lot of hot water.* I shrugged and continued, but it happened again.

Then I heard muffled laughter above me. I glanced up as Bob poured cold water over me from my large glass mixing bowl. I screamed with laughter and moved toward the corner of the small shower to get away from him. *What a joker!*

34

Spring 1970

Everything was so much simpler now that we were married. Bob continued at WKNT. He also returned to Olson's. He got kickbacks when he sold certain speakers and turntables. In the past, he used this money to buy the electronic gadgets he craved. I hoped he would continue to get them, so he didn't cut into our wedding money with his electronics purchases.

I dreamed of working for the local newspaper, the *Beacon Journal*, but the economy had slowed, and they weren't hiring. Besides, I needed to wait until the baby was born.

I kept my appointments with the obstetricians. Stein's partner, Doctor Jurnek, told me I should get used to him, as either one of them could be on call when I went to the hospital.

We applied for June graduation and ordered our caps and gowns. Now, we had to make it through spring quarter without too many glitches.

April 1970 was especially rainy and cold. Happy the apartment was small and easy to heat, I studied at the dining room table that sat in the alcove. Bob set his stereo equipment up. He played "Bridge Over Troubled Water" and every window shook.

Although he had a low lottery number, we felt secure. Nixon promised to end the War and bring the troops home. Funny that just a year earlier everyone hated him and called him *Tricky Dick* during the election. Now we trusted he was trying to bring the War to an end.

It continued to rain hard, almost every day. Then we had snow and more rain. On Thursday, the thirtieth, the weather broke. The temperature soared into the seventies. That night we picked Tim up and took a ride down into the Cuyahoga Valley with the VW top down. The radio played WIXY, 1260, the oldies station, and we cruised the tree-lined roads listening to "Good Vibrations." As we drove along enjoying the warm air, there was a break in the music.

"Nixon invades Cambodia!" an announcer screamed breaking in with a special report. It took a second to realize what he meant. Instead of withdrawing our troops from Vietnam, Nixon was extending the War into another country.

"That bastard!" I yelled over the newscaster.

Tim stood up in the back seat and yelled even louder. Nixon betrayed us. He had promised to withdraw our troops from Vietnam. I was angry. Why did we ever trust him?

We yelled over the noise of the car and the radio. *We must do something before more lives are lost.* As a journalist, I had observed the antiwar demonstrations. Now I was galvanized. We dropped Tim off and headed for home.

Friday, students rallied on the front lawn of the campus to bury the Constitution to protest Nixon's invasion of Cambodia without a declaration of war from Congress. We didn't find out about the rally until too late.

"I wanted to go," I told Bob, disappointed. Frank's taunts came back to me and I found myself agreeing with him. I couldn't stand on the sidelines anymore. Life was passing me by while I watched. I needed to act, not observe.

When the bars closed that night, a disturbance erupted on Water Street. Rioters broke windows and started fires in trash cans. Something big was happening. Another rally was rumored for Saturday night on the Commons. Bob was reluctant to let me go.

"Stay home. You're almost five months pregnant. I don't want you up there getting hurt."

"I'll be all right. I really want to go," I argued.

He relented. He would cover the rally for the campus radio station. "Don't act like you're a reporter," he said. We'd heard stories about reporters and photographers being beaten up at rallies. Bob ran a mike cable down his arm, taped a small microphone to his hand and put on his lightweight jacket to conceal it. He hung his bulky cassette recorder from a strap around his neck and tucked it under his jacket.

A march would form near Music and Speech and wend its way over to the Commons. The protesters congregated as we pulled in and parked. A motley clump of characters with a few protest signs, flashlights and candles formed a line and started walking.

Chants of "One, two, three, four, we don't want your fucking war!" predominated.

The marchers passed Tri-Towers, the newest residence halls, and then walked toward Lake and Johnson, picking up more people as they went. Twilight made it almost too dark to see faces. The march ended on the Commons where the Victory Bell stood at the edge of Blanket Hill. People milled around aimlessly waiting for something to happen. There'd usually be a speaker droning on about Nixon, the War and the loss of lives, but since this march was impromptu, no speaker appeared. Staid professor-types observed while coeds shouted in the carnival-like atmosphere, just happy to be outside in the warm weather. Everybody laughed and cheered at the antics of the crazies who pelted the ROTC buildings with rocks.

Bob whispered commentary into the mike he held in his palm, quietly describing the scene. He was recording a cassette tape he could edit and air later. I stood next to him taking it all in. People gathered in small groups, some around the ROTC Quonset huts and others at the Victory Bell. *What would happen next?* The protest looked like it was losing steam and the crowd began to break up.

Then out of the corner of my eye, I saw someone run toward the closest building. In the twilight, I could barely make out a skinny guy wearing a red headband. He tossed something onto the roof of the wooden building, but it rolled down the slanted roof and dropped to the ground. He raced over and to pick it up. If it was a Molotov cocktail, it was a poor attempt at one.

He threw it again and this time instead of hitting the roof, the bottle smashed a window. The curtains caught fire.

A roar rippled through the crowd. They cheered the fire.

Within a few minutes, a fire truck pulled up and parked on the drive near the building.

Firemen fed out their hoses amid cheers and jeers. The crowd broke ranks to let them through. They closed in on the building and the hose came alive.

Flames climbed to the roof, but the firemen doused them. It looked like they could extinguish it, but just as the biggest part of the wet stream hit the fire the hose sputtered and died. A murmur flew through the crowd. Someone had cut the hose. It slackened. A minute later, the firemen rolled it up. They climbed into their truck and left. The crowd began to break up.

"Let's get you home," Bob said protectively. It was almost midnight and I was tired. We walked the few blocks to our car at Music and Speech. The excitement was over.

⌘

Early Sunday morning I went out to the driveway for the newspaper. I wanted to read about Saturday night. To my surprise, a picture of the ROTC building burnt to the ground graced the front page. Someone had cut the fire hoses with a machete.

I had to see the ruins myself. After Mass at the Newman Center, we returned to the Commons. The area surrounding the building was roped off.

It was still smoldering. I was shocked at the gaping hole in the ground where it once stood. Uniformed men guarded the perimeter. In the distance, a tank was parked on the street behind the Administration Building. It was the National Guard.

"The Guard showed up last night," a gawker told us. That would explain the tank.

The atmosphere was holiday-like around the burned-out building. Lots of students walked about, but there were also families with tots in strollers and baby carriages out for Sunday strolls. Everyone stopped to stare as they walked past. We watched the merriment then left for home. That afternoon Governor Rhodes toured the site and vowed in a press conference to use "any force necessary" to keep the schools open despite the demonstrations.

Later, Bob talked to the news director at WKSU. He needed reporters on the scene in case things deteriorated, so Bob got ready to return to campus.

I wanted to go too, but he said, "Stay home. You'll be safe here." He bent and gave me a good-bye kiss. "I don't want you getting a dose of teargas in your condition." The Guard had used gas during their last assignment, a Teamsters strike. Bob planned to start at Music and Speech and walk behind the crowd just like last night.

I spent a boring evening in front of the TV.

He called after eleven to tell me he'd made a full circle of campus with his tape recorder on and ended up in the parking lot again.

"The Guardsmen bayoneted someone near the front gate," he said excitedly.

I heard a thumping noise in the background.

"That's a helicopter. The blades are beating the smoke down on everybody. It's hard to breathe." He sounded disgusted.

He came home so late I was already asleep. He woke me long enough to tell his story again. He had an acrid smell about him. Teargas.

35

Monday, May 4, 8:30 A.M.

I jumped into the car. I had missed so much on Sunday night. The usual Monday blahs disappeared. Glad to be back on campus, I even wore a new sailcloth dress, a pretty green one I'd sewn myself to hide my pregnancy. The sky was blue, the weather warm—so different from the cold rain of the past few weeks. Bob dropped me off in front of Taylor Hall, where I would take yearbook reservations as part of my job as a *Chestnut Burr* editor.

"Don't go to any rallies today. Stay inside," he warned me.

"I'm just selling yearbooks. Don't worry." Before I went in, I had to check the ROTC building, the one burned on Saturday night. I crouched to peer under the branches of trees dotting Blanket Hill. It was still there, smoldering, and the National Guard was still in place, protecting it.

I set up the reservation table in the Journalism Library but had few visitors. There wasn't much to entertain me.

At 11:30 A.M. the Victory Bell clanged, calling students to the noon rally. I sat listening and wondered what I was missing. Finally, I couldn't resist the clanging any longer and left my post. Outside, Greeks mixed with hippies on the sidewalk behind Taylor, chanting. "One, two, three, four! We don't want your fucking war!"

Shocked, I watched as sorority girls, who in different circumstances might be dating a guardsman, yelled profanities. We were so far away from the ROTC building I doubted anyone could hear them.

Ironic. The Guard's occupation transformed our campus from a quiet Midwestern backwater into a hotbed of anti-war activity. The protesters were angry, yelling for the Guard to leave. The Guard bayonetted students on Sunday night at a sit-in on Main Street, and now they were telling us we couldn't assemble.

Anger gave way to excitement in the warmth of a sunny spring day. All around me students laughed and shouted as if they were at a pep rally. "Pigs off campus!" they yelled in a singsong.

A jeep filled with guardsmen left the safety of the ROTC building and drove toward us. One of the Guard held a bullhorn and as the jeep approached the Victory Bell, he yelled into it. Jeers from the crowd drowned out most of what he said, but I caught a phrase. *Was he saying, "This assembly is illegal"?*

The students stood their ground. "Pigs off campus!" they yelled.

The warning was too late. Hundreds of protesters ranged along Blanket Hill. *No way could a jeep full of guardsmen disperse them.*

I didn't want to go back inside. *What would happen? Could a group of students make the Guard leave?*

After the jeep retreated, a contingent of Guard marched toward us. They stopped. One of them shot off a rocket. *Teargas.* Bob told me what happened last night when the helicopters beat teargas down on the crowd, but I wasn't prepared for its effects. A canister landed near the Victory Bell, shy of the demonstrators, who jeered and hooted. The mild breeze blew the gas away from the hill.

A skinny guy with a red bandana grabbed the canister and tossed it back at the Guard. The crowd erupted in wild laughter and cheers.

But then the wind changed direction, and the teargas wafted toward us. Tears gushed from my blinded eyes. I was afraid I'd miss something, but I had to wash it out. Reluctantly, I ran inside to the first-floor bathroom. Girls trying to escape milled about. I bent over a sink and washed the sting away. *Could teargas hurt the baby?*

Back outside, the crowd on the hill had vanished. *Did they give up?* I walked to the side of the building and looked around. A few stragglers trailed over the crest and out of sight.

Was the confrontation over? Should I go inside? No, I wanted to see what would happen. The heat was beginning to wear on me as I climbed the hill, following the muffled sounds from the other side. At the top, I saw the guardsmen. They had marched through the crowd, toward the practice football field.

They traveled across the field to a fence, which blocked their exit. I laughed, knowing they'd be forced to turn around and come back. With their gas masks and riot gear, they looked ridiculous. This was a college campus, not the inner-city.

I started down the tree root-filled hill as I watched the Guard. At five months pregnant, I wasn't sure-footed and tried not to trip. I worried more about falling than the guardsmen and where they were. When they hit the fence, they turned around and marched back.

In the Prentice Hall parking lot near the end of the field, a rag top VW decorated with stick-on flowers was parked in the first slot. Nearby, a few denim-shirted protesters waved flags as they ran at the Guard, making fools of themselves. For a moment the guardsmen paused, kneeled, and took aim at the flag wavers. *Crazy.* But then the moment passed, and they rose and continued their march. *Were they returning to the Commons?*

As the Guard retreated, the students kept up their taunts. "One, two, three, four . . . Pigs off campus! Kill the pigs!" It was like an out-of-control panty raid, the silly alongside the profane.

I reached the concrete walkway and passed behind the metal sculpture. With my back turned, I lost track of the retreating guardsmen. I kept walking, avoiding the few protesters who surged forward.

As I walked along, I heard a pop behind me and then a long series of pops. *A string of firecrackers?* I looked over my shoulder. My gut seized. They were shooting! The Guard kneeled at the crest of the hill. They were aiming their guns and firing. Smoke puffs erupted from their rifles. *Blanks?*

All around me, people hit the dirt. *Maybe blanks could hurt.* I didn't want to get my new dress dirty, so I continued my walk to a set of stairs. I lay down just as the firing stopped.

After a few seconds, I peeked to see if it was safe. Everyone was still plastered to the ground in eerie silence. No jeering. No chants. I was more angry than frightened. *How stupid of them to fire, even if they were blanks.*

Then people started to stir. I stood and looked around.

A few feet away, a boy lay in the parking lot drive. *Did he trip?* He wasn't moving. A trickle of dark blood seeped from his head onto the pavement. He was on his stomach and it was hard to tell what had happened to him. *He must have fallen.* Other people weren't getting up either. One lay by the metal sculpture where I'd just been walking. There was another person lying by the Volkswagen. *A turned ankle?*

I counted aloud those who were still down. "One, two, three . . ." but every time I got to seven or eight, I shook my head. *Too many.*

Then one of the flag wavers walked over to the guy face down in the driveway. He flipped him over onto his back. His face was a bloody gash. *Oh, my God.* He looked like he had been shot! I was horrified. I started to shake.

Were they firing real bullets? Impossible. My brain wasn't working right. I counted again. *Eight? No, that's too many.* In a haze of disbelief, I took a breath and started over.

36

What am I doing out here? How can I be so stupid? I could have killed the baby. I wanted to leave before anything else happened.

Call Bob, I've got to call Bob! The pay phone in Taylor Hall was free. I fished a dime out of my purse and dialed. He answered on the second ring. *Thank God, he was still home.*

"Turn on the TV. The Guard just shot some students," I said, trying to stay calm.

Bob didn't get it. "They weren't shot. The Guard bayoneted them last night."

"No. Just now! They shot at us!" I yelled. "Turn on the TV." The phone went dead. No matter how many times I tried, I couldn't get another dial tone. He had to come to pick me up.

I wandered back toward the double glass doors that led to the Taylor porch. Chaos reigned outside. Hundreds still milled about. I didn't want to go back out there, afraid of what might happen next. At a loss, I went downstairs to the *Stater* offices. Maybe their phones would work. Paul, the former editor, and two freshmen sat at the horseshoe table revising copy for the next day's paper.

"The Guard just shot some people," I announced. They looked up at me blankly. What I'd said didn't register.

Paul shook his head. "No. They bayoneted students by the Main Street gate last night." Just like Bob. They didn't believe me. They turned back to editing copy. I reached across a desk and picked up a phone. Dead. My mind raced. Why was I wasting time here? *They'll know soon enough.*

Upstairs again, I was torn. I wanted to stay safe but also wanted to see what was going on. I needed to scream and cry, but I was too numb. It was too much to take in. I stuck my head out the door. Sirens blared in the distance. About fifteen minutes had passed since the shooting and the emergency vehicles began arriving.

"Clear a path!" someone yelled, as the ambulances edged through the crowd. I watched as drivers loaded bodies into emergency vehicles, which looked like hearses.

With the bodies loaded, they left. Hundreds stood around, unsure of what to do. A hippie with a homemade flag danced over to the pool of blood that lingered where the boy with the head wound had lain. He dragged his flag through the pool of blood and waved it in the air. People flinched to avoid the splatter.

The crowd drifted toward Blanket Hill. I began to follow them, but as I did a small group of guardsmen appeared toward the rear of the parking lot. They tried to stop us from returning to the Hill. They acted like they didn't know what just happened. People ignored their commands. The rule of law was broken.

On Blanket Hill, people sat bunched together, two or three hundred in a clump facing the Guard. People chanted as the jeep returned. "One, two, three, four!"

"You must disperse!" came the warning through the bullhorn. "This is an illegal assembly. The campus is closed. You must leave."

Nobody moved. The mood changed. The party atmosphere was gone. The protesters were grim. More people streamed around the building then sat on the grass. "We don't want your fucking war!"

Minutes passed, and the crowd remained immobile, except for the chanting.

"Pigs off campus!" Two people sitting beside me, a scruffily dressed boy and girl, talked about storming the Guard.

In the confusion, I couldn't see any leaders. No one knew how many had been shot. Students? Guard? People screamed and yelled with grief. Would this be a long standoff?

The bastards! Why did they fire?

Just then, one of the most respected teachers on campus, a geology professor, Glenn Frank, appeared midway up the Hill. He held a bullhorn and began pleading with the students.

"I'm begging you." He yelled in a voice strangled with emotion, "If you don't disperse, they will move in and there can only be a slaughter. Jesus Christ. I don't want to be part of this!" Tears streamed down his face. His voice broke.

I was bewildered. *How can they shut down our school?* No matter how crazy this command sounded I stood, but I had nowhere to go. The crowd began to disperse. People started walking, so I did too. I didn't know where to go, not living on campus anymore.

I walked down the path leading to Bowman Hall, simply because the crowd flowed in that direction.

Even though the Guard threatened mayhem, the students moved like molasses. Behind me, I heard familiar voices. I turned and saw Lanny and Allan, two yearbook staff mates, carrying their cameras.

"I don't have a car. I need to get home," I said.

"Come with us," said Lanny, "back to our apartment. You can call Bob from there."

Relieved, I joined in with them. They lived a block off campus.

The crowd was deadly quiet as we walked along. In a few minutes, we arrived. Lanny started to unlock the door, but it swung open on its own. There were lots of people inside besides the usual occupants. "Sal left for the *Beacon* and John is on his way back to Pennsylvania." Sal and John were their other roommates, both photographers who probably had footage of the confrontation.

I had seen Sal and John taking pictures outside Taylor right after the shooting. They must have wanted to protect their film.

Good. The photographers got out. The shootings would be recorded for history. People would know what happened.

The phone lines were still dead. It was after 2:00 P.M. I thought of walking the five miles to Tallmadge but feared what might be happening in the streets. Who knew whether the Guard would start firing again?

Students came and went from the apartment. Word filtered in that the City of Kent was shut down. No one was permitted to enter. I couldn't imagine that everyone who had been on campus today had already left. We speculated on how to catch a ride home.

Plenty of others needed to make calls too, so we took turns trying to call out, but the line was still dead. We sat in the living room unsure of what to do next. Someone turned on the radio and TV and everyone listened intently but getting any news beyond "Shots fired at Kent State" was impossible. Reports aired that guardsmen were shot. No one was sure what happened. Even as an eyewitness, I couldn't tell who was injured and who was dead. People focused on getting out of Kent rather than on the shootings.

I called home again around 3:00 P.M. and this time, without me hearing a dial tone or any ringing, Bob answered. Afraid the phone would go dead again, I blurted out information fast.

"I'm at Al and Lanny's apartment. Come get me!"

"Kent is closed," he said. "Nobody can drive in. I can't pick you up. Are you all right?"

"Yes, I'm not hurt." I resigned myself to stay the night in Kent. Luckily all those days of morning sickness and extra peeing were behind me. My body was fine, and I could manage overnight.

The hours dragged by as people drifted through the apartment. This set of buildings was dense with students. With the door open, we watched as a steady stream of people carried boxes and suitcases down the stairs.

A couple of Al's friends dropped by around 5:30 P.M.

"We're leaving for Akron. Anybody want a ride?" the long-haired guy asked.

I jumped up. "I do. To Tallmadge."

Their rusted-out clunker waited in the parking lot. I figured I'd chance it, as it only needed to go five miles. I climbed in and we left. Within fifteen minutes we pulled into our driveway. Bob ran out and hugged me tightly.

"Are you okay?" He didn't let go.

"Yes," I said, shakily, wrapping my arms around him. I told him of my ordeal.

"I was right in front of the Guard when they fired. The guy next to me got shot in the chest. I was so scared! I couldn't get anyone in the *Stater* office to believe me. It was a madhouse. I didn't know what to do." I went on for hours with crazed energy.

Bob held me close.

Slowly it dawned on me. *I am carrying a baby, another life. Today I put that baby, my baby, in grave danger. We are both lucky to be alive.* I shuddered at what might have been. I felt protective of the life growing inside me. *How could I let this happen? I risked this tiny life.* The baby was all I cared about. I felt motherly at last.

Bob focused intensely on me. He didn't let me out of his sight. *He loves me. Everything will be all right.*

I got chills when I thought of what I had done. What was I thinking risking my baby's life like that? May 4 was the day I became a mother. No matter what else happened, my job was to protect my child. I didn't tell anyone about this change in me. Ashamed that I had risked so much, I resolved not to act so foolishly again.

That night I fell into a deep sleep, uncluttered by dreams.

37

May 5, 1970

The school was shut down. Kent was sealed off. I couldn't stop talking about the shootings, reliving them over and over. I kept the part about the baby to myself. I was alive and safe. Going to the rally was a mistake.

Now anger at the Guard overwhelmed me. How could they shoot at unarmed students? There would be no mass catharsis for us because we had been separated and sent home. Left to deal with the aftermath alone we hung on the news reports.

The media exploded with interviews of anyone vaguely connected to Kent. They ran on television. Even if they were miles from campus yesterday, suddenly everyone claimed to be an eyewitness. Reports were that there were two guardsmen and two students dead. It would be another day before there was an accurate count: four students were killed and eleven injured. The dead were Allison Krause, Sandra Scheuer, Jeffrey Miller, and William Schroeder, all students. No guardsmen were killed or injured. No one knew what provoked the shootings. A sniper? An order to fire? A plot? And how many were shot but not killed? It would be months before a reliable account came out.

⌘

With only one car, I sat home glued to the TV while Bob worked. No one knew how long the campus would be closed or whether we would graduate. How would we finish school?

I was left to deal with my raging emotions—overwhelming anger and sadness about the shootings. Surely this couldn't be good for the baby. Bob gave me extra hugs for the next couple of days. He doted on me.

Rallies and protests sprung up all over the country as colleges and universities, high schools and junior highs shut down in protest. I refused to put the baby in jeopardy again. I refused to go to any of them. Then just eleven days later it happened again.

At Jackson State in Mississippi, the police opened fire on another group of students, killing two and injuring twelve. The world had gone mad.

⌘

We were happy to escape the drudgery of our last few classes, but we missed our friends and the connection that going to school provided.

We listened to the news day and night, but the campus radio station, WKSU, shut down when the school closed, frustrating Bob.

Kent was in the spotlight now. Within a few more days the names of the injured were announced: Alan Canfora, John Cleary, Thomas Grace, Dean Kahler, Joseph Lewis, Donald McKenzie, James Russell, Robert Stamps, and Douglas Wrentmore.

Reporters from national publications interviewed local townspeople. "They all should have been shot," was the prevailing opinion. *Chilling that they hated us that much. What about our First Amendment rights?*

We visited my parents a couple of days later. They didn't know I had been standing thirty yards in front of the Guard when they fired.

I started to tell Mom. "I was there. They shot at *me*," but she interrupted.

"You were there? You should have been shot," was all she said.

Stunned, I felt even more alone. "How can you say that? I'd be dead now! Shot with an M-16? Are you crazy? I was just watching—not protesting."

"You shouldn't have been there. I don't care what you were doing." she scoffed.

Bob and I exchanged glances. My parents loved me, and they were Democrats, for God's sake. How could they turn against me? Mom didn't even like Nixon.

I wanted to argue with her and shake some sense into her, but she was adamant. I left that night feeling self-righteous. Somehow student protests were more threatening than the War.

We found out Kent would be closed until Summer Session. A week later, a large envelope came in the mail. It contained a letter from my media professor, Jerry Lewis, explaining how to complete his class. Over the next few days, letters from all our professors arrived. We would do correspondence work to finish our classes.

Graduation would still take place. At Kent, the ceremony was a big deal with thousands of students parading across the stage of the biggest auditorium on campus one by one. We had planned to invite both sets of parents. Now it would be scaled back.

⌘

"I'm so happy they are going to hold graduation," I said bouncing up the driveway from the mailbox. The notice about the ceremony had come in the mail. I waved it at Bob.

He smirked. "Not me. They can shove it. How many people do you think they'll allow in?" He hated Governor Rhodes.

"I'm just glad to be alive," I said. "Anything else is a bonus now."

The *Record-Courier,* the paper I'd worked at last spring, printed letters to the editor about the dirty lice-ridden hippies who had been taken to the ER after the shootings. Local citizens of Kent and Ravenna still voiced the opinion that all the protesters "should have been shot."

I took the moral high ground. Being the one who was shot at, I could feign indifference to Bob's fears.

"I don't care what you think. I'm going to graduation." I would be a silent reminder of the innocence of those students at the protest—a married pregnant lady, not a lice-infested hippie. We could wear our street clothes, not gowns, but I would wear mine as a badge of honor. I'd survived.

"Well, I'm not going. I'll boycott it." Bob was adamant.

I ignored him, certain he'd come around.

⌘

On graduation day I rose early and chose a bright green maternity dress to wear under my gown. Bob relented and decided to go but he wouldn't wear a gown. We drove to campus. Guards were posted at the entrances. We'd been given a half hour to park and get to the gym. The walk between the silent buildings on our way to the gym was eerie. The campus was deserted except for those attending the ceremony, and the guards.

We found a place to sit together among the thousands who showed up for the ceremony. It would take about forty-five minutes. Then we had a half hour to find our car and leave. The campus had been opened just for our graduation.

All we needed was to stand when they announced our college, Fine Arts. No walk across the stage for us. We sat patiently while the doctoral and master's students collected their diplomas. Our turn came. We stood for our half-minute of applause. I saw my parents on the far side in the bleachers applauding.

We left the auditorium together and headed for the car. On the way, Tony Sallet, a reporter for the *Beacon,* stepped in front of us.

"I'm writing an article on feelings about graduation in light of May 4."

We both rolled our eyes.

"How are you?" he asked me, ready to take down any juicy quotes in his notebook.

"I'm angry," was all I said.

But Bob needed to elaborate.

"They tried to kill us and now they expect us to be grateful. Patty was five months pregnant when they fired bullets at her. She wasn't a protester, just an observer. I'm highly insulted."

Now everybody is going to know I'm pregnant. Not too smart.

The next day the story ran on the front page of the *Beacon.* The article referred to me as "expecting." Great. Guess I'd have to live with rumors from busybodies who counted the days between the wedding and the baby's arrival.

38

Summer 1970

With graduation over, I hoped the few months before the baby arrived would be peaceful. The fallout from May 4 lingered. While I hadn't had even one nightmare about that day, I still dealt with the memories in the daytime. I couldn't stop myself from reliving my slow walk to the steps.

Bob came home from work happy. "I found a new sofa and chair. Well, two love seats and a chair. Some doctor is throwing them away."

"Wow. Furniture from a doctor's house?" We could replace Mrs. Miller's disgusting things.

"It's from his office," Bob corrected me, "Not his house. He bought new office furniture."

I didn't care. I was so tired of our ratty burgundy furniture that showed every speck of lint and dust.

"I'll pick it up tomorrow after work."

On Wednesday, I came back late from an appointment. Bob was nowhere in sight, but the new furniture sat in the living room. Orange vinyl, the color of a construction cone, it almost gave off a glow. I shook my head and laughed. At least I could wash it if it got dirty.

⌘

One day, Bob returned from downtown Kent, fuming. "I got a parking ticket. The cop pasted it on top of our peace symbol."

We'd stuck a self-adhesive peace sign on one of the back windows of the VW. Tension ran high between the students who stayed in town over the summer and the townspeople. Rumors flew that hippies were being beaten up on sight. We tried to avoid Kent for the rest of the summer. The university had reopened but with limited access. Guards still checked IDs at the few entrances open.

⌘

A special commission convened in June to investigate the campus shootings at Kent and Jackson State. The Scranton Commission, named for its chairman, Sen. William Scranton of Pennsylvania, would interview anyone who might contribute to an understanding of what occurred.

One afternoon the phone rang. It was the Akron FBI office. "We'd like to talk to you," said the agent at the other end of the line.

I was excited. We would be able to tell our side of the story. Did the FBI know about Bob's tapes? "Sure. We'll be here. Come on over."

We set an appointment for Tuesday. Bob stayed home from work even though we couldn't really afford it.

"Let's record them," he said. "We can hide my tape recorder in the bedroom and tape the whole thing." At 2:00 P.M., they knocked. We rehearsed what to do. I would answer the door as Bob started the tape recorder. I ushered the agents in. Two medium-built men sporting flattops, white short-sleeved shirts, and skinny black ties.

Bob came into the room, ready to answer questions, but they weren't interested in him at all. They wanted to talk to me.

"Were you enrolled in Doctor Lewis's media course this year?" the first agent asked.

"Yes," I said, bewildered at the direction this was taking.

"Did he ever advocate the overthrow of the United States government?"

"What?" I was dumbfounded. "He never said anything of the kind." I hoped I sounded emphatic and truthful.

They acted like they didn't believe me and asked this same question again and again in different ways.

I continued to act surprised. I hoped they understood how ridiculous their questions were, but they wouldn't let go. Was this a preliminary test with the real questions about Bob's tapes coming later?

Finally, they seemed satisfied I hadn't heard Doctor Lewis spout any Communist ideology and moved on. Then the agent asked a rambling question about the torching of the ROTC building. "On Saturday night a person threw a Molotov cocktail onto the roof of the building. Who was that?"

We both shook our heads. I didn't know. Bob didn't either.

"I don't know," I said, a little too quickly maybe because the agent repeated his question. Bob didn't know either.

"We have pictures of the suspect involved in the burning of the ROTC building," he said.

The rumors about informants taking photos must be true. The government had pictures of us.

"Can you identify any of the people who hacked the fire hoses with machetes?"

"No, it was too dark. I couldn't see a thing."

Disappointed, I wondered why they didn't ask about the shootings. The FBI agents were singular in their pursuit of evidence against the students, or agitators, as they called them. I was adamant I couldn't name anyone. So was Bob.

After an hour of questioning, the agents wound down. They closed their notebooks. They shifted around in their seats getting ready to leave. I wondered if they felt absurd interviewing a gigantically pregnant woman about May 4.

I walked them to the door and Bob slipped into the bedroom to stop the cassette recorder. He rewound it and played it back. We could barely hear the FBI over the hum of the living room fan.

⌘

Bob left me alone with the tape and my thoughts while he went to work. He returned that evening with two giant boxes. New Fisher speakers. I was stunned. *How could he spend so much money on himself when we are eating hot dogs and Jell-O four times a week?* I wouldn't speak to him, hoping he'd realize we didn't have money for toys.

⌘

I wanted to take Lamaze classes. Natural childbirth was the rage and these classes taught breathing and relaxation techniques that helped with labor pain.

"I'd like natural childbirth—no drugs," I told Doctor Stein at my next appointment.

He could hardly keep from laughing. "I don't care what you do until the delivery. From that point on, I'm in charge."

I nodded my head, not even trying to argue with him.

As I left the office, I saw a flyer for Lamaze classes laying on a table in the waiting room. The session began in two weeks.

Bob still didn't like doctors and the sight of blood made him queasy. A few weeks earlier I had to yell to get him to go to the doctor when he had a sore throat.

"I would like to take Lamaze classes," I told him one evening, keeping the topic light. He would need to be my labor coach.

Bob was less than thrilled with my idea.

"I faint at the sight of blood," he said.

39

Women had children naturally for thousands of years until the late nineteenth and early twentieth centuries when doctors and hospitals took over. In the 1930s, a natural childbirth movement arose in reaction, emphasizing birth without drugs. Lamaze was one of the childbirth techniques spawned by this movement. A book published in 1959, *Thank you, Doctor Lamaze: A mother's experiences in painless childbirth*, popularized it in the United States. Instructions in Lamaze techniques were offered in community classes.

After I found the Lamaze brochure, I talked to Bob.

"These classes will help me get ready for the birth. I really want to go." I left out the part about him needing to be there for my labor.

Our first class met on a Tuesday night in late June at the United Methodist Church, right across the road from the Newman Center. We walked into a meeting room with an assortment of couples spread out on the floor, each with a variety of pillows and towels strewn about them. We looked for open space.

"Hi, I'm Tina." The young woman sitting next to me extended her hand. "When are you due?"

"Not until September," I said as we sank to our knees and tried to find comfortable positions. I smiled as I awkwardly dropped to the floor. Bob nodded politely. I was happy we hadn't waited until the last minute to take the classes. I'd have time to practice.

The instructor supplied lots of information about what to expect during labor. Panting, shallow breathing and ice chips played a big part in minimizing "the stress of labor" as she called it. Bob said nothing. I could tell from his looks that he wasn't happy to be there.

But me? In my glory. I got the information I needed to be prepared for childbirth.

At the end of the evening, we bid good-bye to Tina and her husband and walked to the car. Bob drove silently while I bubbled with excitement.

"I'm so glad I found a group of people to talk to. I'm not so isolated anymore."

At home, I lay on the floor with pillows and practiced panting and blowing. I tried to imagine myself in pain and made myself breathe through it, whatever that meant.

"Can you help me? I asked.

"I'm busy," he said.

The next Tuesday rolled around and, miraculously, Bob had the evening free. A gorgeous night it was hot enough that all our fans turned on high. We ate supper early and left for Kent. My belly was so big now it almost touched my chin when I sat in the VW bucket seat.

"This means so much to me, for the birth to be natural," I told him as we drove up Route 261.

Suddenly Bob slammed on the brakes. I looked around but didn't see any cars near us. I couldn't imagine what he was doing. While we still rolled, he grabbed the emergency brake and pulled it hard, sending the car into a hundred-and-eighty-degree spin. Startled, I screamed. By then, we'd already spun halfway around and ended up at the foot of a large gravel pile off the opposite side of the road.

"Stop!" I yelled, but he didn't respond. We sat for a minute.

"We're going home," he said coldly.

What had I done wrong? I kept my mouth closed so I wouldn't provoke him further. We rode in silence as the dusk deepened. He spent the evening with his headphones on listening to records. He didn't follow me to bed, as usual, that night.

Bob never mentioned the incident again. What went through his mind? What could I do to fix it? I tried to talk to him, but he wasn't interested. I couldn't imagine what upset him. I was angry he put our lives at risk by spinning the car, but my anger didn't faze him.

He saw himself as an Indy driver or a young Steve McQueen. He must have had a temporary freak out fearing of blood as much as he did. Poor baby. I resolved I wouldn't bring it up again until next week.

Tuesday came and went. Bob had the day off, but he took the car to Cleveland to play poker with his high school buddies and we missed the Lamaze class. Not only did we miss it, but he didn't come home that night. He didn't show up until late the next afternoon.

I was sitting on the living room floor reading *The Godfather*, Mario Puzo's new book, when I heard his key in the lock. He walked in. Even though I was only ten feet away I didn't look up. I ignored him.

He didn't miss a step. He crossed the room toward me kicking the book out of my hand. My adrenaline surged. I was wrong to ignore him, sure, but what I had done didn't measure up to his spending the night away from home, or kicking the book, either.

Now, I couldn't ignore him. I jumped up and ran, but there wasn't much space for me to escape.

I ran into the bedroom, slammed the door and lay on the bed shaking. He'd have to come in to use the bathroom, eventually. I waited. I settled in to watch the *Phil Donahue Show* on the TV, a crazy show about atheists. After a while, Bob came into the bedroom, conciliatory.

"I didn't call you last night because it got to be too late," he said. "We played cards. I stayed overnight with Jerry."

I could choose to believe this story and carry on with our lives or dispute his explanation, at which point our marriage would fall apart. Just then I felt the baby kick inside me.

I let him kiss me. Any alternative to reconciliation would be far worse, but I began to see the downside of marriage.

⌘

Saturday, while Bob worked, I stood in the bedroom folding laundry. As I stared out the window, two motorcyclists pulled into our long driveway. They turned around and headed toward Kent.

One of them was built like Sam, the guy I had a crush on. I walked closer to the window as they made their turn onto the highway. In an instant, I saw myself riding off on the back of his cycle. Funny how such a slight resemblance fired up my desire. I sighed and returned to folding the clothes. I was still pregnant, so escape wouldn't do me much good.

⌘

July turned to August and an envelope from the Scranton Commission came. Inside was a subpoena for me to testify when the Commission met in Kent in a few weeks. There was still confusion about what caused the shooting. I wanted to share any information I had that would explain it. I was excited. But as I read the subpoena, memories came flooding back, visions of the Guard firing, the crowd running and the cries of anguish.

I'd be able to tell my story about May 4. I hoped this time wouldn't be like the FBI interview. It could only help impress them that I was almost nine months pregnant and looked like I swallowed a beach ball. What would a pregnant lady be doing at a demonstration?

40

My subpoena was for early August. I was getting huge. I hoped I could testify before the baby came.

I wore my green dress, the only maternity dress still loose enough to cover my enormous belly. A lot snugger now than on graduation day, maybe it would gain me credibility with the Commission.

Apprehensive about who I might see at the hearing, I wondered how much animosity there would be among those waiting to testify. Two months later conflict still ran high between townies and students.

Bob drove me to the Holiday Inn on the outskirts of town. An assortment of townspeople and students sat in the anteroom. Everyone stared at the floor, ignoring each other. I didn't see any-one who looked like Guard though I didn't know how I would recognize them without their gas masks.

After a few minutes, they called me into a small meeting room set up like a courtroom. Men in suits and ties sat at tables along the sides of the room while Commission members sat behind a long table. "Mrs. Turner," they called me up to the dais and asked a set of questions like those the FBI agents had asked.

I told them I couldn't identify any of the protesters. This was still true as I didn't know them beforehand and had not learned their identities since. Again, I said I never heard Jerry Lewis advocate the overthrow of the government.

Even if a professor had used seditious speech, it didn't give the Guard a license to kill innocent people. My answers didn't seem to have any impact. Was this just a charade? I left, hoping their report would provide enough evidence to bring the Guard and Governor Rhodes to justice.

⌘

I drove Bob back and forth to work a few times a week, so I would have a car during the day. One day we drove past the hospital where I'd deliver the baby.

"There's Akron General." Bob pointed to City Hospital in the distance. Out of fear he would again do something crazy, I let it slide. I didn't want another fight.

With my growing size, going to the laundromat was too hard. I took our wash to Mom and Dad's late on a Monday night in early August. I complained about constipation and backache.

Mom studied me. "The baby dropped. You'll have it soon."

I laughed off her comment. I wasn't due until September, almost a month away.

I confided in my mother about the changes in Bob's behavior. "We're having some problems." I didn't mention his crazy driving or that he spent money we didn't have.

Mom stared at me. "You made your bed, now lie in it."

I was shocked. Mom could be brutal. I decided not to pursue this conversation any further. I told myself I'd have to live with my own mistakes.

⌘

The weather was hot, and I was tired of going up and down the basement stairs with the laundry basket. Bob showed up, and we waited for the laundry to dry so we could go home.

"My back hurts," I said, rubbing it. "I'm going to call the doctor when we get home."

When we got home, I went into the apartment and climbed into bed, forgetting about the doctor. Luckily, I fell asleep. I woke at midnight feeling worse. Bob slept beside me. My back hurt more by the minute. I reached for the phone.

The answering service took my call. They found Doctor Jurnek. "I want you to go to the hospital," he said.

Surprised, I didn't want us to run up an additional hospital bill just for them to send me home. He turned down my request for a laxative and hung up.

"They want me to go to the hospital," I told Bob, who had woken and lay there listening. He got up and dressed. I grabbed a red nightgown from my top dresser drawer and threw it into my overnight bag.

City Hospital was only ten minutes away. The streets were deserted. Bob dropped me off at the Emergency Room door and parked. An orderly found a wheelchair for me. Seemed like a lot of trouble for constipation, but I didn't complain. At the desk, the worker asked for my insurance card.

"We're paying ourselves. We don't have insurance," Bob said.

The triage nurse turned to the orderly who lurked nearby, "Take her to the maternity ward."

Wait a minute. I was shocked. I thought they would check me and send me home. Bob followed me. We rode the elevator up to the fourth floor.

They quickly put me into a room.

"Put that gown on." The nurse pointed to one on the bed. I did as she told me, still convinced they would check me and send me home.

Another nurse came in and shaved my pubic hair, too soon in my opinion.

I protested, but she kept on.

"You're not leaving," she said.

I was confused. I thought they'd just check me. Now it sounded like they were keeping me.

About then, things settled down in my guts and the pain stopped. Bob came into the room. We waited. Whatever the doctor thought was happening had stopped for now.

"I want to go home," I said to the next nurse I saw.

"You can't. You'll have to wait. You're right where you should be."

Why wouldn't they let me leave?

Bob looked tired, more uncomfortable as the night dragged on. He slumped in his chair, sighing. His work started in a few hours. I was convinced they would send me home soon, shaved pubes and all. Finally, I told him to go home and rest.

"I'll call you to come to pick me up."

Bob left, and my wait began. At 3 A.M. they brought another girl into the room. I couldn't see her behind the closed curtain. After a couple of hours, her moans got louder. They took her to the delivery room. Meanwhile, nothing was happening with me. At six, a doctor checked me.

"You're only dilated three centimeters. We'll induce you."

Afraid of what this might mean, I argued with him. "I thought you would send me home."

"Nope. Not now. We'll break your water and give you a shot of Pitocin. You'll deliver by noon."

Since this was my first labor, this information didn't mean much to me. With no phone in the room, I couldn't call Bob to tell him. The doctor broke my water with something that looked like a button hook. The nurse gave me a shot.

"Now we wait. Do you want some pain medicine?"

"Oh, no thanks," I said with bravado, "I'm having a natural childbirth."

She shook her head and left.

I wondered how I could do the Lamaze exercises by myself. I hoped Bob would come back after he slept. Or maybe he'd call and they would update him. Even though he was scared of blood, he'd be back. It was his baby too.

My contractions started again. This time they were closer together and much harder, a lot more painful. I tried to do Lamaze on my own. I watched the clock on the wall, timing the contractions. I panted and blew but I wasn't dilating very fast. Two other women had gone to the delivery room since I'd been there. I must be doing something wrong.

A doctor with a retinue of students following him came in to check my progress. Behind him, each one of them lined up to stick his hand inside me to feel my cervix.

I couldn't believe this was happening. After the fourth one, I yelled, "No!" and refused any more.

Labor had lasted twelve hours so far. Bob was nowhere in sight. The contractions hurt even when I panted through them. I began to wonder about this Lamaze method. I'd ask for pain medication the next time someone came into the room.

A new nurse showed up to check me.

"Can I have some pain medication now," I said in between moans.

"Oh, honey, it's too late for that. How about something to take the edge off?"

She came back a few minutes later with a hypodermic.

Great. This will help. Frantic, I wondered where Bob was. The new medicine did help, but it made me drowsy and I fell asleep.

The pain medicine threw my timing off, something I hadn't realized. I slept through the beginning of each contraction. I didn't wake up until the contraction peaked. Then it was too late for me to benefit from the panting and blowing that helped with the pain. Now I either slept or was in so much pain I screamed with each contraction. I couldn't help it.

"Mom!" I screamed instinctively. Not that I wanted my mom, but it was the easiest thing to yell out.

"Mom!" I cried again, as loud as I could.

"Your mother's not here," said the nurse, smugly.

Embarrassed, I tried to quiet down but why was it taking so long? I remembered seeing TV shows where women gave birth in less than an hour and then went back to work in the fields. I couldn't figure out what was different with my body. I gave up on Bob.

41

My labor went on for hours, without any apparent progress. The doctors who came in to examine me called out "Three" and then later "Five." They meant the centimeters I dilated. Ten was when I would be ready to deliver.

At 7:00 P.M. the doctor who'd been checking me decided my labor was taking too long. "Take her to X-ray."

The nurse helped me climb onto a gurney. I didn't know what the problem was, and nobody told me.

As we began the trip downstairs to X-ray, I got an overwhelming urge to push. The nurse watched my face and as I started she said, "Don't. Don't push."

I learned from the Lamaze classes that if I pushed too soon, my tissue would tear, but the urge overwhelmed me, and I couldn't stop it. I pushed again, this time as we entered the elevator. She reached over and slapped me across the face.

"I told you to stop!" she yelled.

Those around us looked shocked, but I didn't care.

I was X-rayed, but something had changed on the trip downstairs and as quickly as they took me down, they took me back to Labor and Delivery. The contractions came much closer together now. I moved back to the bed, and the doctor checked me again.

"You're going to Delivery," he announced, and I breathed a sigh of relief.

This would soon be over. As we approached the delivery suite, we ran into a traffic jam in the hallway. So many gurneys were parked along the walls, we could barely get through.

At 8:00 I went into the delivery room, was prepped, and given a saddle block. Suddenly everything went dead down below, and the pain stopped. What a relief. I thought the baby would be here soon, but everything else stopped too.

"Doctor Stein isn't here yet. He says he'll be here at 8:30."

"Sit up, dear." Someone behind me gave me a little push in the small of my back.

They helped me scoot toward the end of the table and I sat with my legs dangling. I sat on the baby's head. I hoped I wasn't smothering it.

Everyone came to attention as the doctor walked in, gowned and ready to go.

"Push," he said as someone propped me up. A couple more pushes and the baby popped out.

"It's a boy!" the nurse said, cleaning him off. She laid the baby on my chest for a few seconds before taking him away. I was surprised. We thought it would be a girl. I saw a mass of wet black hair. My baby was here! After all that pain, now I felt intense joy. The doctor finished sewing me up and then I was wheeled into the hall. That's where I lay when Bob found me.

"Hey." He approached the gurney.

"It's a boy."

"A boy?" Bob was surprised too. "Is the baby all right? Somebody said one of the babies died."

"Not ours. He's in the nursery."

"Why are you out here?" Bob took my hand tenderly. I was parked in a row of gurneys lining the hallway.

"I don't know."

A nurse walked by. "No bed for you yet. We had twenty-three deliveries tonight. We usually only have fifteen or sixteen. We've been really busy."

Shortly after midnight, a bed in a ward became available and I was wheeled into a room. Bob was still there. He'd spent the day calling the wrong hospital, Akron General Hospital, not City.

"No one could find you," he said. "I didn't know what to think. A nurse finally asked what floor you were on. When I said 'third,' she told me to call City."

"Did you go to work?"

175

"No, I just stayed home trying to find you."

None of this made any sense to me, but I was so tired I didn't have the energy to argue. I lay back in the bed and tried to quit shaking. A sense of peace arrived now that the hard work was done.

Bob's tiredness from the night before vanished and he stayed by my side while I fell asleep. I woke around 3:00 A.M., famished. It had been more than thirty hours since I last ate. Bob asked the nurse for food.

"There won't be any until breakfast," she said.

We saw a Red Barn sign across the street. I told him to ask if I could eat takeout.

"Sure."

He left to buy me a Barnbuster, fries and a chocolate shake. A nurse brought the baby in early in the morning for feeding and laid him on my chest. "Are you going to breastfeed, dear?"

I nodded. "Of course, I am."

"Your milk won't come in for a few days, but you can practice while you're waiting." She showed me how to get the baby to latch on.

We didn't have a boy's name picked out. Since that night in the Chinese restaurant in Arlington, we thought we would have a girl. We had settled on "Patricia." Now we started over.

Bob went to work, leaving me alone. My parents hadn't visited yet. The nurse took the baby.

"You need to move around. You have to pee on your own before we can let you go home." I slid myself to the side of the bed to sit up. As I raised myself up, a blinding headache struck.

I told the nurse. She asked what kind of anesthesia I had.

"A saddle block."

"Oh, you have a spinal headache. Lie down. I'll tell the doctor." Thus, began a series of attempts to help rid me of the headache.

The doctor prescribed codeine for me, in pill form. Each time I swallowed a pill I threw up almost immediately. Vomiting made my headache worse and so I was stuck in a vicious cycle. Though the maternity ward was overcrowded, and I was in a room with five other mothers they kept me.

Bob visited that night. He was bewildered by my state. "The baby looks fine. I can see him through the nursery window."

We still didn't have a name picked out. Our attention turned to boys' names. For every name one of us suggested the other thought of someone with that name they didn't like.

I pleaded for Bob to contact my parents. He told me he would. "Why haven't you called them?" I was desperate to get out. Maybe mom would be able to help.

"I wanted some private time with the baby before your relatives descended."

The next day my parents came with nightgowns for me and a little outfit for the baby. Very cute.

Mom was solicitous. "A spinal headache? I had one too. It hurts. Just lie flat."

Not very encouraging, but at least they'd come to visit.

The madness with the codeine pills continued. On the fifth day, I woke with no headache. First, the nurse then the doctor came in. They were happy with my progress.

"You're out of here," the doctor said.

I dressed as soon as the nurse left to call Bob. We'd decided on a name we both liked, David. The baby looked like a Davey. An aide brought him. I dressed him in his going-home outfit, an aqua-checked onesie that he swam in. My fingers felt huge as I fumbled with the tiny snaps.

My heart swelled. *My baby! The start of our new life together.* Though by all calculations, Davey wasn't due until September, he was here now, and he was normal weight and length. I wondered whether I figured the date wrong.

Bob arrived at noon. The orderly wheeled me out the same emergency room door I came through five days earlier, this time with Davey cradled in my arms. Bob pulled the VW up.

It was a sunny August day. The fresh air rushed in through the gaps in the rag-top roof as we drove home. It was great to be alive. I clutched Davey. I'd held lots of babies, but this was different. My twenty-third birthday was the next day. The world was just beginning for me. We spent a quiet day, me caring for Davey and Bob taking care of both of us. We celebrated my birthday quietly.

I didn't expect any presents, mostly because we were broke. But I already had the best present of all, Davey.

⌘

Our life settled into a routine. Bob worked the Sunday morning shift at WKNT. I went to my parents for laundry and to visit. They set up a crib in the corner of their own bedroom where I could put Davey down for a nap.

One afternoon, Davey felt a little feverish. After putting him down I looked for a thermometer. Mom kept one in the upper drawer of her dresser. I didn't find it in the left drawer, so I pulled open the right.

I didn't find a thermometer there either, but my fingers found a piece of paper pressed against the front of the drawer. *Strange.* I pulled it out. It was a yellowed, brittle piece of stationery, folded in half. I read the letter. I was stunned.

It read like a suicide note. "Give the baby to Gert and Jerry. Take care of the kids. I'm sorry."

It wasn't signed, but it was Mom's handwriting. It went on for about a page, explaining how she couldn't go on living and gave instructions for handling her affairs.

My mind reeled. *Why would she keep this? Did she want someone to find it? Why was she going to kill herself? Who was the baby?* Guilty that I had such a laser view into my mother's soul, I hastily refolded the paper and put it back.

As I did, I was thrust into the past. Again, I was back in the kitchen watching as Mom grabbed Tim around the neck and choked him. I was so afraid I almost wet my pants. In a few seconds, it was over. Mom shook her head to clear it. Tim continued to sob, but the rest of us ignored him.

Did she write this yellowed note back then? If she did, why did she keep it?

I didn't tell anyone what I'd discovered, not even to Bob. I acted like I'd never seen this piece of paper. But I couldn't stop thinking about it. When did she write it? After one baby, me, or after several? Did she have the baby blues?

178

I was torn between scorn that she couldn't handle her own life and sympathy for how alone she must have been. Too scary to think about. I was glad I'd never had to deal with anything so bleak.

As I held the note, I remembered Dad checking with me about Mom's mood when he came home from work. I was around eight or maybe ten. I was used to him looking for me when he came home from work. He'd pull into the driveway and give me a look.

"How's Mom?" He wanted to know if she was angry or tearful or just acting crazy before he went inside.

If I said "good," he continued into the house, all smiles. If I shook my head, Dad paused a minute to compose himself before he went in.

This didn't seem strange to me. I was flattered that he relied on me. I was important. I thought Dad and I shared a secret.

But I got a creepy feeling when he took me out in the car alone. He always talked about Mom, how he loved her. He wondered aloud how he could make her happy. I knew the answer.

"She wants you to spend more time at home and help her," I told him.

Dad couldn't fit that into his reality. "I have to work. Otherwise, we'll end up in the poorhouse."

But I was unrelenting. "Mom wants you to stay home at night, not go to your second job. Stay home on Saturdays. Don't volunteer at the Knights of Columbus."

I had been thrust into the role of a marriage counselor.

⌘

I alternated between the bliss of new motherhood and frustration with Bob's spending habits. I discovered he took some of our wedding money to buy a new reel-to-reel tape deck that showed up one day. I confronted him angrily.

"How could you spend money like this? We need everything we have to pay bills."

He walked away, ignoring me. I bristled. A few days later he brought this fight up again.

"Why can't you be the way you were before we got married?" he asked.

A chill went down my spine. Why was I the bad guy?

Should I be more easy-going? Non-accusatory? Fun loving? I stewed in silence. He was the one who wrecked our finances. Why did he blame me?

42

Fall 1970

I ignored Bob's outburst. After that, time passed peacefully for us. I learned how to care for a newborn and Bob adjusted to having another mouth to feed. We had subsisted on hot dogs and Jell-0 to stretch the wedding money, but I thought about what babies needed and bought more meat and vegetables. Bob left for work at noon and returned at nine. I was usually up half the night with Davey and slept in when I could.

⌘

Still in my housecoat, I went out to the roadside for the mail at noon one day in late August. As I sorted through the letters, I found something from the draft board. In the past, Bob had been I-A (available for military service) and avoided being drafted by re-enrolling at Kent. Now, with graduation and the lottery, those safety nets disappeared. I held the letter up to the light, but it was opaque.

When Bob got home, I gave him the draft board letter. We were apprehensive, expecting this to be his draft notice. It was. He looked worried, but I reminded him of what we had discussed last year during the lottery. He could become a conscientious objector. That meant convincing the board he was against all violence, not just the war in Vietnam.

Bob used to say, "I wouldn't mind the Air Force if I were in a plane."

That didn't sound much like a conscientious objection to me, but I wasn't about to argue.

"What do you think about CO status?" I asked again. "Is that what you want to do?"

This time Bob liked the idea. "I'll find out."

Since he hadn't changed his address, his draft board was still in Cleveland.

He said he would contact the board and proceed. Things were out of my hands. I worried that if he procrastinated or skipped a step, he might still be drafted. In 1970 most draftees went to Vietnam. A sick joke circulated that they were all cannon fodder.

The CO application came in the mail. It consisted of some questions, an essay for Bob to write and a request for reference letters. Then he needed to submit it to the draft board for review. Afterward, he might get a hearing.

Bob worked on the questions and the essay. I busied myself with the baby and stayed out of his way. He needed to complete the application in between his work at Olson's during the week and at WKNT on the weekends.

Davey grew quickly and soon slept through the night. I spent my days bathing, nursing and rocking him. After just a few weeks reality hit me. Motherhood was a lot like babysitting. I never liked babysitting. Now I did it full time for free. A job suddenly sounded good.

⌘

Bob's schedule changed and now he worked nine to five, so we ate dinner together as a family. One Saturday night we got a surprise. While Bob was still at work, his mom called. Mary asked if we would be home later.

"Of course." I was eager for them to come for a visit. She said they'd be there at 7:00.

I let Bob know his parents were on their way. He left early and walked in on me cleaning the house. Davey had been fussy all day, and I was upset. We ate supper hurriedly and cleaned up the dishes. At 7:00 there was a knock. The Turners. Mary picked Davey up and cuddled him. All went well until he fussed. Feeding time. I readied myself to nurse him, sat down as usual in the living room rocking chair and lowered my top, but I felt embarrassed in front of my own in-laws. I teared up.

Davey wasn't interested in nursing. He stared at the newcomers. After several attempts, I gave up and took him into the bedroom. When I closed the door, I broke into sobs. I was surprised. Maybe I had the baby blues everyone talked about. I stayed in the bedroom a while, then dabbed my eyes dry and came out. Mary and Bob stood by the door, about to leave. Relieved, I mustered a smile and said good-bye.

"What's wrong?" Bob asked, but I shook my head. I didn't know. I hoped this sadness would pass.

⌘

By Labor Day, Davey was almost five weeks old. His baptism would be at the Newman Center with Father White officiating. Our college friend, Pat Larson, and my brother, Tim, would be godparents. I invited the whole family and my own godparents, Aunt Gert and Uncle Jerry.

Bob called to invite his parents.

"We're busy," Mary said abruptly. "We're going camping over Labor Day."

I was secretly glad, but Bob looked hurt. They'd only seen the baby once. I bet he wondered why.

The baptism went smoothly, with a party at our apartment afterward.

⌘

We worked on the CO application. We kept this to ourselves. If he were designated a conscientious objector, Bob would have to find employment—alternative service—at an approved job. No point in upsetting the parents until we knew what the draft board decided.

I still tried to figure out breastfeeding. At the hospital, the nurses told me to supplement my breast milk with formula and now I had a hard time getting Davey to nurse. He preferred the bottles. My nipples were raw and sore and so I gave up and switched him to formula.

⌘

We'd been waiting since mid-August for the findings of the Scranton Commission. Finally, there was a news report that it would be published. The news was good. The Commission found:

> Even if the guardsmen faced danger, it was not a danger that called for lethal force. The 61 shots by 28 guardsmen certainly cannot be justified. Apparently, no order to fire was given, and there was inadequate fire control discipline on Blanket Hill. The Kent State tragedy must mark the last time that, as a matter of course, loaded rifles are issued to guardsmen confronting student demonstrators.[1]

Wonderful news! Now we just needed to wait for the government to indict someone. My testimony had been worth it.

⌘

Bob finished his CO application. I typed it while he gathered reference letters. He mailed it to his draft board and then we waited.

In November, Bob received two pieces of mail from his draft board. The first reclassified him from student status to I-A. Now he could be drafted. The second letter informed him of the date of his CO status hearing, set for early December at the draft board office in downtown Cleveland.

As December approached, I worried he would be drafted before the hearing. Bob ignored things, while I dwelt on everything awful that could happen.

---

1. *Report of the President's Commission on-Campus Unrest.* President's Commission on Campus Unrest, Washington, D.C., 1970.

43

December arrived. We were both excited, but Bob was worried too. He asked Tim to go with him to his CO hearing. There were storm warnings that night. An Alberta Clipper, a storm that blows across Lake Erie picking up heavy snow and moisture as it goes, was predicted for the next day. If they were lucky, the storm would dump snow inland and miss the draft board location, a few blocks from the Lake. They might have to drive through lots of snow in the snow belt south of Cleveland, but downtown should be clear. They took Tim's car since the VW had problems.

The next morning, they left early. The hearing was scheduled for 1:00. The trip to Cleveland usually took an hour, but traffic would be crazy with the snowstorm.

"I love you," I said and gave Bob a kiss. "Good luck!" I only wished I was half as confident as I sounded.

At noon, I turned on the news. A huge sailboat being taken into dry dock had blown off its flatbed truck near the draft board and hit the side of a building. It crushed a couple of cars in its wake. The worst of the storm hit downtown Cleveland directly. I fed Davey and played with him until naptime. As he slept, I stared out the picture window in the living room. The trees bent in the wind, waiting for the storm to hit. Bob and Tim could stay in Cleveland overnight if the weather got too bad.

At six, a car turned into the driveway. Bob came in the door.

"How did it go?"

"Oh, the roads weren't bad. It only took us three hours to drive home," he said sarcastically.

"No, I mean the hearing."

"The wind was so bad the draft board office closed," Bob said. "There wasn't anyone to answer questions. I guess they will re-schedule it."

I was crestfallen. The wait began again. I checked the mail every day. Finally, Bob got a letter telling him the hearing would be the following week. The day dawned clear and cold. No snow-storms to contend with.

"I gave them my support letters. I answered their questions as truthfully as I could," Bob told me. "Now we wait."

I didn't know whether to prepare for a drop in income or for a husband who would be inducted and sent to Vietnam. Either answer was preferable to having to wait over Christmas.

⌘

Dad offered to take the VW off our hands and replace it with a Ford Fairlane. On Sunday Pauly and Caroline planned to get a Christmas tree. That sounded like a good idea and so I asked if we could join them.

After church, we changed clothes, then drove the Ford to the outskirts of Kent. We met them at the entrance to a field encircled by a beautiful glade of tall pine trees. The field was right across from John Herning's house. We didn't know who owned it. Betting they wouldn't be caught, Bob and Pauly walked toward some big trees at the edge of the woods. They both brought axes and saws.

I strapped Davey to my back in the baby carrier. I was top heavy and almost tipped with every step I took.

Bob looked like a lumberjack on speed as he climbed one of the pines. They planned to cut the tops off two pines, tie them to the roofs of the cars and drive home. Pauly and Caroline lived only a few blocks away. With no one else around, I imagined they could get a tree back to their apartment safely, but we had three miles to drive. The sawing began and soon one treetop fell to the ground. The other followed. Bob pulled out some ropes. The next thing I knew, he stood on the roof of our car. Pauly and Bob tied the trees to the car and off we went.

The minute we reached the main road and could drive over twenty miles per hour, it flopped around. I screamed. Bob yelled at me to grab it from my side window. Luckily, Davey slept in his plastic car seat in the back. We yelled and laughed as the tree flapped above us all the way home.

Carrying the tree into the house was no problem. Bob carried it straight in from the parking lot and down the hall to our apartment. It didn't fit into the living room, so Bob trimmed it in the front yard. We used a stand Mom and Dad loaned us. I moved the sofa and playpen so we could stand the tree in the corner.

It brightened the room immediately, but we didn't have any lights or ornaments. We didn't think to borrow either from my parents who'd saved hundreds over the years. For sure, we wouldn't ask the Turners for anything.

We were avoiding them because they asked about Bob's draft status. Jim knew Bob's status had converted to I-A when he graduated. Bob's number, 120, had already been passed in this year's call-up. Before I met him, Bob's father told him they would disown him if he ever became a conscientious objector. While that hadn't happened yet, Bob still wanted to avoid his dad's questions.

We played a waiting game with his parents. If we told them the truth, Bob would be disowned. If we didn't talk about it, tensions rose.

When Bob first told me they'd disown him, I laughed. "Your parents don't own anything. They're not rolling in dough. They don't have property." This was a ridiculous threat.

"What are they disowning you from?"

But for Bob it meant something. Even though the Turners mocked his cousin, the first lieutenant who was supposedly fragged by his own men in Vietnam, they were deadly serious about wanting Bob to serve.

In the past, I tried to reason with them about the possibility he might be injured or killed, but they were adamant. Better dead than disgraced. How they could prefer their son to be killed rather than work peacefully at home made no sense. Jim had been in the Philippines during WWII. Surely, I thought, he must remember the horror of war.

Things were different with my own parents. They didn't approve of this CO idea either, but they still wanted to see the baby, so they kept their opinion to themselves.

187

44

I took a hard stand earlier on Sunday, saying I didn't want to spend any money on Christmas tree ornaments. By four o'clock, Bob began to wear me down.

"We can put them on our charge card," he explained, very rationally. "We won't need to pay it until January."

We had run out of our wedding present money about a month earlier and the reality of our one-income family hit me. With the economy still bad, I hadn't found a job. There were no newspaper jobs. Bob's Olson's job paid minimum wage without kickbacks for selling big-ticket items. He still worked Sunday mornings at WKNT, but management acted like he should pay them for the privilege of working there.

"Let's go to Ace Hardware," he said when he stood back to look at the tree. "Their ornaments are half price."

I relented. The tree was bare without ornaments.

We picked out a string of old-fashioned red, blue and green lights, a couple dozen red, silver and gold ornaments and tinsel. By the time we got home, it was dark. Inside, the apartment smelled like a pine forest. We ate a quick supper, I fed the baby and then we decorated.

I cracked open a bottle of Boone's Farm Strawberry and we each downed a few slugs to get in the mood. Bob laced the lights around the tree and plugged them in. They glowed softly, marking the best places to hang the ornaments.

"Lay those icicles over the branches, Patty." Bob assumed the role of an art director.

By nine o'clock we'd hung every ornament.

Bob and I stepped back and admired our work. We fell into each other's arms and embraced. We made love as Davey slept in his crib at the foot of the bed.

⌘

We split Christmas between the two families. For some reason unfathomable to me, we were back in the Turners' graces and they invited us to eat dinner with them. We made the trek to Cleveland, then finished up the day with my family. We didn't buy presents for ourselves because we were broke.

Ironically, our best Christmas present came in January. Bob received another letter from the draft board, this time designating him I-C.

"What does that mean?"

"Conscientious Objector, CO."

We hugged happily. We rejoiced. Along with the letter came a list of acceptable employment. Several listings were for hospital jobs. Bob would have to give up his job at Olson's because the CO rules wouldn't allow him to work two jobs. I needed to look for work myself.

Becoming a CO was a long process. Bob was quickly hired as an orderly at Barberton Citizens Hospital. But with all the paperwork required by the board, he couldn't start work until the end of May. He passed his physical, had the training and began working in surgery. What irony. Bob fainted at the sight of blood. He regaled me with stories of the bloody happenings in the OR. "You won't believe what I had to clean up today—a leg in the corner of an operating room. Just laying there."

Wide-eyed, I listened raptly. "You're not making this up, are you?" Hard to believe some things he told me. Undaunted by his duties, he reported for work every day. I couldn't figure out how someone so afraid of his own blood could work at this kind of job.

Our wedding anniversary was coming soon. We would leave Davey with my parents while we went out to dinner. That night when Bob came home from work he handed me a single rose.

"One rose for our one-year anniversary."

How sweet. Touched, I gave him a hug.

45

Spring 1971

I heard the *Beacon Journal* might be hiring, and I drove down-town Akron to apply. None of the friends I graduated with had found journalism jobs. Most settled for other work. One wait-ressed. One worked as a deckhand on a Great Lakes ore ship. Some moved back home to live with their parents and some went on to graduate school. Lucky for me, Bob had been able to continue working while I took time off to care for the baby.

I completed the *Beacon* application and the next week the State Desk Editor, Pat Englehart called me in for an interview. Pat was a wiry, middle-aged guy with a receding hairline and a cigar dangling from the side of his mouth. He had the gruff manner of an old-time newspaper editor, like in a 40s movie. Pat told me I could try out for a reporter's job. A tryout meant working with no pay for a while until he decided whether I was good enough for the job. Then they might hire me.

"I'm going to try out for the *Beacon*," I announced, and Bob looked at me skeptically. I didn't tell him it only paid $3.20 an hour plus mileage.

He laughed. "What do you mean 'a tryout'?"

The next night I covered a Zoning Board of Appeals meeting way out in Medina County, 30 miles away. I didn't even care about the long drive.

The boring meeting consisted of homeowners pleading for variances for their sheds and TV towers. I drove back to the *Beacon* office after dark. The newsroom was deserted, except for a bunch of people sitting around an island of desks. I walked over. A few young people pounded away at typewriters.

"Hi," I said and a couple of them looked up. I tried to explain myself in a way that sounded nonchalant and experienced.

"I'm Patty. I covered a meeting in Brunswick."

A man with longish red hair and a handlebar mustache looked up. "Oh, I cover Medina County too. I'm Jim. You must work for Alesky."

I was a little confused but smiled and tried to fake it.

"He's one of the State Desk editors," Jim explained.

"Where should I sit?" I glanced around the cavernous room, the far reaches of which were almost dark.

"You can sit over here by me. Alesky asked me to help you. Grab a free desk when you come in. Write up your story and leave it on top of this pile here." He indicated a wire basket filled with a stack of newsprint sheets.

I started to write. Luckily, the Zoning Board of Appeals issues were simple, and I finished the story in forty-five minutes. Everyone else was still working, so I quietly put my story on the pile and stood to leave.

As I began to walk out, Jim called me over.

"Here," he said. "Alesky wanted me to give you this." He handed me a typewritten list of meetings scheduled for the next week. I must have seemed puzzled, so he added, "He wants you to cover these."

Elated, I broke into a smile. I was a working journalist.

I was so excited I woke Bob up. "I think I have the job. They gave me a list of meetings to cover next week."

Half asleep, Bob just mumbled, "When will they pay you?"

I shrugged my shoulders. He laughed and fell back to sleep.

Next Monday, I covered the Brunswick City Council meeting. This meeting lasted until almost 9:15 and with the long drive back to the office, I didn't start writing my story until 10. By the time I finished at 11:30, I was falling asleep. I made a mental note to try to sleep later the next morning.

Bob laughed again when I told him I had work assigned four nights in the coming week. "How do you know if you're hired?" he asked again, clearly amused.

I admitted I didn't, but I showed up for work and waited to see what would happen. Jim acted surprised when he saw me on Monday night and then on Tuesday.

"You keep coming back," he joked. "Did somebody say you were hired?"

"Not yet." But on Thursday night I was vindicated. An envelope addressed to me lay on one of the desks. There was a paycheck inside. For ten dollars. I guessed I had the job.

⌘

I loved my job at the *Beacon Journal.* Even though I worked nights and was a part-timer, I got to know the late shift characters who lurked in the newsroom. Fran was a fifty-something woman who was fatter than almost anyone I'd ever met. She wore men's overalls and spent the night on a couch in the ladies' restroom, using newspapers for blankets. She wrote a popular column about the goings-on in Akron's outer suburbs. She was eccentric, even compared to the rest of the late-night staff.

Another reporter, Bill, was the first openly gay person I'd met. Bill regaled me with stories of the hemorrhoids he suffered, his many loves and his life's ups and downs. I sat there typing, acting like all this was normal fare for a 23-year-old to hear. I nodded at what I thought were appropriate intervals.

A few more full-timers sat off in the shadows on the periphery of the State Desk. They did their work and went home. Then there were the part-timers, mostly young, right out of school and eager to prove themselves.

The economy was failing, and we were happy to have jobs. We showed up hoping to be noticed and hired full time.

Bob watched the baby at night. Since I didn't leave for work until 6:00 P.M., I spent the whole day with Davey. I looked forward to my evening job as a real reporter though most of my beats encompassed sleepy little towns in rural counties. *Mayberry RFD.*

Our relationship didn't improve much with this arrangement. We saw each other around 5:00 for a quick supper. Things went okay until late one Saturday afternoon in June.

I was still mad at Bob for holding me down when I tried to pick up a crying Davey in the middle of the night. He thought that picking up a crying baby was bad parenting. Davey rarely cried at night but that night he started screaming without any warm up. It sounded to me like he was in pain, so I tried to go to him.

With three of us in the same bedroom, his screams were hard to ignore. But Bob put his arm across my chest holding me down. Surprised, I struggled with him. He was a lot stronger than I, so I ended up under his arm, flat on my back, listening to Davey's pitiful screams.

"Stay here," Bob whispered to me. "You'll spoil him."

Shocked at his sudden concern about spoiling, I was speechless. *What had gotten into him? Had he been talking to his mother?* I couldn't get out of bed if he held me down. After a while, Davy stopped screaming and fell back to sleep. I lay there crying silently. *What's bothering Bob?* Our relationship was primitive. With him regulating my every move, what kind of partnership did we have?

I was still mad the next day. Bob asked me to make his lunch and rather than doing it, I whispered under my breath. "Make your own goddamn lunch."

That was it for him. He grabbed Davey out of my arms and pushed me out of the apartment into the hallway. He chain locked the door.

Ridiculous, but I felt like a little kid being punished and reacted badly. None of the other tenants were home, so I knocked on our door. Well, knocked at first and then pounded.

Bob laughed. He opened the door a crack but left the safety chain on. I snaked my hand around the door to unlock it but couldn't quite reach it. I wasn't strong enough to push my way back in, so I decided to reason with him. He laughed at me.

"What are you going to do?" he jeered.

I tried to grab him through the crack in the door, but he smashed it into my arm.

"Let me in!" I whispered crazily. I didn't want to alert the other tenants. Bob slammed the door on my arm. I couldn't figure it out. I sat down on the linoleum dotted with dust bunnies and hairballs. Disgusting.

No one else was home. It would be too humiliating for me to knock on random doors. I didn't have the car keys, so I couldn't drive anywhere for help. Maybe I could use one of the neighbor's phones if they came back. Reluctant to leave the hallway, I wondered if Bob would come to his senses and let me back in. I waited him out, resting my back against the wall.

After a while, our catty-corner neighbors came in from the parking lot and unlocked their door. Still frantic, I wondered if I should ask to use their phone. I didn't know who to call. The police would think this whole episode ridiculous and probably not respond. Mom already told me that I'd made my bed and now I must "lie in it." No use calling my parents. I was too humiliated to call anyone else.

Explaining my predicament to the neighbors would make me sound insane. What would I say? Every version I rehearsed as I sat there on the floor sounded like a squabble between five-year-olds.

The neighbors gave me a strange look. I smiled and waved. I bet they'd never seen anyone sitting among the dust bunnies before. I decided to go talk to them, but as I rose, our door opened a crack and Bob peeked out. Then the door opened all the way. I forgot about talking to the neighbors and rushed back into our apartment.

I ran into the bedroom and slammed the door. After an hour, I got so hungry I came out. In the kitchen fixing dinner, I slammed things around. Until now there'd been a truce between us, but now I couldn't stop thinking about the sorry state of our marriage. *What was wrong?*

For his part, Bob kept reminding me that in our wedding ceremony I promised to "love, honor, and obey him."

I couldn't bear it. I taunted him. "I didn't actually say the word *obey.*"

"You're not funny. You must obey me."

He'd changed from a fun-loving anything-goes kind of guy to someone who forced his will on me. Any sign that he was asserting his authority made me rebel.

I couldn't figure out what had changed. How had I failed?

"Why can't you go back to the way you used to be?" Bob asked.

What did he mean by this? Should I go back to being sweet, cooperative and unchallenging?

I panicked whenever he said this. *Go back to how I used to be?* Who would pay the bills? Maybe he didn't want me to challenge his spending on toys and trinkets. We were at an impasse and I didn't know how to move beyond it.

⌘

Weeks passed, but our anger at each other persisted. Bob escalated almost every disagreement into a physical confrontation. He turned his back on me in bed.

I was afraid of him and worried about making him so angry. *What changed?* I spent hours wondering about it.

Was he jealous? I did find a job as a reporter while he had to do Alternative Service. If that was the problem, I couldn't change it. We needed all the money we could earn. I resolved to curb my smart remarks.

One Saturday morning, I slept in, but Bob had other ideas. He'd been up for a while. The baby stirred.

"Get up," he said flatly, as he walked by the bed. "We're going to clean." I pulled the covers up. I was drowsing when I heard water running in the kitchen. He was filling something with water. As I lay there, Bob came into the bedroom.

I opened one eye. He stood above me dripping water from a mixing bowl onto the back of my neck. Before I realized what was happening, he tipped it, pouring water on me. I jumped up screaming. He stopped.

"I want you to help me clean," was all he said.

A chill went down my back as I dressed.

"We're cleaning the house today," he announced again.

I was surprised. I had just dusted and run the sweeper two days ago. Something else must have been bothering him. I couldn't imagine what.

I gave him the dirtiest look I could muster. He caught it and in a rare instant of connection, he stared at me, holding my gaze like he could read my mind.

He laughed derisively. "You'll never be able to make it on your own."

He was one step ahead of me. I hadn't even thought about leaving, at least not until today. I shrugged. I didn't want him to provoke me again. I had never thought about making it on my own, but he planted a seed.

I tried not to react and continued with the housework. *Could I divorce him? If I left, I guess he would keep the baby. That would be horrible.* His nasty remark triggered a doomsday scenario for me.

Was he right that I couldn't make it on my own? I didn't know any other single mothers, but I would be more worried about him stalking me than whether I could make it financially. And I did love him. Why was I even thinking about this?

⌘

In the meantime, I continued to work evenings, reporting for the newspaper. Bob worked days, and we split the childcare. It was a blessing we didn't spend much time together. The marriage wasn't much, but at least when we worked different shifts we weren't fighting constantly.

⌘

In July, Bob came home with news that a nearby school district had an opening for a telecommunications teacher and radio station manager. He pulled the ad out of his pocket. "This is perfect for me."

"Would the draft board accept that kind of job as alternative service?" I asked. I didn't want to challenge him directly. Most of the jobs on the Selective Service list were menial, designed to humiliate rather than elevate the CO.

196

Our friend Rick Alexander, the chief engineer at WKSU, taught at Roosevelt, a nearby high school.

"I'll talk to Rick," Bob said excitedly.

⌘

The job was in Streetsboro, a small town ten miles north. They were looking for someone to build a radio station at the high school and teach broadcasting classes, adding a strand to their vocational program.

Bob interviewed and landed the job. He was happier than I'd seen him in a long time. His contract began at the end of August and after a month he would have health insurance and other benefits. We'd been putting off the hernia surgery Davey needed and now we could afford it.

"Building a station will be easy," Bob said. He talked to Rick about what he had done at Roosevelt. Bob had always been mechanically minded, but I worried about the teaching part. *What if he can't handle the students?*

We celebrated Davey's birthday and mine almost as an afterthought, we were so focused on the beginning of the school year. He'd be teaching classes and building the station simultaneously. He was so happy to be done with the hospital this didn't faze him. His last day at the hospital was the Friday before school opened.

He had a surprise for me too. He found a townhouse in Kent we could afford with his pay increase. Thrilled we could ditch our tiny apartment, we moved at the end of August.

⌘

We heard lots of horror stories from friends who'd been teaching. The social revolution of the late sixties had filtered down to the junior and senior high schools.

Kids came to school with marijuana, cigarettes, LSD, you name it. The idea of sit-ins and protests arrived too.

Bob's first days at Streetsboro High were memorable.

"You won't believe what kids wear to school these days. I had a girl come into my class wearing only a T-shirt and underpants. Oh, and some flip-flops."

I laughed at how ridiculous this sounded but decided to play along. "You couldn't send her to the office?"

"What for? They can wear anything they want. It's the seventies, you know."

These kids were not the sharpest. Bob told me he tried to get them excited about the radio station construction and how they would soon be able to broadcast to the entire school. He had them plan programming for the school day.

We were finally making enough money to live on. Our townhouse was on a back street in Kent, about five minutes away from Mimi and Chip. We didn't have much furniture, so the move was easy. On Labor Day weekend, we carried the final load of boxes into our new home. It was twice the size of our old apartment. The townhouse had air conditioning and a space for a washer and dryer. There was even a carport.

We'd yet to meet our neighbors, but Bob noticed a car with a Streetsboro High sticker on it as we took Davey for an evening walk. The car belonged to Cheryl, one of the high school math teachers. Bob stopped by to visit her and her husband Roy and was soon spending his evenings at their house while I worked. Bob told me he'd even been to a party there.

"What did you do with Davey?" I asked, thinking he'd kept Davey up all hours of the night.

"Oh, I left him in bed. I put the phone in his crib and called from Cheryl's. Then I ran back home to pick it up, so the line was open. I could hear his every peep."

Crazy. I debated whether this was worth fussing about and said nothing.

I took Davey for daily walks in his stroller. The weather was warm, perfect for September. The leaves were turning yellow and orange. The sun created an amber glow as we strolled along. We even bought a grill and cooked out.

"The radio station is going great. It should be finished and on the air by January," Bob told me.

Things improved between Bob and me although I was still cautious about what I discussed with him. Our schedules kept us apart on most days. I could relax at work.

Bob's CO status had begun in January. Since then he'd been employed for almost six months. That left only eighteen months to go until his military duty was finished and he'd be free to live a civilian life again. He dreamed of owning a radio station.

If not for the FCC and its rules barring felons, I was sure our life would be quite different by now. If only he hadn't gotten involved with that stupid telephone scheme.

46

Fall 1971

I continued working at the *Beacon*. One night as I pulled into the parking deck, I noticed I was almost out of gas. The Fairlane was a gas hog.

I finished my story in record time and left the newsroom by 10:15 P.M. I got onto the freeway that would take me through rural Portage County back to Kent. As I crossed into Portage County, the gauge sank to empty. The engine sputtered, then the car slowed to a crawl and died. I pulled off the road. I was between exits with no service stations nearby.

I sat for a minute, trying not to panic. It was a clear, cool autumn night. Traffic was light, so it didn't make sense to try to hitch. I grabbed my purse, locked the car and started walking on the berm in my clunky heels, not made for hiking. After a few hundred yards, my feet began to hurt. I hoped a car would come along.

Within a couple of minutes, a battered white Pontiac drove past, pulled off to the side of the road and backed up toward me. There was a guy behind the wheel. He came alongside me and rolled down the passenger's window.

"I ran out of gas. Could you give me a lift?"

He looked older, with a crew cut and a white T-shirt.

"Hop in," he said.

He eased back into traffic, then off at the next exit, only a minute ahead by car. He glided down the ramp and into the gas station parking lot.

"Thanks." I reached for the door handle.

He slowed, but as I started to open the door he hit the gas, floored it and zoomed up onto the freeway again. A chill ricocheted through my spine. He was going too fast for me to jump out.

What is happening? After a few seconds, I realized he meant to keep me. I opened my mouth to protest, but he reached over, grabbed me by the neck, and forced me down on the seat beside him.

This is not good. My mind raced in sheer panic, but I couldn't figure out what to do. I needed to calm myself. He held me down with his right hand and steered with his left. I froze. He was too strong for me to fight. I couldn't free my head. I struggled to talk to him.

"What are you doing?" I tried to sound as normal as possible. "The gas station is back there."

He answered in a low, gruff voice.

"I know. You're coming with me."

I had to pause to steady myself. "Where?" I tried to be calm even though my heart raced. I pretended I didn't understand. "Huh?"

"I'm gonna take you somewhere and have sex with you."

At least he's not calling it rape. Don't panic! I wildly searched for something to say to him. "Where were you tonight?" I asked innocently. Anything to keep him talking.

"I bowl at Colonial Lanes on Waterloo. I'm in the Tuesday league."

He'd driven east toward Kent so far but suddenly veered off at an exit, made a couple left turns and reentered the freeway going in the opposite direction, toward Akron. *This wasn't good.*

"My family is expecting me home," I said.

He grunted. My head rested on his right thigh. Now he tried to press my face into his crotch, but there wasn't enough space between his fat gut and the steering wheel. With his right hand, he pulled up my skirt and shoved his rough fingers inside me.

Disgusting. I squirmed and tried not to panic.

"Where are we going?" I asked, but that upset him too.

"A motel," he said flatly.

I returned to the family tactic. "Are you married?" I asked, in my most innocent voice.

Incredibly, he answered me.

"Yes." He was abrupt.

I ventured a little more. "Do you have kids?" I hit the jackpot.

"Three girls. Teenagers."

I thought about this for a minute. Then I chanced it. "How would you like it if someone took one of them?"

With that, he let me loose and I sat up. An electric silence permeated the car.

"You spoiled it for me," he said gruffly. He pulled off at the nearest ramp and into the first station.

The car slowed to a roll. I grabbed the door handle, opened it and leaped out, too scared to look at him or catch the license plate number. He floored it again and sped up onto the freeway.

I couldn't stop shaking. When I looked around the gas pumps were deserted. There wasn't a pay phone outside. I'd need to use the attendant's. Inside a teenage boy sat behind the counter.

"Can I use your phone?" My heart pounded in my chest. I tried not to cry. "My car broke down," I said, keeping it simple. I called Bob, and he finally answered, sounding like he had been asleep.

"What?"

"Can you come to pick me up? I'm stranded at the Gulf station at the corner of 532 and 76." I didn't want to go into detail.

He hesitated, so I had to explain a little. "I was abducted," I whispered, hoping the attendant wasn't eavesdropping. Bob needed to retrieve our car which was still parked on the side of the freeway.

"Patty, I'm calling the police."

"Can't Pauly give you a ride?" I asked hopefully. He hung up, and I waited. Within a few minutes, a cop car pulled into the parking lot. The attendant gaped at me as I walked past him toward the cruiser.

Breathlessly, I told the officer what happened.

"Get in the car. I have some emergency gas. I'll take you back to your car."

He poured the gas into the tank then followed me back to the house. The lights were on downstairs and Bob was waiting.

"I'll take a report," the officer said, but when I explained in detail what happened, he got a strange look on his face.

"Ma'am, you are alleging incidents in Tallmadge, Akron, Mogadore, and Kent. Two different counties. You need to file reports with all those agencies. They'll investigate."

I sighed, but Bob spoke up. "So, you're saying the guy probably will get away with it?"

"Yes, unless you have the license plate number or a better description of the car. There are hundreds of white Pontiacs out there."

I shook my head. I just wanted to go to bed. I wondered what Bob thought of me. Mom's voice echoed in my head. *You brought this on yourself.*

After the cop left, Bob took me in his arms. I felt dirty.

47

I tried to erase the abduction from my mind, but it was hard. I wasn't sure if I imagined it, but Bob seemed less interested in sex. We hadn't made love in days and I wondered if he thought I was ruined. I worried about our lack of intimacy but was afraid to ask him. I didn't want to upset him again.

⌘

In early November, I took Davey to the Penney's store on State Road to have his picture taken. A couple of weeks later the pictures were ready. Bob got home early. I had the day off. We decided to pick the photos up before dinner.

We piled into the Ford, Bob driving and me holding Davey on my lap in the front seat. The pictures were darling, perfect for Christmas. Davey wore red overalls and a red-and-white checked shirt. His blond curls framed his crimson cheeks and cherubic smile.

We were back to the car in minutes. Bob drove through the parking lot toward the street, down a lane of parked cars. I looked at the photos, not paying much attention until we reached the end of the row. Instead of driving out the exit, he started to drive over the curb, directly into heavy traffic.

I gasped as we narrowly missed hitting another car. I clutched the baby to my chest. Bob sneered at me and proceeded into traffic, jolting us as he did. Just a minor incident. I leaned back in the seat. I pulled Davey close. Nothing to worry about.

Suddenly, Bob speeded up to the stop light and slammed on the brakes. The car jerked to a stop and Davey and I flew into the windshield.

"What are you doing?" I screamed, scared.

"I'm going to kill us all," he said flatly. He accelerated and then slammed on the brakes again hard. I shook, terrified at what he might do. *Has he snapped?*

"I'm going to kill us all," Bob growled again under his breath. When the light changed, we started rolling, accelerating faster and faster until we came to the next stoplight. Bob slammed on the brakes and Davey and I hurtled forward, this time hitting the dashboard before I could work my hand loose to catch us. I didn't have time to reason with him or try to calm him down.

He's trying to kill us? I need to get away fast. I tried to jump out but couldn't with the car moving forward. *When he stops, I'll jump.*

Bob sped up to the light at the next corner. I had to escape before he hurt us. We were in the middle lane surrounded by cars and he revved the motor, waiting for the light to change.

If I jumped out and ran down the side street, he wouldn't be able to follow me. He had to go with traffic. Maybe I could run fast enough that we'd get to safety before he circled back. My throat burned with fear, but I couldn't let myself scream. I didn't want to upset him further.

My eyes scanned the street as I frantically searched for a safe place to run. I'd have to jump before he really did hurt us. It was 5:00, the beginning of the rush hour and we were boxed in by other cars. He proceeded through the intersection.

My chance came at the next stoplight. As the car slowed to a stop, I popped the door open, grabbed Davey tightly and ran through the traffic to the sidewalk. It was too late for him to change lanes and follow me. I half ran, half walked away from him, juggling the baby in my arms.

My stomach convulsed, and my breathing was ragged from the strain of carrying Davey. I looked over my shoulder as I ran down the street. Bob hadn't found us yet.

I reached the middle of the block and had to choose. I could run to the library, half a block away or try to make it to a house where someone was home.

The library might be best. I could call Mom from a pay phone there. I kept going. *Almost there.* Just then, Bob rounded the corner, coming from the opposite direction. He had gone around the block. I wouldn't make it to the library. I cut across a lawn and ran to the nearest house, up the driveway to the door. With Davey wriggling, I knocked.

An older lady in a housedress appeared, stared out at me and pushed the screen ajar, a questioning look on her face. I panted, out of breath, listing to one side from the weight of the baby. I opened my mouth to ask for help. But as she opened the door, Bob pulled into the driveway. He rolled down his window.

"Get in," was all he said. His threatening tone told me he wouldn't tolerate this silliness another minute.

Frantic, I tried to imagine what would happen if I walked into the house. My fear won out, and I turned, shoulders drooping and walked back to the car. I sank into the seat and Bob peeled out of the driveway.

We rode home in silence. My stomach catapulted, and inwardly I verged on hysteria. Sweat ran down my forehead into my eyes. Davey fell asleep while I sat there, took some deep breaths and tried to keep from sobbing.

At home, Bob dropped us off, then left. *Where was he going?* I was glad I didn't have to be alone with him. My heart wouldn't stop pounding.

I was desperate to leave him now but didn't know how. *Where can I go? What can I do?* My parents already told me to deal with my own problems. The police would laugh. I imagined the conversation.

"Has he hit you?"

"No," I would admit. "He hasn't beaten me. He hasn't laid a hand on me, but I'm terrified of him. I'm not making this up. He's dangerous," I'd tell them, but it wouldn't make a difference. We were married.

If only I could figure out what I did that provoked him, I could stop it. I resolved to be doubly careful in what I said and did. No more smart remarks. No more sarcastic jokes. I alternated between thinking of ways to appease him and ways to escape. *Where would I go? Who would take care of the baby while I worked?* He tracked me down in the past. He followed me. He lurked outside the house on Allerton. Now that he threatened to kill us all, I knew I must leave, but how? This threat to kill us was much worse than anything he'd done before.

I sat on the living room floor, distractedly playing with Davey, turning things over in my mind. After an hour Bob returned. I heard his key in the lock and my heart leaped. I shook and sweated. My head pounded. *Calm down, calm down.*

He walked into the living room, looming over me. I didn't know whether to take cover or to embrace him, so I just sat there, frozen. Davey played on the floor between us, unaware. His presence diffused the tension. Bob carried a big box under his arm.

"You'll like this," he said pushing it toward me. Inside was a brand-new vacuum cleaner, something I needed.

I shivered in terror as I opened the box. *He thinks this will make things better. Is he trying to atone for what he did?* I was so scared of him I shook as I stood. I didn't want to seem like I was cowering, letting him know he'd won, so I smiled a little and thanked him.

"This will help a lot," I said.

"Well, I knew you needed one, so I bought it for you." He left us in the living room and went upstairs.

I didn't think I could fix supper, but I pushed myself up from the floor, put the baby in his playpen and fried some hamburgers. *I'll keep things as normal as possible. Try not to upset him again.* It seemed futile though as I didn't know what I'd done to set him off this time.

Afterward, it wasn't the same between us. We never talked about the car ride. *Does he blame me for being abducted? Am I ruined?* I couldn't figure it out on my own, and I was too afraid of him to ask.

I was nervous. I jumped at my own shadow. My only escape was work. I was so ashamed of what happened, I couldn't tell anyone.

48

After the car incident, I changed from a fun-loving coed to a cowering rabbit. I jumped at the slightest noise. When he pulled into the driveway, my heart pounded. I forced a smile to my lips when I talked to him, but I couldn't stop thinking about the day he tried to kill us. I begged Bob to go to counseling.

He laughed. "How could that help?"

Catholic Charities had an office near us. I set up an appointment and went alone, keeping it secret.

"Can you get a ride to school with Cheryl? I need to pick up my paycheck at the *Beacon*," I told him and dropped Davey off at Mom's.

My hands shook as I completed the intake form in the storefront counseling center. The counselor stepped out to greet me. Tall and angular, he sported a bushy beard.

"I'm Jerry," he said as he ushered me into his office. "What brings you in?"

I told him about Davey, my parents, the Turners. I worked up to the threats and the violence. He didn't push. "Where's Bob? Why didn't he come?"

"Oh, he thinks everything is fine. The problem is me. He wants me to act like I did before we got married."

Soon, our forty-five minutes ended. I hadn't gotten to the frightening things yet, the threats, the violence. It'd been more than two weeks since the car incident. I still hoped Bob would change.

"It's getting better," I said, hopefully. I would tell him about Bob's threats the next time. We would meet again in December. Glad the appointment was over, I walked out the door, but my stomach somersaulted. I had betrayed our marital secrets. I was so humiliated by Bob's violence, I couldn't bring myself to tell the counselor about it that first time. In the car, I was full of recriminations. How could things improve if I wasn't honest with Jerry?

Even though I had doubts about our marriage, Bob was on a campaign to reassure me.

"Why don't we apply to the Telecom master's program? We'd find better jobs after we graduated."

"Who have you been talking to?" I asked, warily.

He pulled out two applications, surprising me.

"We need to submit them by December. Then we'll hear from them in January."

Even though this seemed like a crazy idea to me, I did want to work with him. Maybe this would better prepare me. He had already done the groundwork. We completed the applications and sent them in.

⌘

We spent Thanksgiving with Bob's parents. Davey had learned to walk and was talking more. They delighted in him. A lot of the tension I'd felt in past visits melted as we watched the baby's antics. We drank wine with dinner and Mary fell into a pensive mood.

"When my father died, I had to leave school," she reminded me. "My mother couldn't afford the tuition to Ursuline anymore."

"Yes. I remember. I wondered about that."

"I was the only kid still living at home. The others were grown and on their own"

I nodded as she continued. At the other end of the table, Bob and his dad talked about a problem with the radio station construction. Davey pounded the high chair tray with a spoon and shoved Jell-O into his mouth.

"My father was with his secretary. A train hit their car out in Lake County. They were both killed."

I tried to make sense of this. "Were they there on business?"

"I don't know. He had a receipt from the Lakeside Inn in his pocket. I guess we'll never know."

Her lips quivered with sadness. I shook my head. She rose from the table. "Let's do these dishes. Bob, you and Dad can clear, and Patty and I will wash."

⌘

Bob was back to his old joking self. "The station is coming along. The kids love me." He was elated. None of the petty conflicts he had on other jobs arose at the high school.

With only two weeks to go before Christmas, my job slowed. The weather held up and no major snowstorms kept me from driving to assignments in far-flung counties.

⌘

"I'm thirsty," Bob said one night as I readied for work. He always drank lots of cola. Now he was up to four bottles a day. He said he peed a lot more than usual. He couldn't have a bladder infection, or he'd be doing more complaining. I remembered a *Reader's Digest* article about thirst and diabetes. Could this be the problem?

Good thing we had health insurance. Bob's complaints were bullets on the diabetes checklist: Increased thirst, increased urination. He would fight me if I asked him to go to the doctor. I waited for the weekend as we both relaxed.

The next time he complained of being thirsty, I said, "You could be checked for diabetes. I think it's just a blood test."

Bob didn't buy this.

"What do you mean? I'm not sick."

I was still terrified of him no matter how calm things were. I backed off.

I changed the subject. "Let's talk about Christmas."

"I'm not going to any doctor," he said emphatically.

Now I just wanted to avoid escalation. I didn't take the bait.

"I want to buy Davey some toys and clothes." I kept my voice level. "Should we get a tree?" Anything to prevent another argument.

"Oh, I can pick up one on the way home from work," he said.

He calmed down when I stopped pressing him about the doctor.

With one more week of classes before Streetsboro's Christmas break, I hoped his thirst would improve once he stayed home. Things were going so well, I canceled my appointment with the Catholic Charities counselor. *Why rock the boat?*

⌘

Davey tore into his Christmas presents, mostly soft plastic trucks from the nearby discount store. He loved them.

"You missed one, buddy." Bob pointed to a package hidden behind the tree and Davey crawled to get it. He brought it over for Bob to unwrap.

We laughed as he lined up his trucks in a row. He was so happy. He zipped them around the floor and parked them under one of the orange love seats.

⌘

We ate Christmas dinner with Bob's parents. Davey, at sixteen months, was still the source of entertainment. He laughed at Grandpa Turner's antics and toddled around the table. The aroma of turkey, gravy, and dressing filled the air. I helped Mary with the food, then called the men to eat.

The conversation turned to Vietnam and the protests at home.

"Are you a bra-burner, Patty?" Mary asked with a smirk.

Why did this interest her? Was she jealous because I graduated from college while she couldn't? Why was she so nasty to me?

"Oh, no." I must have sounded defensive because she persisted.

"The news is all about young women who won't wear their bras. I hope you don't turn into one of them. These hippie girls disgust me. Nobody wants to see them flopping in the breeze."

My face flushed. I barely needed a bra, but I hadn't learned to ignore her gibes. I couldn't decide if Mary truly disliked me or whether this was just dinnertime entertainment for her.

⌘

We stopped by Mom and Dad's on the way home. The party was still underway. Though they'd eaten, there were lots of leftovers.

I set Davey down in the living room and he crawled over to his cousin. Tim, Jenny, and Roy were there, as well as an assortment of Scott cousins.

A cluster of kids unwrapped small presents brought by the aunts and uncles. The smell of freshly brewed coffee wafted through the air. In the dining room, people jockeyed for seats at the table, hoping for a second helping of turkey and dressing.

Dad visited with Uncle Dick and Aunt Rita, who'd stopped by with their whole family. Mom offered a tray of apricot bars and cutout cookies from the kitchen.

I sat and tried to follow a conversation that revolved around dirty hippies and how they had no respect. *I thought I escaped this when we left the Turners.*

I missed Bob and looked for him. He was at the kitchen table, sitting with his head down on his folded arms.

"Are you okay?"

"I'm exhausted. Can we go home?"

I was surprised. He was usually the center of attention.

"Sure," I said, although I wanted to stay.

"I mean now. I want to go now," he insisted even though he didn't move a muscle. *What had gotten into him?* I brushed the back of my hand across his forehead, but he didn't have a fever.

I retrieved Davey and gathered his things, but Bob still sat where I left him with his head down.

"Let's go. I have our things. Just find your coat." For once we parked on the street, so we didn't have to move five other cars to get out.

At home, Bob fell into bed while I changed Davey. He was different and a little scary. He was never this tired, even if he was drinking, so I was puzzled.

49

Winter 1972

The baby slept late. We spent a lazy New Year's morning at breakfast then drove to the Turners' for dinner. Mary served ham, potatoes, and salad. She'd already made a shimmering red Jell-O with Queen Anne cherries.

"We'll eat a bit early, about three," she said, "so you can get home before dark."

Afterward, we helped clear the dishes. I struggled with how to bring up Bob's symptoms. I hoped his mother would make him go to the doctor. In the kitchen cleaning up, I told her how worried I was.

"He says he's sick. He drinks too much Coke. He's tired. He's lost weight. He won't see a doctor." I rambled.

She brushed aside my worries. "He always drinks a lot of Coke in the winter. The air is so dry. Leave him alone. Stop being such a bitch."

Stung, my feelings were hurt. *Is that what they think? I'm a bitch?* I was angry. I was done with them. I would handle this myself.

We drove back to Kent in silence. I fumed. Bob didn't know what to make of me. No way would I tell him about my discussion with his mother.

On Monday, he went back to work, and I left Tuesday night to cover a zoning board meeting.

Life returned to normal, despite my fears. Bob watched Davey while I worked, and I cared for him during the day. But Bob's symptoms continued. I studied his face during supper, trying to figure out what was wrong. He was thinner now, and he hadn't been that heavy. On the weekends, he dragged around the house. I cleaned up the television parts he'd left strewn on the living room floor, so Davey wouldn't mess with them.

"Leave those alone!" Bob yelled. "I'm fixing that TV." He didn't lay them out again. Unusual.

Though we fought and worked opposite hours, we had managed to have a good sex life. But that disappeared too. Bob hadn't been interested in making love for a couple of months.

I couldn't stand waiting any longer. He had to see a doctor. Desperate, I came up with the idea to tell him I would leave him unless he made an appointment. An ultimatum.

"I'm leaving you and taking the baby if you won't go to the doctor."

He looked at me like I was crazy but nodded his head. "Okay. I'll go."

Gee. That was simple. Why hadn't I tried it before?

He picked up the phone, called and made an appointment for Monday morning. He'd have to miss the first hour of work, but I was adamant.

On Sunday night, Bob complained that he felt sick.

"I'm going to bed. I feel like I'm catching a cold."

By morning, he was sneezing and coughing. I gave him a dirty look when he asked to stay in bed, so he pulled himself together and got ready.

"How'd the doctor go?" I asked when he came home that evening.

"He ordered tests for Thursday morning," he said curtly. "I'm still sick. I'm going up to bed. I feel terrible. I think I have the flu," he moaned as he climbed the stairs.

He was obviously in no shape to take care of Davey.

"I'll drop the baby off at my parents' house, so you won't have to watch him tonight." I got ready for work and loaded Davey into the car with me.

⌘

"Why don't you stay overnight, Patty?" Mom asked when I showed up. "Then you don't need to wake Davey."

I finished early with the zoning board and was sitting at the State Desk by 9:30 writing my article for the next day's paper. The phone rang, and Bill picked it up.

"It's Bob, Patty."

He never calls me at work.

"I spilled milk on the floor," he began in a rush. "A whole gallon."

He was crying. A chill went down my spine. *What is wrong with him?* In the six years I'd known him he'd never cried. I sat there frozen. My heart sank into my stomach. *What is happening? Why is he so helpless? Why cry over something that trivial?*

"I tried to clean it up, but I'm too sick."

"Don't worry," I told him. "I'll handle it when I come home."

50

I slept fitfully on the living room couch at Mom and Dad's and woke a little after 6:00 A.M. Davey and I ate a quick breakfast and drove back to Kent. Bob still lay in bed sick.

"I threw up last night. I'm not going to work today."

I panicked. "I'm taking you to the hospital," I said, but he threatened me in a guttural voice like something out of *The Exorcist.*

"Get out of here or I'll kill you," he growled.

I turned and ran from the room. Downstairs I started cleaning up the milk. I was so worried about his odd behavior I couldn't even be mad at him for leaving such a mess.

He improved during the day. When I checked with him at 5:00 P.M., he said, "I feel better, but I don't think I can watch the baby."

I took Davey back to Mom and Dad's. We couldn't afford the drop in pay my missing work would mean. I sat at the State Desk writing my city council story. That night, Bob didn't call. He must have been asleep.

I finished my article and turned it in, then returned to my parents'. Davey slept upstairs with everyone else. At 1:00 A.M. I wasn't going to wake him. I spent the night on the couch again.

I couldn't figure Bob out. He said he had a cold, but I didn't know what to make of his crying. *Is he having a mental break-down?* Wednesday, Davey woke early. I packed up, and we left.

The fields gleamed after last night's snowstorm. The sky was azure without a cloud. When we got home at 9:00 A.M., everything was quiet. Bob was still in bed though he'd promised to go to work.

"How are you?" I called out as I climbed the stairs to our bedroom, but he didn't answer. He moaned softly when I peeked in.

"Leave me alone! Close the door."

My insides somersaulted. I'd never seen him like this. He looked so sick. He didn't want me bugging him, so I got Davey ready to go for a walk. It would be cold, but worth being outside.

I dressed Davey in his snowsuit. Given Bob's threats of yesterday, I decided not to bother him and put the baby in his stroller and left the house quietly. Outside in the brilliant January air, I couldn't calm myself. *What should I do?* He wouldn't go to the hospital. His blood tests weren't until Thursday, two days away. I'd have to wait.

In my rush to leave, I forgot my house key. When we returned, I banged on the front door for Bob to let us in. The door was directly below our bedroom, but I had to knock loudly for at least five minutes before Bob came to the window. I waved frantically to catch his attention, but he stared off into the distance. Couldn't he see us standing right below him?

"Come open the door," I yelled as loudly as I could, and he left the window. After about ten minutes, Bob opened the door a bit. I lifted Davey out of the stroller and shouldered the door the rest of the way open. As I did, Bob crawled slowly up the stairs on his hands and knees. I was stunned. *What is happening?*

I set Davey down and ran upstairs after Bob. By the time I caught up with him he'd closed himself in the bathroom. I heard water running. I opened the door and found Bob bent over the sink, drinking from the overflowing basin.

"What are you doing?" I screamed. *He's like an animal.*

I grabbed him from behind by the arms and tried to guide him back to bed. My heart sank. His skin hung from his body. He looked like he was starving to death. His muscles wasted. I half carried him to the bed and helped him lie down. *Am I crazy?* He seemed dreadfully sick.

Despite his claims that he was getting better and his threats for me to leave him alone, he had gotten dramatically worse. He could hardly walk. His strength was gone. His six-foot frame, shrunken. Thin as a prisoner of war, his face was drawn and gaunt.

"I'm taking you to the hospital now," I said, and jostled him, trying to wake him from his stupor. He shook his head no, refusing, and fell back onto the bed.

Desperate, I left the baby in his playpen and ran outside to find anyone who could help. A neighbor emptied the trash.

"Please come look at my husband," I pleaded with him. "He's sick." The guy eyed me skeptically but followed me to the house and up to the bedroom.

He took one look and turned pale.

"How are ya doin', buddy?" he asked

"Fine," Bob mumbled and then sat up to prove it.

"Well, lady, I don't know what's wrong with him, but he's mighty sick," he said and backed out of the room and down the stairs.

I was on my own. I called the doctor Bob saw on Monday while Davey played at my feet. The receptionist answered.

"If his tests are scheduled for Thursday, the doctor won't see him until Friday," she said and hung up.

Bob couldn't wait until tomorrow for the blood tests. With the shape he was in, he wouldn't make it to the lab.

⌘

Tim knocked at the front door then stood at the window gesturing for me to let him in. He was on his way up to campus for an afternoon class.

"Is everything okay?" he asked. I shook my head.

"Bob is still sick. I don't know what's wrong with him. Come upstairs and talk to him," I pleaded.

By the time we climbed the stairs, Bob was awake and talking. "St. Timothy!" he yelled as Tim walked into the room. "How are you?"

He propped himself up on one elbow.

For the life of me, I couldn't decide whether he was fine and just joking or if he was out of his head. He wasn't making any sense. He bantered with Tim like he always did but his eyes were blank.

"He's lost a lot of weight," I told Tim. "He was lapping up water out of the bathroom sink before you came."

Tim was in pre-med at John Carroll before he transferred to Kent. I hoped he could figure out what was wrong. I needed a reality check.

"I called the doctor, but he won't see him until after he gets blood tests on tomorrow."

Tim shook his head. Downstairs, he said, "I don't know what's wrong with him," and left for his class.

I ran back upstairs and found Bob talking gibberish. "Hi, Billy," he said to me. Billy was his neighbor in Euclid. A chill ran down my spine. I was taking him to the hospital, no matter what. Bob was taller than I and sixty pounds heavier. I couldn't handle him and the baby by myself.

I called Chip and Mimi who lived a mile away and asked them for help. Chip hadn't left for his afternoon shift at the post office yet. He offered to come over.

Minutes later, I showed him upstairs where Bob looked like he was unconscious. Neither of us could wake him. We decided to take him to the hospital. Sitting Bob up, we each took an arm of his shirt and tried to dress him.

He'd lost so much weight in the past few days his clothes almost fell off. His strength was gone but as we put his pants on, he roused again.

"I told you to leave me alone," he mumbled. "I'm not going anywhere." I gave Chip a wild-eyed, pleading look. We ignored him. We dragged him down the stairs and out to the car.

"Patty! I'm going to pass out," Bob cried and he did. We had to get to the hospital. We left Davey with Mimi and raced to St. Thomas, ten miles away. Nobody thought to call an ambulance.

The ride took forever. It was rush hour. On the way Bob regained consciousness.

"I can't see!" he yelled.

I cradled his head in my lap as he lay across the back seat of Chip's Camaro.

"Hold on. We'll be there soon." I wanted to scream and escape this horrible scene. How did things deteriorate so fast?

At the emergency room door, Chip and I pulled Bob out of the car and into a wheelchair.

"You can leave," I told Chip. "I'll call you when we need a ride." I was confident they'd give Bob a shot and send him home.

A little after 3:00 P.M., the triage nurse asked me a few questions then called for an orderly to wheel Bob into the treatment room. "Go to the waiting room. We'll get back to you."

The orderly wheeled him away and I sat helplessly waiting. A few minutes later a nurse came out and ushered me into an office.

"The doctor wants to talk to you."

"What kind of drug is he on?" the doctor demanded as he walked into the room. I shook my head. "Nothing."

"He's delirious. He's on something."

I was astounded. "He's not on anything," I insisted. "He won't even take an aspirin. I think he might have diabetes."

"Well, he could have diabetes," the ER doctor countered, "but we want to figure out what's wrong with him right now. What did he take?"

"He's not on any drug." I was crying now, I was so scared.

Al, Anna's brother-in-law, a resident in Internal Medicine, walked in. I sighed with relief. Al knew Bob. At least he would understand. I told him about Bob's thirst and other symptoms.

"Maybe he has diabetes," I said again.

"We've already done tests and his blood sugar is very high. We'll try to help him."

I began to make plans to go home. The nurse came back.

"Now, dear, I don't want you to be alarmed." Her voice was soothing. "They always give patients the Last Rites before they take them to Intensive Care."

"What?" I screamed. "Last Rites? Intensive Care? What's happening?"

51

I started to shake. Then Anna walked in. How did she know to come? She grabbed my arm and pushed me into the hallway. They'd gotten Bob onto a gurney and were wheeling him toward the elevator. I was terrified. He was out of his head, yelling and screaming.

"Help me! Help me!"

I ran to his side and took his hand. "You'll be all right," I whispered. "They're taking you to a room."

At the foot of the gurney, a chaplain walked backward, anointing him, and praying. I didn't understand. I thought they'd send him home. It was a Catholic hospital, so maybe they gave everyone going to ICU the Last Rites.

⌘

I stood on my tiptoes outside the ICU door with Anna right behind me, watching the faces of the doctors and nurses who passed in and out. I tried to figure out Bob's condition from their expressions. I pushed the door open, but the nurse told us not to come in.

"Visiting hours start at six."

At 6:00 P.M., we walked in. Bob opened his eyes and smiled at Anna. He didn't notice me.

"How're you doing?" She joked with him and he tried to smile.

I decided not to kiss him. I didn't want him to know how scared I was. I was trying not to overreact. "You'll be out of here soon," I said, not wanting him to worry.

A nurse appeared and ushered us out. "Go back to the waiting room. You can come in at 8:00 P.M. " We stood outside discussing a place to eat supper.

Al saw us through the window and came out. "I'd rather you didn't leave the hospital. He's in critical condition."

Critical? That didn't sound good.

We found the cafeteria. When we returned a half hour later, Bob's parents had arrived. They looked stricken.

"What happened?" Mary asked.

"I don't know. He caught a cold, and then it got a lot worse."

We sat silently, waiting. Eight o'clock was a long way off. My parents arrived. They had panicked looks on their faces. I stationed myself by the ICU entrance, trying to see what was going on.

At 8:00 P.M. I pushed the swinging double doors expecting to be let in.

Three doctors, a nurse, and two orderlies squeezed into the cubicle, all working frantically. A stream of water flowed from Bob's bed onto the floor. The nurse wouldn't let me enter.

Al came out. "His temperature is up to 108 degrees. He might have some brain damage. We packed him in ice to try to bring the fever down. Those are the ice blankets dripping."

Al gave me a worried look. He turned to go back.

I stared out the window at the falling snow, trying to calm myself. I imagined visiting Bob in a nursing home. Brain damage. That's not so bad. I can handle that.

The on-call was Doctor Mader, my own doctor. He and Al had been working on Bob for more than four hours. After a few minutes, he stormed into the waiting room.

"Where are this boy's parents?" he yelled. The Turners looked up guiltily, and he zeroed in on them. "Don't you know he could very well die? Why wasn't he brought in sooner?"

They looked down sheepishly.

I hoped they remembered that conversation I had with Mary on New Year's Day.

With that, Doctor Mader turned on his heel.

Die? Impossible! Twenty-four-year-old men don't die. One part of my mind screamed while another imagined Bob lying in state in a funeral home. My troubles would be over. I would be free. I was horrified at my own thoughts.

At 9:00 P.M. heartrending moans started coming from the ICU. Al came out again. "This is good," he said, meaning Bob's moans. "He's fighting for his life."

Good. He'll survive. Brain damage wouldn't be too bad a price to pay.

I planted myself in front of the door again. I begged each person who walked through for information on his condition.

Various doctors ventured guesses.

"Well, if his next blood sugar is lower, he might have a chance," one said.

"If his fever goes down, he might improve," offered another.

My hopes were up, and I began making plans to go home so I could sleep and come back in the morning.

At 10:00 P.M., they let me in again. I was stunned and almost fell over when I saw him. He was gasping for air. His eyes were glazed over and crusted. With every breath, he lunged upward off the hospital bed, moaning. I stood by his side, staring, horrified, unable to even touch him. I turned and ran from the room. My God! He looked like a monstrous fish flopping around, mouth gaping, eyes bulging. What was happening to him?

Outside in the waiting room, a nurse shoved a plastic medicine cup filled with liquid at me.

"Drink this. You'll feel better."

As the sedative took hold, I started feeling optimistic. I went back to my station by the ICU door. Bob's parents begged me to stay in the waiting room, but I ignored them.

At midnight, Al came out and sat beside me.

"Bob has the second highest blood sugar I've ever seen. It's 1350. A person usually goes into a coma at 500. We can't figure out what to do for him. We've already given him 850 units of insulin, and he still isn't responding."

He sounded desperate.

"If the next thing we try works, he might pull through."

He'll respond. I know it. I was hopeful again. I made plans to go home and rest. I sent my parents home.

At one o'clock, Al met me at the doors.

"Bob's kidneys failed. He has no blood pressure. We gave him a shot of adrenaline directly into his heart. It might help."

No blood pressure? I ignored that and focused on the adrenalin part. I told the Turners, "They're trying to raise his blood pressure."

I peered inside. The nurse shoved more of the sedative at me. Two A.M. was the next time I could go in.

At two, Al came to the door. "He's dead," he said.

My brain didn't compute. "He's getting better?" I asked, hopefully.

"No. He's dead. Now we just have to wait for his heart to stop beating."

I couldn't believe what I heard. "Can I see him?" They made a mistake.

Bob's eyes were covered but his color seemed better. The heart monitor still beeped. He's alive. I reached under the sheet and touched his arm. It was still warm. He's still alive.

I caressed his face. I kissed him on the forehead. I squeezed his hand and waited for his response. But there was none. I started to cry quietly.

Just then, Al came back. He'd been with Bob ever since we brought him to the ER. "It takes a long time for a young heart to stop beating," he said. Then he began crying too.

52

The head nurse came in. "Do you want an autopsy?" She sounded official.

"He's not dead yet!" I screamed.

"Yes dear, but we need your signature on these papers. You should order one, especially if you have a child."

"I can't sign them here. Not in front of Bob." He was still breathing. That would be a sacrilege.

"We'll do it in the waiting room."

In the waiting room, the Turners sat still as death.

"They want an autopsy," I said.

"No!" Mary yelled. "You can't cut him up!"

Torn, I started sobbing. How could I keep them happy and still do the right thing? What if an autopsy gave us information important for Davey's survival?

The nurse set the papers in front of me. I took a deep breath and signed.

When I returned to the ICU, Al was unhooking the monitors.

I eyed him accusingly. "They're still beeping."

He shrugged.

"You must go now," the nurse whispered as she took me by the shoulders and guided me toward the door. "He's dead."

"But the machines are still beeping," I cried, pointing to a blip moving across the screen.

"Oh, don't worry. That can happen even after a person dies." She led me back to the waiting room.

I sat between Jim and Mary, sobbing. My parents were coming back.

Signing for the autopsy was the first time I'd openly defied the Turners. I didn't want this kind of terrible thing to happen to Davey if I could help it. "I want to know what killed him," I said, but they ignored me. I could barely think. After a few minutes, Mom and Dad returned. They sat beside me, edging the Turners out.

I wanted to get out of there. After a minute, I stood and walked toward the elevator. My parents followed. They drove me back to their house where Davey slept.

"Go lie on the couch," Mom said as we took off our jackets. They went to bed, but I lay there wide awake, unable to close my eyes. Past the point of tears, I couldn't turn my brain off. *Maybe there's been a mistake. Maybe Bob is still alive,* I wondered as I tried to fall asleep.

Sometime after 4:00 A.M., I fell into a fitful sleep. A little after 7:00, I heard someone in the kitchen. Mom was making coffee. I rolled over, so my face almost touched the back of the sofa, but I couldn't sleep, so I just lay there. *Was Bob really dead?* I sat up, thinking about who I should call.

First would be Streetsboro High. Bob was expected there shortly to begin his school day. I wasn't sure I could get through a conversation with the secretary, but I wanted to be the one to speak to them. I waited until 7:30 A.M. then dialed the number before Mom realized I was up. If I talked to her, I knew I'd start crying, and if I started crying, I'd never be able to stop.

"This is Mrs. Turner," I said when the secretary answered, with as much dignity as I could muster, my voice catching. "Bob won't be in today. He died early this morning." I spilled it all out in one breath, choking back the tears.

53

The next few days blurred together. I wanted the funeral mass to be at the Newman Center. I hoped people would notice the irony. We had been married there just twenty-two months before.

I cried at the hospital but now was afraid if I started again I would never stop. What good would I be then? I plowed grimly through each day, hoping no one would say anything to make the tears flow. People tiptoed around me carefully. We focused on the superficial things, the flowers, the casket, what clothes to bury Bob in.

His only suit was the one he wore for the wedding. He should be buried in that.

"I don't know what to do with his ring," I told Mom. "Should I keep it? Should I bury it with him?" I loved it with its gold and platinum bands. I tried not to think about it, but I couldn't stop focusing on these little details.

I decided to bury it with him. Still afraid, I wanted to be done with him. Burying the ring was symbolic.

Jim called. "We bought burial plots a couple of years ago at All Saints Cemetery. There are four of them, one for each of us, me, Mary, Bob, and Kitty."

Strange they bought one for Bob. Where did they think his wife would be buried?

The next time I saw the Turners, Mary rushed to comfort me.

"You're so young. You'll get married again. You can buy a burial plot with your next husband."

Next husband? What a horrible thing to say. The thought hadn't crossed my mind. Married again? Not me.

But I was glad I didn't have to find a grave on top of everything else. Bob died on Thursday, leaving little time before the weekend to arrange the funeral. His parents wanted his calling hours to be in Euclid where he grew up.

Friday, Mom drove me to the mortuary to meet the Turners, pick out a casket and then to the florist.

Brickman's Funeral Home was a colonial-style building with white columns, lit by floodlights even during the day. One of the black-clad workers ushered us in. The fresh-cut flower smell hit me. Inside, Jim and Mary talked with Ed, the funeral director, a friend of theirs.

We sat in Ed's office as he presented the various options. Like buying a car, there were different combinations of services. I didn't know what to select, but Jim and Mary had ideas and nodded their heads in sync as he flipped through his binders.

Was I paying for the funeral? I didn't know how I could afford it, so I hoped to keep the cost low. How much did a funeral run, anyway? I would have hospital bills to pay too.

I didn't want to seem too cheap to the Turners, but I didn't want to sink myself with debt. I brought home ninety dollars a week from my *Beacon* job. I couldn't be too extravagant on that kind of money.

Mary said they took out an insurance policy on Bob. "You can use it. It pays five thousand dollars."

Small comfort. That would cover the funeral. Bob had life insurance through Streetsboro High. I hoped it would come through soon.

The Turners wanted two days of calling hours. Things had happened so fast. They needed a longer time to say good-bye to him.

We went downstairs to the casket showroom to pick one out. Everything from cheap wooden caskets to elaborate steel and bronze inlaid models were displayed around the room.

Upstairs, I'd already gotten the talk about the liner, about which kind would hold up better and which might leak. I began to question the whole idea of preserving the body, so it could rise again. What help would a cement liner be if there were just bones inside? I nixed it. I didn't want Bob rising on the Last Day.

I was at a loss as we strolled along the rows of caskets. Some had pillows, some tufted satin linings. *Who are they kidding? He's dead.*

As we walked slowly down the aisles, Jim cried, quietly at first. He was like a Geiger counter. He sobbed louder and paused longer by ones he liked. He paused longest and sobbed the loudest in front of a lustrous bronze casket. I tried to sneak a look at the price. Thirty-five hundred! Double the caskets I liked.

I looked around for Mom, hoping she'd be able to temper Jim's sobs. She hovered in the corner, but she didn't come when I motioned to her. I wouldn't get any help from her.

Finally, I resigned myself. *What's the point of keeping it cheap if this casket is going to make Jim happy?*

"This one," I said, pointing to the bronze one. "We'll take it." Jim sobbed louder. My stomach sank. How could I pay for all this?

After the funeral home, we drove to the florist in Willowick.

"I don't want carnations on the casket. Carnations remind me of death," I told Mom in the privacy of the car.

"Roses would be nice," she said, "but they're expensive." She humored me.

I caved into Jim on the casket, but now I decided to stand firm on the flowers. I wanted something light and spring-like. The florist was in a tiny brick Lego building. By midafternoon the icy ground had thawed a little. I jumped over the giant potholes with little icebergs floating in them. We gathered at the front counter, us on one side and the florist, an older lady, dressed in black with black stockings, and long black hair on the other.

She opened a picture book filled with arrangements. There were free-standing heart-shaped monstrosities chock-full of carnations, wavy scrolls of roses with golden ribbons and riotous bouquets shoved into giant wicker baskets. I was desperate to keep this from becoming a money trap like the casket.

"Do you have any spring flowers?" This was the middle of January. The florist gave me a strange look.

"I mean something lighter. Not carnations. How about gladiolas?" She nodded and pulled out another book.

Now it was my turn to sob. She showed me cascades of yellow,
orange, and white glads, meant to perch over the open casket.

"This one," I cried.

"What about a heart from Davey?" Mary asked. I'd not thought
of it. *Gross. How could a 17-month-old give flowers? He doesn't
understand Bob is dead.*

She persisted. "It could read, 'Love, from your son.' We'll order
one from Kitty too."

Disgusted, I went along to keep the peace. The autopsy
was important, the flowers weren't. By 2:00 we'd accomplished
everything we needed for today. There was one more free day
before the calling hours on Sunday.

⌘

"Why are you up so late?"

I sat in Tim's favorite chair in the den. It was after midnight.
I didn't want to admit I was afraid to go to sleep. That would be
ridiculous. Tim watched *Johnny Carson* every night. I planned on
staying up with him.

"I'm just hanging out."

He shrugged.

I imagined I would toss and turn as memories of Bob's suffering flooded back if I went to bed too early. In every down moment,
reminders of him rose like monsters—the doctor yelling, Bob's
eyes bugged out and dilated, waiting for his heart to stop. It was
torture. I tried to keep myself from shaking. I didn't want to be
alone with my thoughts and night was the ultimate alone time.

When it felt too bad, I repeated to myself, *He's dead. I escaped.*
But when I was alone, I wondered if he were really dead. *Did the
hospital make a mistake? They had unhooked the monitors before
his heart stopped beating. Maybe he was still alive.* In my saner
moments, I reasoned that, of course, he was dead. No one could
survive what he suffered.

I couldn't bear to pick Davey up. He looked so much like Bob,
even at seventeen months, I cried each time he came near. He

reminded me of what I'd lost. I repeated my mantra. Nobody knew what I thought.

I found some Valium Doctor Mader had prescribed for my stomach. I took it at bedtime, a quarter pill at a time, with a swallow of the whiskey Dad had stashed away in a kitchen cupboard.

Late at night while I waited for the Valium and liquor to kick in, I talked to Tim. He had switched his major to psychology once he transferred to Kent.

I badgered myself and Tim too. *What if I had called an ambulance, would he still be alive? What if Chip had driven quicker? What if I had divorced Bob? What if he were drafted?* At twenty-one, Tim didn't have any more answers than I did. I pinned my hopes on the autopsy. It would at least tell us why he died.

⌘

With no answers to the important questions, I focused on the mundane. I needed to find something to wear to the funeral home. I'd bought a dress last fall for job interviews, muted gray with a filmy Navy-blue coat attached. That would have to do. But I needed some shoes. I owned nothing but white tennis shoes and the clunky brown platform heels I wore for kicking around the rural counties, covering stories for the *Beacon*.

Anna came over early Saturday morning. "What's happening?" she asked as she walked in. She sat at the breakfast table with Mom and me.

"Let's go to Chapel Hill," I said. "I need dress shoes." Anything was better than sitting looking at my parents' sad faces.

Chapel Hill was quiet. Most people were still sleeping off Friday night. I felt raw. When the teenage shoe salesman flirted with me I let him have it.

"Are these for a party?" He was helping me into a pair of Navy blue strappy pumps. I ignored him. He persisted. "Where will you wear these?"

I stared him dead in the eye. "I'll be wearing them to a funeral. My husband just died." I said this for myself as much as for the witless salesman. Bob had been dead for thirty-six hours now. I still couldn't believe it. Anna giggled beside me.

He flinched. "I'm sorry," he muttered.

Outside, we dissolved into gales of laughter.

"Did you see his face?"

I found a new source of power, making people uncomfortable. We finished buying the shoes, and it was barely 10:45 A.M.

We walked the length of the mall, looking for something to do. The crowd was growing. Ahead, I spotted a man's head. He had sideburns and longish curly dark hair. Bob! I gasped in surprise and Anna looked at me quizzically. I managed to stop myself from running to him.

"I thought I saw Bob." I began crying, and it took me a while to recover. *Bob is dead. It couldn't be him.*

⌘

I was doomed to spend the rest of the day with my parents. Mom sprang into action as I walked in. Neighbors had brought casseroles. Dad wiped off the extra folding chairs in the base-ment. Davey sat in the high chair, eating orange sections while Mom did the breakfast dishes. Davey stretched his arms out for me to pick him up, but I just couldn't. I handed him his bottle instead.

"I need your help," Mom said. There'll be lots of people here.

Thank God, I had something to do. Mom picked Davey up. He wiggled to the floor and ran toward the den. Roy was in there watching cartoons. He was a source of endless fascination.

"I'll clean the living room." At least I would be far enough away to avoid any sad glances Mom might cast my way.

"I want you to make a dessert," Mom said. I was secretly glad. In the role of a kid again, I didn't have to decide anything until tomorrow. It was like getting ready for a party.

⌘

Saturday night Aunt Katie arrived to watch Davey. It would be too hard for me to care for him at the calling hours.

I hadn't told anyone that taking care of him was too painful. I cried at the thought of holding him or changing his diaper. I silently acquiesced to this plan. Katie would stay with him and everyone else would go to the funeral home.

Brickman's was on the shores of Lake Erie—an hour away, but this was what Bob's parents wanted. They were taking back the power they'd lost over him during our marriage. I sat numb and prayed the ride would end soon.

I hadn't seen Bob's body since I left the hospital early Thursday morning. *How could they possibly clean him up?* The last time I saw him alive his eyes bulged, his neck arched from the strain of breathing and his skin was blue. I dreaded seeing him again. *But I must look at him. I must prove to myself he's dead.*

54

Dad dropped us off at the front door. As I reached for the handle it opened from the inside. One of the Brickman brothers dressed in black held it for me.

"Would you like to view the body?"

The body? I startled. *It's my husband, not a body.*

"Bob?" I asked, mean-spiritedly. I guessed he was used to grieving widows. He didn't react. He ushered me into the viewing room where the bronze casket lay against the far wall. The gladiolas were glorious. I steeled myself and walked forward slowly, trying to prepare for the sight of my dead husband. Alone with the casket, I took on the role of witness. Bob's parents didn't want to look at him. In my mind, I was now the brave one, the unflinching one. I needed to play this out, no matter how much it hurt. I approached the casket. A stabbing pain tore through my heart as I saw the outlines of his wedding suit come into view. He looked relaxed, not contorted in pain anymore.

The purplish cast was gone from his face. With his eyes closed, he looked peaceful, almost alive. He wore his ring. I resisted the urge to shake him awake. I took a gulp of air and knelt. I inspected his face and hands. *Not too purple. His parents would be happy.*

I'm finally free of this monster. I didn't want anyone else to be able to see the relief on my face. I must play the grief-stricken widow. I pushed myself up off the *prie deux*, turned and walked back to the lobby.

⌘

At 1:00 P.M., the crowds started arriving. A steady stream at first, it became a rush, with people backed out the door. I stood in front of a chair with Mom on my right and Dad on my left. People said crazy things.

"At least he didn't suffer."

"You're young. You'll remarry."

"What happened?" people asked as they bent to greet me. The truth was I didn't know. The doctors weren't sure. I'd tell a simple version of the months-long agony.

"He wouldn't go to the doctor. He got sicker and sicker and we took him to the ER." No matter what I said it didn't sound good and didn't make any sense. How could a twenty-four-year-old man go from seeming fine one day to dying the next? I couldn't explain it. Not cancer. Not a heart attack. People shook their heads in disbelief.

There was entirely too much talk of God.

"This was God's will."

"God watches over you."

Why would God want me to suffer like this? I began to wonder if there really was a God, so different from my earlier life when everything focused on my love of the Almighty.

After a while, I got into a rhythm. I figured out how to shake someone's hand without bursting into tears. *Don't look in their eyes.* Focus on the person in front of you. I stood zombie-like. My friends appeared at the end of the line. I was surprised because our graduation from Kent was almost two years ago and everyone had moved away.

Jack Nickles inched forward in line. I didn't know him well at school, so wondered why he was here. He bent, reaching for my hand. As he did, he whispered in my ear.

"Call me if you want to get together," he said, innocently.

Disgusted, I couldn't imagine anything I might want from him, but I nodded my head politely.

Next came Pauly and Caroline. Caroline cried. *I can't do this if people cry in front of me.* I steeled myself as they approached. If I started crying I wouldn't be able to stop. Then what? Would they take me away? Give me a sedative? It wouldn't end well. *Don't think. Don't feel.*

I wanted to get away, but there was no place to go. The January wind blew off the lake, so outside wasn't an option. I'd been avoiding the viewing room since I looked at him earlier. *Will this ever be over?* I tried to disappear into the crowd in the foyer but that didn't work. One of the morticians appeared at my elbow.

"Can I get you something?"

Yeah, how about a new husband?

I needed to take a break. I hid in the ladies' room. Mercifully, the calling hours ended before I screamed at anyone. Everyone eyed me as we walked to the car. I couldn't let myself ruminate. *The Turners are stupid and clueless. They let their boy die and now they're reaping all this sympathy.*

I begged them for help just three weeks ago. Not only did they ignore me, but they ridiculed me. They got what they deserved. They wouldn't be seeing much of me or Davey.

I was so tired by the time we got back to my parents' I was almost asleep. Katie had put Davey to bed and waited in the living room.

"How did it go?"

I shook my head and went upstairs. Mom would fill her in after I fell asleep.

⌘

The forecast for Monday was snow. The service was at 10:30 A.M. at the Newman Center where we were married just twenty-two months ago.

Katie had tired Davey out, so he would sleep until morning. I couldn't face getting up with him if he woke crying. I didn't bother to set my alarm. He would wake me up at 6:00 A.M. That gave me more than four hours until the funeral mass. I closed my eyes and fell into a deep sleep.

At 6:00 on the dot Davey called for me.

"Mama. Mama." I picked him up. He jumped down from my arms and clambered downstairs. Dishes rattled in the kitchen. Mom.

She hit me with one of her stares.

"Stop! Stop staring at me."

She was hurt. She couldn't help it. She was only trying to read my mood. No matter what, it would be bad. Bob's funeral was today.

We talked about how after the service we would ride in a limo to the cemetery. It wouldn't be fun as it was a thirty-minute drive with the Turners in close quarters.

I imagined breaking down and screaming at them. *You let him die. This is all your fault! How could you be so stupid?* This was the fastest way to rid me of them. But I knew I wouldn't scream. I would hold it together and try to pretend they didn't exist. They didn't even notice my snub in the limo. They were miserable enough on their own. I replayed the New Year's Day kitchen scene in my head. I told Mary Bob was sick. He wouldn't go to the doctor.

What did she do? Did she recognize the danger and urge him to make an appointment? No. She lashed out at me. My anger at them took my mind off my loss.

55

As we pulled into the Newman Center lot, I flashed back to our wedding day, less than two years ago—walking out of our reception and being surprised by the red Volkswagen convertible. It was a much happier time.

A cold wind blew, sending a chill down my back. January in Ohio was brutal. A light lacing of frost covered the ice-encrusted piles of dirty snow, improving their color.

I walked up the hill ahead of Mom and Dad. Roy and Jenny straggled behind. No one waited in the vestibule to escort us down the aisle, but I knew I should sit in the first row. The casket rested between the two communion rails. *How will I ever get through this?* I hit on a strategy. I wouldn't look at the coffin. I would pretend he was someone else.

I sat between my parents, so that would be tough. I could count on Dad holding it together but if Mom started crying, I might lose it. The church filled. I didn't see many of the Turner cousins in the pews although Mary and Jim were right behind us.

Mimi played the organ, and we rose. Father White, who married us, and baptized Davey would officiate. I wanted to sob. My throat ached and my eyes burned, but again I was afraid I couldn't stop. *Don't think. Don't feel. Don't cry.* That would be my motto. I only needed to last a couple more hours before I could collapse. The mass began.

I hoped there wouldn't be incense. It still made me sick, like in the first grade. I gripped the front of the pew and pulled myself up. Soon Bob would be buried and gone. My life could start over.

I'd be ashamed if anyone knew what I thought. I kept my head down hoping no one could see my face. This wasn't about me. I tried to put myself in a trance, but memories came flooding back, the hospital room with Bob gasping for air, the ride in Chip's Camaro. I wavered and a tear leaked down my cheek. Then I remembered the November day Bob tried to kill us. That steeled my resolve. I could do this. I stole a glance at the coffin. The lid was closed. He was still in there. He was still dead—the bastard.

⌘

The service was almost over. We stood for the final prayer while Father waved the censer over the casket. I swayed, but Dad grabbed me. I could make it if I stopped inhaling that damned incense.

The priest finished, and we followed the coffin out to the hearse. Tim, Bill Donaldson, and Bob's cousins were pallbearers. They loaded him into the back between piles of flowers. The funeral director ushered us into the limo. I looked down, so I wouldn't have to talk. *No smart remarks or cutting gibes.*

Mom glared at me. I could read her mind. *"Keep your mouth shut."* No problem.

Jim started to cry.

⌘

The cemetery lay along a sweeping ridge at the edge of Cuyahoga Valley. The view to the west revealed a bleak winter landscape. Like everything else in the area, it was named for the crooked river that wound its way south, and then north toward Cleveland, dumping into Lake Erie. A source of endless fun and entertainment with its ski runs and hiking trails, now it would hold a harsher memory.

A white canvas tent billowed about shielding people. The ground on the twenty-yard walk from the car was snow covered and frozen. Inside, brilliant green artificial turf draped around the gaping hole. *Who comes up with these things?* Guess they didn't want us thinking about the icy dirt underneath.

The wind brought the temperature down to fifteen degrees. Beneath my coat, I broke into a cold sweat and shivered. A small group of mourners had followed us. Now we waited as they parked and found their way to the grave. Father White hurried up the incline. He started his prayers even before the last of the people arrived, too cold to wait.

He sprinkled holy water on the casket as we said an "Our Father." Then, it began to sink. I didn't want to watch. I turned away and Dad, beside me, caught my shoulders again. Things were heart-wrenching enough, especially with Jim's sobs.

I walked back to the car with Dad holding me so I wouldn't slip.

⌘

The house on Meriline was big, large enough to hold at least thirty guests plus the family. It overflowed today. I opened the side door and Davey ran to meet me.

"Mama!" he yelled and held out his arms for me to scoop him up. He looked like Bob. He acted like Bob. It hurt my heart to hold him. I grabbed him and cried softly. This was going to be harder than I thought.

Rafts of relatives from both sides of the family joined in the luncheon. I couldn't avoid them. Everyone held back. No one wanted to be the first to talk to me. I understood, but it made me crazy. Afraid I would cry, they had no way of knowing I was still numb. No bursting into tears today, at least for others to see. Tim was in the corner of the dining room, so I dragged a chair over and sat with him. Davey came to play at our feet. He had lost so much too.

It was a little after noon. I needed to hold myself together until 4:00 P.M. By then most people would leave. After a while, I couldn't sit still anymore. I walked into the living room. Davey followed behind, cranky because he missed his nap. He shadowed me, hanging on my legs.

Out of the corner of my eye, I saw Mom whispering to Mary and nodding my way. I seethed inside. *She's telling her I'm crazy. Nobody's going to talk about me behind my back.*

I crossed the room to call her on it, but as I moved in her direction, I took a deep breath and regained control. *Mary will leave soon.* I tried to ignore them. My moods and emotions were open to public comment now.

It wasn't the typical Irish funeral with laughter and stories. Nobody played poker over in the corner or drank until fights started. Nobody sang "Danny Boy." Everyone talked quietly. Nobody had the heart to laugh. He was too young.

The crowd dwindled. I sat down on the couch in the living room. Someone turned on the television and the *Three Stooges* ran through one of their silly routines. At the other end of the house, dishes clattered in the kitchen as the aunts cleaned up.

I wanted to close my eyes but couldn't while Davey was awake. He was starting to stink. He needed to be changed, but I was too tired to do it. After a few minutes, Katie walked by. She took a whiff.

"You stink!" She grabbed Davey and carried him upstairs for a diaper change.

I hoped the Turners would make their good-byes and head for the door. They didn't belong here with people who loved Bob. They'd disowned him. They ignored all the danger signals. They wouldn't go into the ICU while he was still alive. They didn't want an autopsy. Now they wept and sobbed. My anger at them was boundless. Here they sat taking up space. I couldn't believe Mom was still talking to them. Dad, sure. He talked to anybody. But Mom? Come on. She was just being polite.

I drank all day in little sips. Now I planned on getting drunk. I wanted to pass out. After Mom and Dad went to bed, only Tim would be up. I'd drink more then. With no nap, Davey would surely go down early. I hoped he wouldn't be too tired to fall asleep.

It would be over soon. I helped put the dishes away and ate some of the leftovers. In the kitchen, I checked the time. It was only 3:30 P.M.

56

Even though the throngs were long gone, and Davey had fallen asleep, I couldn't relax. Everyone else was exhausted. Mom and Dad flopped down in front of the television and stared until the news came on, then dragged themselves to bed. Tim watched the news and waited for Johnny Carson. Good. I sat but couldn't keep my mouth shut. Suddenly, everything I held back all day came rushing out.

"He didn't need to die. He wouldn't go to the hospital." I felt compelled to relive it. Tim didn't say a word, he just listened.

"He looked so terrible at the end. He was suffering. But I'm glad he's dead. I couldn't have taken care of him." I rambled on. "What if Chip had driven faster?"

I flipped from intense grief to intense relief in the same breath. My emotions couldn't catch up with my words.

I wasn't sure what Tim made of this, but he didn't stop me. *The Tonight Show* played on. I desperately sipped the last of the whiskey I poured to knock myself out. Sleep was the hardest thing, and I feared it. I couldn't shut my mind off.

I'd picked whiskey to drink because I didn't like the taste. I figured there would be less chance of being hooked if I drank something I didn't like. I thought about the bottle of Valium Doctor Mader gave me last year and that I still carried in my purse. I wasn't sleepy yet, and I didn't want to be awake by myself. I took the bottle out and started counting out the pills. If I bit them in half, I might have twenty days left. Forty if I managed to bite them into fourths.

I bit off a quarter of a pill and washed it down with the last sip of whiskey. Pretty soon, the mix of the two washed over me. My eyes started to droop. I said goodnight to Tim and climbed the two stories to the attic.

I didn't wake until Davey stirred the next morning. *Thank God. I made it through the night.* I lifted Davey out of his crib. He rubbed his eyes, raring to go. He wasn't going to fall back to sleep.

"Mama," he cooed. He broke my heart. He didn't understand any of this. How could I explain it? How could I make him understand his father wouldn't be coming home?

Downstairs in the kitchen Mom was busy. She greeted Davey lovingly and then turned to me. Again, she stared, trying to figure out my mental state. I ignored her. I refused to give her a blow by blow report of my night.

⌘

Our townhouse in Kent still needed to be packed and cleaned. I focused on that. I called our landlord. He understood when I told him what had happened. "I can't pay February's rent. Would you let me out of the lease?"

He took pity on me. Now I had a week to pack everything and move out.

"How about Tim and I go up to Kent and start packing? Can you watch Davey?"

Mom nodded her head. She hadn't returned to work yet.

"All right but wake Tim now."

I was humiliated enough losing my husband. Now I had to worry about money too. I wouldn't have enough to cover my expenses, at least not until the Social Security money started coming in. I still couldn't find Bob's life insurance policy. How would I get the money I needed? I woke Tim.

⌘

In Kent, things were quiet. Snow still covered the ground. The lifeless hulk of the Fairlane still sat in the carport.

"I don't know what's wrong with that stupid car," I said as we walked past. "I hope Dad will take care of it."

My heart rose to my throat at the back door. No one could imagine the terrible things that occurred there. Every room held a different frightening memory.

Inside, we surveyed the mess. That god-awful orange vinyl furniture still sat in the living room. I'd leave it at the curb and hope the garbage men would haul it away. That left the bedroom furniture, Davey's toys, Bob's electronics, and record albums to pack.

We had ordered a new mattress, a Christmas gift from Mom and Dad but it hadn't arrived yet. Maybe I could cancel it and get a refund. For sure, I didn't need a new double mattress.

Upstairs, blankets were still strewn across the bed, the way Chip and I left them when we took Bob to the hospital. A chill went down my spine. I stopped myself from crying, but my thoughts returned to those final few hours. I shook my head trying to make the memories go away.

I searched through piles of paperwork on the desk. Bob's grade book and the rent notice lay there. Out of the corner of my eye, I saw some insurance papers off to the side.

Looking closer, it hit me. This was the life insurance application, completed and signed, but still sitting there. He hadn't turned it in. I stared in disbelief. *He didn't take it back? No life insurance? This can't be right.*

57

I couldn't sleep without the Valium and the whiskey. My mind wouldn't shut off. I thought about Bob's ghastly look as he lay dying, the insurance, the mourners whispering behind their hands. Numb was better.

At times I longed for Bob. I missed his body and the comfort of physical closeness to another human being. Hugging a toddler couldn't replace that. At other times, I was glad to be rid of him. I didn't miss his threats to kill us and I sure didn't miss the walking on eggshells. Now my shells were all broken.

I lost my future—owning a radio station, working beside Bob, having a second child. I ached. My whole identity revolved around our dreams, the life we would build together. How could I go on? I'd lost everything. At night I lay in bed sobbing. Then it hit me. I could kill myself.

Suicide? It was a new idea. Comforting. I'd be with Bob again and my husband in the afterlife would be certainly better than my earthly one. How could I do it? I didn't want anything messy Davey might find or that would freak out my parents. But it was an answer.

I used to be such a devout Catholic. I believed in the Church teachings, heaven and hell, limbo, purgatory. Back then, when I wanted to join the convent, suicide was a mortal sin. You couldn't be buried in a Catholic cemetery. But now? I didn't care. It would solve all my problems. But the irony hit me. I had scorned my mother for her suicide note and now my thoughts went to the same solution. How could I leave Davey? *That* would be a tragedy.

How could I ache from missing Bob and be happy he was dead? Emotions swirled through my brain as I struggled to fall asleep. They made me crazy. On the outside, I appeared stoic, not crying, able to handle every task. I wouldn't tell anyone what I thought. I smiled half-heartedly when I sat down to breakfast. Mom continued to stare.

But time did help. As the days passed it was easier to be around Davey. He delighted me though his resemblance to Bob was eerie. He banged his spoon on the high chair tray. "Mama, mama."

How could I ever leave him? My parents would end up caring for him, or worse yet, he could go to Bob's parents.

I called for an appointment with the Catholic Charities counselor I abandoned last fall. I wanted to tell him what happened and get his support. I wouldn't mention my thoughts of suicide.

I'd been off work for a week, without talking to anyone at the *Beacon* about returning. Would I feel better if I went back? I still waited to hear about my application to Kent, but I needed money fast. Ironically, with Bob gone, there would be less competition to get into the graduate program.

Had Alesky, my boss at the paper, heard about Bob's death? As morning dawned, I dragged myself out of bed determined to call the State Desk to find out when to come back. I couldn't just show up. I needed an assignment—a meeting to cover. I would give them time to quell the 8:00 A.M. fires before I called. Mom fixed breakfast for Dad. She eyed me again like she did every morning. I ignored her and made some toast with strawberry jam.

"What are you doing today?" She thought my life unfolded in an orderly way.

"I'm going back to work." I tried to shock her into butting out. "I'll call the *Beacon* today."

"Who'll care for Davey while you're at work?"

Oh, no. Now she was giving me trouble about that. I hoped she wouldn't make me beg her to watch him or worse yet find a sitter.

She forced me to play my hand. "I hoped you and Dad would, or maybe Tim will do it."

"I'm going back to work too. On Monday," Mom said.

"I don't have to leave for these night meetings until 6:00 P.M. You'll be home by then." I bargained with her. She wasn't giving me any breaks just because I lost my husband. Now I was angry.

I didn't tell her about my thoughts of suicide or my plan to quit the newspaper and go to grad school at Kent. Bob had wanted to keep everything secret. Now I was mad.

We'd planned to finish master's degrees and find jobs in broadcasting. We hoped the poor job market of the past couple years would improve while we were in school. Was this foolish now? Possibly, but it would give me a two-year cushion before having to decide what to do with my life.

"I need to talk to your father about babysitting," Mom said.

I resented her delaying tactic, but I knew Davey and I were a burden.

I took a deep breath and dialed the *Beacon* number.

Alesky answered the phone. "State Desk." All official. He seemed pleased it was me. "How are you?"

I didn't go into detail about my life. "I'm fine." Not true, but I couldn't figure out how to explain things without falling into pathos. "I mean, I'm ready to come back to work."

He sounded relieved. He was probably glad I wasn't crying.

"Great!" He rushed on. "When?"

"How's Monday?"

"Good. Good. Why don't you start with the Brunswick Council meeting? I'll have a schedule ready for you when you come into the office. Nice to have you back."

I'd be in the swing of things next week. Suicide could wait. I had something outside myself to focus on.

⌘

Still cold and blustery, it was a typical Ohio winter. The snow was so deep I couldn't take Davey outside for more than a few minutes. Though he'd been walking since eight months, his little legs were no match for the snowdrifts. We stayed in the living room with his toys spread out on the floor. I was so tired I just sat and watched him play with his trucks.

I spent my time in front of the TV, numbing myself. At night, after everyone else went to bed, Tim still listened to me ramble about the hospital, what Bob looked like and how scary it was. I couldn't turn my mind off. Now it took a little more booze and half a Valium to put me to sleep.

Tim and Dad helped me move out of the townhouse. I waited for the deposit from our landlord. That, plus the $265 death benefit I expected from Social Security was all the money I had, so buying another car was out of the question.

Dad had junked the Fairlane. The water pump was broken. It hadn't run since the Monday before Bob died. I hoped I could borrow one of the family cars.

Now, I just needed to survive the weekend. Anna went back to Toronto. My friends had moved away after college and I'd lost touch with everyone else from high school. By the time Bob and I graduated, our only friends were from the radio station.

None of them had contacted me since the funeral, except when they showed up to pick through Bob's electronics and record collection. I kept all his *Playboy* magazines, model cars, and train sets. Davey would like those later. Bob's clothes went to Goodwill. The furniture went into the trash.

Ten days had passed without him. I still had doubts that he was dead. I couldn't stop myself from reliving those last few hours in the hospital. What if we had driven faster? What if I had divorced him? Could anything have saved him? I needed the distraction of work.

58

My mind played amazing tricks. I heard Bob's voice or caught a glimpse of him in a crowd. I'd gone down the rabbit hole again, so I tried to calm myself. *That's crazy. Of course, he's not alive. They embalmed him. He's buried. He's in the ground. The ground is frozen.* This became my mantra.

My parents tiptoed around me. Tim listened but didn't say much. I dumped it on him every night, afraid I might scare anybody else with my thoughts. *You're lucky to be alive,* I repeated over and over.

Even though I loved him, I was glad he died. When I thought about our future, I got chills. *He stalked me. He tried to kill us.* I imagined what a divorce would have done to him. He wouldn't let me go. *God did me a favor.* I just needed to believe it.

Every night as I fell asleep, I repeated it like a prayer: *I'm lucky. We got out alive.* Sure, I loved Bob, but I hated what he did to us. I hated him for scaring me, for threatening us and most of all for dying. We were better off now.

I devised a cover story, one for people who said, "Oh! He was so young! Was he killed in Vietnam? In a car accident?"

I had to stop them before they got carried away with their guesses. The truth was much more mundane. "He was afraid of the doctor. They couldn't save him. He died." This produced more gasps, but thankfully evoked more pity than horror.

People closer to me asked harder questions. "Did he know he was diabetic?"

"He had all the symptoms," I said, "but I couldn't make him go to the doctor." Many of them gave me a funny look, sensing a gap in my story. I left out his attempts to kill us. I was humiliated that I was so afraid of him I let him die.

⌘

Monday morning finally dawned. I stored our boxes in the attic cubby holes behind the beds. Davey had been up for a few minutes and I heard him downstairs, two stories below with Mom, probably eating toast with grape juice. By evening I'd be back at work.

I loved the drive to Brunswick. Route 303 ranged up and down tree-covered hills through the Cuyahoga Valley and onto the flat plane where Brunswick sat. At twilight snow still glistened on the ground. As I turned onto 303, "American Pie" came on the radio. I sang as I zoomed along.

It felt great to be out of the house, free of Davey, free of Mom's stares. The simple things I looked forward to now astounded me. No more plans for owning a radio station. My happiness was defined by how many minutes I kept myself from dwelling on Bob.

No one in Brunswick knew of his death. Preoccupied with Council matters they ignored me.

The meeting dragged on with the usual business: paving a few roads, paying bills. Mercifully, it adjourned before 8:30 P.M. I hoped I could write my article and be home in bed by midnight.

I composed the story mentally as I drove, keeping me from thinking about myself. The parking deck was almost deserted. I found a spot by the door. Good. The wind blew hard and cold.

I made a run for the door that opened onto the newsroom. I hoped there wouldn't be too many back from their nighttime assignments yet. Only Doug and Bill were there so far. I dreaded telling people about Bob and what I went through.

My coworkers had overheard his late-night phone call. Even with my made-up stories, I hoped no one would ask about his death. If I started crying, they might think I wasn't ready to return. But I desperately needed the income.

Both Doug and Bill were engrossed in their stories. They barely noticed as I took a seat, interspersed my three newsprint pages with carbon paper, and rolled them into the typewriter. I pulled out my notepad, reviewed my notes and typed my lead.

Bill shook his head. He said, "I'm sorry."

Doug gave me a wry smile and continued typing. Over the next hour, the rest of the night crew drifted in.

"I'm all right," I told each one of them in turn. I wanted to write my article and leave before I had to answer too many questions.

I finished my story and laid it in the wire basket on Alesky's desk. I was out the door by 10:30 P.M. At home, Tim waited for Johnny Carson to come on.

For once I was tired. I said goodnight to him and climbed the stairs to the attic. Davey slept, and I was determined not to wake him. I undressed quietly in the dark. I stared at the ceiling for an hour before I went downstairs to the kitchen, took a bite of one of the few remaining Valiums and gulped it down with a half a glass of whiskey.

59

Weekends were the hardest. With no work to occupy me, I sat and stared. Mom still cared for Davey. It grated on me though. *He loves her more than he loves me.* She grabbed him up and put him in the high chair for a snack. She caught him in mid-run and laid him on his back for a diaper change. She laughed when he called her "Mama."

I couldn't stand it. After caring for five kids of her own, she was a much better mother than I. She made it seem so easy. Even though I couldn't bear to care for him, I watched the two of them like a hawk, sensitive to their closeness. I couldn't take it any longer.

"Stop!" I yelled as she laid him down to change another diaper. "I already lost my husband," I screamed crazily. "I'm not letting you take my baby away."

The room grew quiet. Everyone turned and stared. Now they knew I was crazy, even Roy and Jenny who had been absorbed in *The Little Rascals.*

Mom gave me a look that said it all. She didn't know what to expect from me. "Are you nuts? You don't appreciate anything I do," she said with a hurt look.

She let go of Davey. He jumped up and ran to me, a toddler soothing a crazy woman. I wasn't crying yet, but I choked back tears. *I can't cry now.* I was afraid I wouldn't be able to stop.

I swallowed hard. Davey still needed to be changed. Mom threw the diaper at me. She rose from her knees with tears in her eyes. She hated crying.

I bent down to tend to Davey and immediately felt guilty. Guilt mixed with self-righteousness, though. *Who does she think she is, anyway? Davey is mine.*

I finished pinning the corner of the diaper and he squirmed away. I lifted myself up from my knees and as I did, I noticed all eyes on me. Mom stormed into the kitchen, but now Dad and the rest of the kids stared at me. I grabbed Davey and made a beeline for the door. *I'll take him for a walk. I need to cool down.* I helped him into his red snowsuit and little boots.

The cold air smacked me as I opened the front door. Not many people about. Walks hadn't been shoveled since last night's storm. I sat down on the porch steps and cried. Davey, who'd been occupied eating snow climbed the steps. He patted me on the arm. "Mama," was all he said.

Thank God, I had an appointment with Jerry the Catholic Charities counselor. He might help me make sense of this. I had to get through the weekend and two nights of work until my appointment on Wednesday. I focused my attention on Davey. It hurt. He was so like Bob. But I needed to find the strength to take care of him; otherwise, I'd lose him.

Wednesday came, and I readied myself for my appointment. I wanted to take someone with me for support, but everyone had work or school, except for Tim who volunteered to watch Davey.

A sunny winter day, it wasn't too cold. The snow melted again. I sweated nervously as I sat in the waiting room. I planned to tell him exactly what happened, not holding back like I did last fall. He'd be the first person to hear the whole story besides Mom and Tim.

He poked his head around the corner and called my name. Did he remember me from November? He ushered me into his office and began with small talk.

I was so glad to see him. He could give me something to hang on to, to fight off the thoughts of joining Bob, of killing myself. I rushed right into my story.

"I'm here to tell you what happened to Bob." I launched into the story I'd rehearsed. I told him about Bob's threats and his attempt to kill us, his illness and his sudden death. Jerry's eyes widened. At the end, he shook his head. I expected him to tell me I should return for more therapy.

"How are you doing?"

I decided to be honest. "I'm torn. I'm so relieved he's dead. I feel free. I'm happy," I said, though the happy part was an exaggeration. "But I miss him. I still cry at night." I didn't tell him about my thoughts of suicide, afraid he might lock me up.

He shivered like he wanted to escape the burden of my story.

"Well, great! You don't need to return."

I was stunned. For some reason, the fact that Bob's death was a two-edged sword had escaped him. I stood and shook my head. Less than a half hour had passed since I entered the room. "Well, thank you."

"You don't need another appointment," he added in case I didn't understand.

I drove home in silence, the radio off. I turned his words over in my mind. *Am I really okay?* I didn't think so, but he was the expert. He must have known what he was doing. *Was my story too scary for him, too raw?* Somehow, I didn't convey the depths of my devastation.

I thought about what he said. *Was I okay? No. Goddamn him. How could he be so blind to my desperation?* If I ever saw him again, I'd . . . I'd what? I was so angry. I'd show him. I could survive without him. By the time I reached home, I was seething, but the nagging thoughts of suicide had gone away. I'd show him. I could survive without his help. And God? Well, He sure wasn't any help either. I needed to take this step by step, to figure it out on my own.

⌘

It had been more than three weeks since Bob's death. All my hopes lay in the autopsy report. To me, his death was senseless. A twenty-four-year-old in good shape? Who ever heard of such a thing?

I still had moments when I doubted he was dead, but they didn't come as often. I kept remembering the scene at the hospital, in the ICU. He looked so deathly ill. I couldn't shake the image of him gasping for air. Then the funeral, the grave. I could see the casket being lowered. I still wondered if it was a mistake.

I told myself that my mind played tricks. I replayed the same reassurances over and over. *He's buried, his body has been drained of blood and fluids.* This worked when I was wide awake, but as I was falling asleep, I doubted it.

I hoped the autopsy results would help me stop this thinking. Everyone I talked to was shocked by Bob's sudden death. There must have been some hidden condition that caused his death. When I told people an autopsy was done, they almost smiled. It would provide some answers to the mystery.

I listened for the phone. I hoped Doctor Mader's office would call to tell me the results came in. He was my doctor too, the same one who yelled at Bob's parents in the waiting room.

Doctor Mader had shown his humanity that night before they unhooked Bob from the machines. I hoped the pathologist would find some illness, some brain abnormality that tied everything up in a neat bundle, explained Bob's behavior and cause of death.

I hoped they would give me information about what to watch for in Davey, so this wouldn't happen again. The Turners opposed the autopsy, but my rights as his wife superseded theirs.

On a Thursday, almost four weeks to the day after Bob's death, the phone rang. Doctor Mader's receptionist was on the line.

"Can you come in for an appointment next week?"

"Of course. When do you want me?"

She set an appointment for Tuesday. Mom and Dad both worked. I would go alone. Finally, the mystery would be solved. My hopes ran high. Bob would still be dead, but I wanted to put my fears for Davey to rest. After this, I could get on with my life. Would Doctor Mader refill my Valium prescription? I was almost out.

Tuesday dawned cold and snowy. Gloom and sleet were followed by slush. I dressed in my best work clothes, settled Davey in front of the TV to watch *Sesame Street* with Tim and left.

⌘

Doctor Mader offered me a seat. The office was dark with rich brown leather chairs. A single table lamp glowed on the desk. I leaned forward expectantly.

He was all business and as I waited, he riffled through a file, looking for the report. He pulled an onion skin document out scanning it quickly like he'd read it before. He took a deep breath.

"Well, there isn't much here, Patty," he began, apologetically. "It says he had a bit of pneumonia in one lung, but the diabetes is what killed him."

"There's nothing else?" I asked, stunned. This couldn't be. My heart raced. I fought back tears. "That can't be it."

"I'm afraid so. I hoped there would be something else too," he admitted. "I guess we'll never know."

I shook my head and cried, too stunned to ask any sensible questions. They didn't find a brain tumor or something else that would explain his crazy behavior?

"But why did he die? It couldn't be diabetes."

Doctor Mader became fatherly. "The diabetes was too advanced. He waited too long to come in." He shook his head sadly.

I was too humiliated to explain why he didn't go to the doctor sooner. In every version I'd tried so far, I sounded like a cowering rabbit.

He handed me a copy of the autopsy report. "Read it yourself. Is there anything else I can do for you today?"

It sounded like he would continue as my doctor. I remembered the Valium.

"Could you refill the prescription you gave me last year?" I asked casually. "The Valium?"

He studied me for a minute. "No." He said with a note of finality.

He stood, and our meeting was over. In the parking lot, I found Dad's car. As I unlocked the driver's door, a tear left my eye and rolled down my cheek. What was worse, the autopsy report or his refusal to give me Valium?

I cried the rest of the way home. When I pulled into the driveway, I had more control of myself. The autopsy was supposed to answer all my questions. How could I go on?

Davey and Tim were still in front of the TV. Tim glanced up expectantly. I shook my head in despair.

"They didn't find anything," I said dramatically. Tim gave me a weird glance, disbelieving. Again, I held back tears.

"What are you talking about?"

"The autopsy found diabetes. Nothing else."

"What do you mean?" He was incredulous.

"It was diabetes. He had a slight case of pneumonia, but the doctor said that wasn't enough to kill him."

I couldn't explain this twice more today. It was hard enough to bear my own grief, but the stricken looks of my parents would devastate me. Still, I needed to tell them.

60

There was something particularly painful about watching Mom cry. She'd held up well during the funeral. I only saw her tear up a little once or twice. Before this, the only time I remembered her sobbing was when Kennedy was shot. I wanted to tell my parents about the autopsy report that night. I wouldn't call her at work like I usually did. I didn't want to break down again.

I fed Davey lunch, then got him ready for a walk. The chilly temperature would tire him, so he'd nap this afternoon. By 1:00 P.M., the stormy weather passed, and the air turned balmy for mid-February, almost thirty-eight degrees.

The sidewalks were too rutted with frozen slush to push the stroller. We stayed in the front yard where he played in the snow while I thought.

What did the autopsy mean to me? Bob was still dead, but the report did tell me whether I could have done anything else. Now for sure, no one was to blame, except for him and his parents. I remembered when he was trapped in the health center on Pill Hill that first summer. He told me he didn't like doctors. Who knew it would lead to this?

Then there was the time when his throat was so sore he couldn't talk. I yelled to get him to see a doctor. Turned out he had strep. A warning, if I had only known.

⌘

One good thing about our large family was our connectedness. I only needed to explain the report to my parents and they would tell my aunts and uncles.

Davey picked up the snow, tossed it and watched it glisten. There was a light dusting around his mouth. A snow eater. I gathered him up and took him in the cellar door. I removed his boots and snowsuit. Wrangling that stupid snowsuit exhausted me. He was ready for a nap.

I helped him climb the stairs, three floors, all the way to the attic. I didn't remind him of his impending nap. I lifted him into the baby bed and turned to go, determined not to trigger his protests by kissing him night-night.

He lay down quickly. The outdoor air worked its magic.

Downstairs was quiet. Tim had gone to an afternoon class. In the living room, the television was still on. I flipped through the channels and found the *Phil Donahue Show*. Falling into an armchair I stared at the TV, or rather past it, too tired to think.

Minutes later, I heard the door. Mom. I hadn't started dinner. I jumped up, but she had taken her boots off and gotten as far as the kitchen. She gave me a questioning look as she came into the room. I bet she wondered why I hadn't called.

I shook my head. "The autopsy didn't find anything else. It was diabetes."

She scoffed. I had pinned my hopes on the wrong thing again. It was not the reaction I expected from her, but at least she hadn't cried, which meant she wouldn't make me cry either.

She didn't even yell at me for not cooking. She retrieved her apron.

"Get some carrots out of the refrigerator and peel them." She was all business, a relief. "We'll have leftover stew meat and salad. We'll talk more when your dad gets home."

⌘

Dad smiled as he came in. As always, he checked Mom's mood as he stuck his head into the kitchen. We both worked on supper. Davey crawled around beneath our feet.

"How are you, big boy?" Dad crooned to him. Davey jumped to his feet and ran into his arms.

"I have some news." He boosted Davey up on his shoulders. "I found a car for you."

My transportation problem had been ongoing, ever since the Fairlane broke down right before Bob died. With no money to buy a new car, I borrowed one of Mom and Dad's for work. There'd always been at least one car sitting idle.

I dreaded telling Dad about the autopsy, so this was a distraction.

"What kind is it?" I asked, not that it mattered. It just needed to run and be affordable.

"A '70 Comet. A Mercury with a Ford engine but a different body." Dad loved the inner workings of cars.

Thrilled, I didn't care about the make.

"It's outside. Do you want to look?"

Yeah, anything to avoid the autopsy discussion. We went to the door. Outside sat a beautiful, fire red Comet. Could I afford the payments?

"I can't pay for this now," I said. "Maybe when the Social Security check comes through."

Dad shook his head. "Don't worry. I'll cover it until you get your money. You just need insurance."

The door was unlocked. I sat in the driver's seat. I loved it.

Mom called from the doorway. "Let's have supper." She went up the steps and called Roy to come to eat.

I rushed through dinner. I was hot to try out the new car. While we ate, I casually mentioned the report to Dad.

"They didn't find anything. I mean they didn't find something new or surprising."

Dad nodded his head in despair. Davey banged on the high chair tray. Dad saw my disappointment.

"I'm sorry," he said. Then, without missing a beat, he added, "Let's go for a drive after dinner."

61

We finished eating. I helped Mom clear the dishes and grabbed my coat. She entertained Davey while Dad and I took a test drive.

It was dark now, but the streets were dry. I drove down Second Street and onto the expressway, so I could give it some gas.

"How much is it?"

"Twenty-five hundred. I got it from one of the car dealers I work with."

Dad worked in the Loan Department, funding loans for used car dealers who wanted to replenish their stock.

"You can get a loan from the church credit union," he said. "You won't need to pay for another couple of months. By then Social Security should come through."

I breathed a sigh of relief. I hadn't told anyone that I only had sixteen dollars left in my bank account.

"I'll go by the credit union tomorrow."

The five-hundred-dollar loan I took out for my first car helped now. When I walked into the credit union, the loan officer was ready for me. He asked me a couple of questions and granted me a loan based on my payment record. It didn't hurt that Dad volunteered there either.

That night, getting ready for bed I hummed "Let It Be." Things were looking up despite the autopsy.

I loved the car. It was fire engine red and went fast. More than a car, it restored me to adulthood. No more asking permission to use a family car. No more driving under the speed limit so

I wouldn't get a ticket. We could come and go as we pleased. I thought about the other ways I'd lost myself with my move back home.

Besides losing my husband, I'd given up my independence too. My parents didn't intend it, but that's what happened. I resented their generosity but didn't have the guts to tell them. I was so broke I needed to rely on them. Work continued at the same pace, which meant I wasn't earning any more money.

With lots of bills to pay, I worried I wouldn't have enough money for the mortuary bill. The timing was wrong to look for a higher-paying job. Anyway, I worked at the best newspaper in Northeastern Ohio and, the economy was still so depressed that many college grads were jobless.

⌘

My friends disappeared in the weeks after the funeral. It hurt me, and I couldn't understand why they'd left. I wasn't any different from when Bob was alive. Did they think my bad luck would rub off on them? I was heartsick. Not only had I lost Bob but also my connection to the adult world.

It was still mighty cold outside, so I couldn't even sit with other mothers at the playground. I'd lost touch with my high school friends one by one. I didn't know their addresses or phone numbers anymore.

Davey was the center of my world. Every decision I made was for his benefit. Of course, this fit with Mom's thinking. Her generation stayed home after WWII to raise kids while the men worked. When she saw me moping around the house, she couldn't contain herself.

"You just need to get married again." She nodded knowingly.

I scoffed, but she played right into my fantasy. I was only twenty-four years old. Surely, I'd be married by twenty-five, twenty-six at most. I missed Bob so much it was physically painful. Most days I occupied myself with Davey, but at night my body ached for Bob. My single bed in the attic was a sad reminder. *Why did I let Mom talk me into buying it?* I longed for his touch. I took a second pillow to bed with me and clung to it all night.

⌘

My fellow reporters left me alone. I could hide in the newsroom banging out stories about sewers or school dress codes. I wished Kent's Telecom department would call with news about the graduate assistantship. Then I could either make plans to escape the *Beacon* or get serious about advancing there.

In mid-February, an envelope arrived from Social Security. Maybe it held Davey's survivor's money. I tore it open and scanned it. The benefits were approved. Inside was a check for two hundred sixty-five dollars. I jumped for joy. Another step forward. Davey would get a monthly check starting in March. There was a widow's benefit too. I'd also receive a retroactive payment for January. Now I could afford the car.

The next day, the funeral bills arrived. I gasped. The combined total for the funeral home and the cemetery was more than five thousand dollars. Then the hospital bill showed up. Seven hundred dollars for eight hours in the ICU. I couldn't believe it. It was the same amount we paid for Davey's birth less than two years ago when I stayed in the hospital for five days.

Mom comforted me but didn't offer any money. "Don't worry, things will work out."

Her tough love killed me. I pinned my hopes on the graduate assistantship at Kent. At the start, it had been a dream. Bob wanted it more than I did. I went along, thinking it would help launch us toward owning a radio station. Now it took center stage in my fantasies. Not that I disliked the newspaper, but an assistantship could be a way out of my low-paying cellar-level job.

I'd call Doctor Wiser tomorrow morning. He might be able to tell me when they would make their decision.

At 8:00 A.M. I phoned and for once, I got some welcome news.

"We decided to award you one of the assistantships," he said very formally.

"Wonderful! When do I start?" I couldn't wait to quit the *Beacon.*

"Oh, it won't be until the end of August. We'll send a letter explaining everything. And the stipend is twenty-five hundred dollars a year."

"Wonderful! What will I be doing?"

"We haven't decided yet. You'll find out in August."

I was so excited. Twenty-five hundred dollars! Half of what Bob and I earned last year. The acceptance letter would come soon. Overjoyed, I was saved. I could quit my job.

I ran into the kitchen to tell Mom. "I got it," I said, self-satisfied. She nodded approvingly.

"Got what?"

"I'm going back to Kent in Telecom. Bob and I applied to the program last year. I'll be a grad assistant. I'll get a stipend—twenty-five hundred dollars a year."

To Mom, all education was good. She wouldn't fight me. Now I had another source of income besides Social Security. I wouldn't be tied to the newspaper anymore.

Things were improving for us. I grabbed Davey up and swung him around.

"I'm going back to school," I sang. I had sworn to avoid Kent ever since May 4. I guessed I could overlook that for money and security for a couple of years.

Davey laughed and clapped. I sat him down in the high chair and he took another bite of toast. Both he and Mom stared, not sure what to make of this sudden change. True, I didn't have much experience in broadcasting aside from the volunteering I did at WKSU. If my assistantship focused on news or reporting, I'd be fine. I knew about those things. I returned to the *Beacon* with renewed vigor.

"I'm going back to school!" I almost sang to anyone who would listen. My classmates who couldn't find jobs in the recession were just finishing their graduate work. Being in school was normal.

The Telecom letter came, signed by Doctor Wiser. The incoming graduate assistants would meet in August for assignments. I was nervous about what I'd be doing, but Bob would be proud. The whole idea of returning to school was his so I could help when he bought his own station.

That dream was dashed, but he would be happy for me. I drove up to Kent to thank Doctor Wiser personally. He didn't know he'd saved my life by simply doling out a little of the university's money.

I took Davey, and we piled into the Comet early one wintry afternoon. The drive was a pleasure, not onerous like when I commuted. I carried Davey over the puddles in the parking lot. I let him loose inside and he bounded down the hall, hooting to hear his voice echo. We took the stairs to the third floor. He'd tire out.

The heavy double doors to the station were still there although now a new sign read *WKSU AM-FM*. The handle was too high for Davey, so he waited for me. Most of my friends were gone except for staff members John Herning and Rick Alexander. Doctor Wiser and a couple of other professors from our undergrad days were still there too. I peeked into his office. Empty. Davey stamped his feet and listened for his echo, so I picked him up to quiet him.

Right then, I saw Doctor Wiser coming out of the music library. He recognized me and kept on until he was just a foot away. This was the first time I'd seen him since Bob's death. I opened my mouth to thank him for what he'd done, but before I could, he spoke.

"It's been hell on wheels for you, hasn't it?"

I was so shocked I couldn't respond. *He's talking about Bob. How could he guess?* I hadn't told anyone outside the family about his behavior. I was too humiliated.

"Trust me, I know." He nodded and stared into my eyes, laser-like.

Tears formed. I swallowed hard but not soon enough. My eyes flooded with tears. For a moment I felt an intense connection with him. *He knows. He understands what I've been through.* I was both relieved and mortified.

"I want to thank you," I stammered.

"Don't worry. This will be right for you. It would have been bad for Bob."

Again, I was shocked and amazed. I heard rumors his wife had a mental illness, but it wasn't discussed openly. That must be why he understood what I'd been through.

I drove home. I hadn't expected to find someone so understanding. I turned it over in my mind. On one hand, I felt comforted. On the other, I wondered if Doctor Wiser's view of me would color my return to Kent State.

62

Spring 1972

I continued at the *Beacon.* I planned to give them two weeks' notice before I quit. Late Thursday afternoon, Alesky called to tell me there'd been a change in policy and now part-timers must come in each morning to write obituaries. Were they trying to make work so odious the part-timers would quit? I couldn't function on four hours sleep.

I was glad I would earn more money but what if I collapsed from the lack of sleep? This new schedule didn't start until summer, so Mom could watch Davey. I guessed I could do it for a while.

Even if Englehart, the big boss, wanted us to quit it didn't make much difference. I was leaving by mid-August, anyway. I only hoped my body could stand this new schedule. When August rolled around, I'd be dancing out the door.

Seven weeks after Bob's death I stopped wearing my wedding ring without telling anyone. I didn't want the reminder of what I had lost. I rambled on to Tim but only on the weekends. I still drank and took Valium, but because my supply had dwindled, I resorted to biting off smaller and smaller bits of the pills.

My despair wore me out. I was too tired for suicide now. Besides, how could I leave Davey? My worst times were when everyone else was asleep. I still took an extra pillow to bed with me and held onto it. *How could he leave me like this? Was he so unhappy he wanted to die?*

I couldn't stop the questions, but when it got too bad I tried to think about the positives. *We're lucky to be alive. He might have killed us if I'd stayed with him. I must stay alive for Davey.* It was exhausting.

While I was dating and married to Bob, the sexual revolution and the women's movement began. I told myself I'd missed out on so much. I could date and experience new things. Make up for the lost time.

We were too poor in college to go to Woodstock or the March on Washington, but now I could try everything I'd missed. Crazy? Maybe, but it helped for a while.

I explained this to Tim during one of our nightly talks and he looked at me like I *was crazy.* Then he laughed. He thought I was kidding. I didn't care. I just needed to believe in the plan myself. I wanted the mourning to be over.

The next Saturday, Tim decided I needed to resume my life. "We're going out tonight. I'm taking you up to Kent. You can put your theory into practice."

Water Street was where students hung out on weekends. I hadn't gone anywhere except to work since Bob died. I waited for my friends to call and ask me out, but they'd forgotten me.

"We'll just go to the bars," Tim said. He meant the student hangouts in downtown Kent. "I'll be with you."

"I'm so much older than the students, almost twenty-five," I argued.

"Well, you have to get out."

I couldn't argue with this logic, but I was still nervous. "Could we go to a movie instead?"

A George C. Scott movie, *The Hospital* was getting rave reviews. We decided to see it. Tim said we'd stop at one bar afterward. Mid-March, it was almost time for spring break. There'd be lots of people out. He was trying to distract me from my woes.

Mom didn't approve, but she did agree to watch Davey for the evening. Sometimes it was like I lived with my great-grandmother in the nineteenth century.

We went up to the mall to catch the movie. The movie was about young people dying of unknown causes in a hospital. The first went into a diabetic coma. I cried softly to myself. If I made it through this, I could handle anything. By the end of the movie, I had regained my composure, though my eyes were a little red.

"We're still going to the bars," Tim said firmly when he saw my eyes.

We found a parking place on Water Street and walked down the block. First, the Water Street Tavern and then around the corner on Main, The Loft.

We strolled through the Tavern, Tim leading the way. "Brown Sugar" played on the jukebox, strobe lights flashed. We didn't recognize anyone among the throngs milling around inside. We moved on and ordered a beer at The Loft. If only The James Gang was playing tonight. I gulped the beer and set the empty stein onto the bar.

"Let's go," I said. "I'm done."

Tim stared at me incredulously. He laughed. "We're not leaving yet."

This must be one of his psychology tricks. My brain worked overtime, figuring out how to escape. Was it wrong so soon after the funeral? Everywhere I looked, couples close danced and necked. I wanted to get out of there. I had nothing in common with these kids. What would I say if a guy talked to me? My husband just died? That would screw up everything.

I would wait Tim out. This would pass, and I would be home in bed. Tim only made me stay a few minutes longer. We walked back to the car in silence.

"What's wrong?" he asked as we climbed into the car.

"I guess it's too soon." I wanted to cry. "I shouldn't have come with you."

63

Back home, I hugged the pillow and cried. I missed Bob so much it ached. I couldn't stop myself from seeing him in crowds, behind me in the mirror or when I glanced over my shoulder. I kept telling myself he was dead. When I missed him, it was best to remind myself that I was afraid of him. Then I could comfort myself with the thought that he was dead. Twisted, but it worked.

I didn't want to meet somebody new. I slid into the depths of depression. It was hard for me to wake up. I lost my appetite. I moped around. This was what everybody was waiting for: me to fall on my face. I cried myself to sleep.

The 7:00 A.M. start time at the *Beacon* was draining. Still dragging from the night before, it was hard for me to get my brain functioning. My morning routine changed. I woke up before Davey and left.

A different segment of the newspaper staff worked in the morning. The editors were there. Our boss, Englehart, was scary, barking orders out of the side of his mouth while he chewed on a cigar. I could see how the State Desk staffers respected him.

I longed to be hired full time, but I didn't have the amount of energy I'd have to expend to compete for a job. Davey and I couldn't survive on the $90 a week I was earning now until I could prove myself.

My plan to go back to school had centered on helping Bob while he was still alive. Now my motives were different. School would be a welcome change. Returning to Kent would give me time to decide what to do next. It would buy me time to recover. My heart wasn't in broadcasting anymore, now that Bob was dead, but I didn't have to tell anyone.

Thinking I wouldn't be stuck at the *Beacon* comforted me. It allowed me to write obituaries swiftly and not worry about mistakes. Who cared? The copyeditors would catch them. I wouldn't be there much longer.

I still covered the far reaches of Medina and Stark Counties at night. One night as I sat at my typewriter someone new came in from the parking garage. The other reporters sitting around the clump of desks seemed to know him and nodded hello.

"Who's that?" I whispered to Bill, motioning toward the door.

"Oh, that's the new guy, Mike. He's on the Falls beat now."

I went back to writing my city council story, lost in my own work. Soon Mike walked by, on his way to the candy machine. Everyone else ignored him, so I kept typing. On his way back, Snickers bar in hand, he made a purposeful detour past my desk.

"Hi," he said, nodding. "How are you?" He didn't exactly leer at me, but his eyes lingered a bit too long.

A little flustered, I nodded and smiled. "I'm fine." That was the end of it. I finished my story quickly and tried to leave earlier than usual. I needed to be back again at 7:00 A.M. As I walked toward the door, Mike rose and brushed past me in the narrow aisle.

"When are we going out?" he said quietly, smiling. Shocked, I just laughed and shook my head in wonder.

Later, on the ride home, I began to think. This was my chance. He was different. For starters, he was black. From what the others had told me, he was a street-smart ghetto kind of guy. I let my imagination run wild.

It wouldn't do Davey much good for me to get involved with him. Then, there were my parents. Though they never said anything against other races, they did stop Jenny from dating a black guy.

But this was different. I was out of college and an adult. My own person. I could date him and see where it might lead.

The next time he walked past my desk, I decided to smile. Climbing into bed that night, I grabbed the extra pillow to cling to but fell asleep easily.

⌘

After my morning shift with the obits, the rest of the day dragged as I cared for Davey and readied myself to go back to work. I was pretty sure I could handle Mike, street smarts or not. I dressed up in a purple, formfitting mini-skirt and top, hoping he would like it.

I checked the mail. There were two envelopes from Social Security. One was addressed to Davey, the other to me. Was it Davey's benefits? I tore open the first envelope. Inside were two checks for almost $800—more than I expected for one month. An enclosed letter explained this was a lump sum payment to catch up on money Davey was owed.

I crossed my fingers before I opened my envelope. Maybe mine contained a lump sum too. I couldn't believe it. Mine had two checks. Altogether, I had gotten $1,600 from the government. I could make the car payment and pay the rent money I owed my parents.

That night, I cruised through my meeting, not listening to the zoning appeals people drone on. My mind was on Mike as I drove back to the office. *Would he be there? Would he talk to me?*

As I came in from the parking deck, carrying my notebook and oversized purse, I was met by silence. The newsroom was half-deserted. True, I did finish a little early and did speed back. Everyone else was still in the trenches.

I looked around. No Mike. *Don't worry. He'll show up.* I focused on my story. If I finished too soon and he came in later, I'd miss him.

I immersed myself in the story. Like a prairie dog, I popped up each time I heard the door open. Now, the night crew was hacking away at their typewriters. I couldn't stand the wait.

About 9:30, the door opened again. Mike sauntered in. *Not too eager.* I tried not to stare at him. I was so cool I was almost comatose. I barely smiled as he walked by. He did an immediate turnabout and came back to my desk.

"What's up, Mama?"

Settle down. I bit the inside of my cheek. I tried not to fall all over myself smiling and nodding. *Get a grip!*

"When are we going out?' he asked like we were old friends.

I started to shake my head no but then plunged ahead. "You tell me. When are you available?"

He didn't miss a beat. "How about Saturday? I'll pick you up."

Oh, no. I didn't anticipate this. He couldn't come to the house. Dad would have a fit.

"Why don't I meet you somewhere?" I batted my eyelashes. Two could play this game.

"No. I'll come to your house. What's your address?"

So, it was set, my first date since Bob died four months ago. I was nervous. I couldn't fall asleep. Thank God, Saturday was two days off. I worried about what to wear, what to say and whether my parents would overreact.

⌘

I asked Jenny to watch Davey. She was sixteen and still home most weekend nights. Saturday came, and Mike arrived at the curb at six, like he promised. I gave Davey a quick kiss good-bye, ran to the car and jumped in. We discussed going to a movie.

I tried to turn off the dialogue running through my head:

Too soon?

No, I think not.

Why are you with a black man?

It's just a date, nothing more.

We made small talk. Mike told me he lived in Cleveland. He was from Philadelphia where he had worked on a black newspaper. He didn't ask about me. I felt relieved. I didn't want to go into the details of my story.

Two B-movies and *A Clockwork Orange* were playing. Mike liked *Clockwork Orange* and I didn't care. I only knew Stanley Kubrick from *2001*, and I had liked that. So, in we went.

Turned out *Clockwork* wasn't a great first date movie. I squirmed in my seat as the rape scene unfolded. *I can't ask him to leave, can I?*

Afterward, Mike wanted to eat. We agreed on pizza. He wanted to go to a parlor near his apartment.

I gave myself a pep talk. *This is an adventure, right? I'm doing all the things I missed out on.* "Sure, let's go."

On the way to Cleveland, he held my hand. *How romantic.* The first time a man had touched me in four months. I was starved for affection. I sighed and sank back into the seat. We ate a quick bite at a neighborhood pizza joint.

Then Mike asked innocently, "Would you like to see my apartment?'

I hedged a little. "On our first date? Not tonight."

Mike was a skilled negotiator. "We're in the neighborhood," he said sweetly. "Only one street over. Let's stop by. You can see where I live."

I couldn't argue. I was twenty miles away from home and it was late. I couldn't jump out of the car and hitch back to Akron.

"Okay. Let's go."

Mike lived in a walk-up apartment on the second floor of a storefront building. Judging by the freeway exit he took, we were somewhere on the south side of the city.

"I'm looking for a place closer to Akron," he told me. "I came here for a tryout with the *Plain Dealer.* I didn't make it, but the *Beacon* was hiring."

Things began to make more sense. That's why he lived in Cleveland. Upstairs, the two-room apartment was sparsely furnished. I sat on the couch, tugging down the hem of my short skirt. Mike sat next to me.

"Would you like a glass of water?"

I sat there, nursing it. When I set the glass down for a minute and he made his move, lunging for a kiss.

I drew back instinctively. *Settle down. This is a new experience. You're trying to make up for lost time, aren't you?*

My fantasies of free love failed to consider the realities of how it would happen. Too late, it occurred to me Mike's plan for tonight was a lot different from mine.

He held me for a little while and we kissed. Slowly, his hand dropped down to my breasts and then to my thigh. A war raged inside of me. I wanted to leave, but I wanted to have this experience too. I had been afraid thoughts of Bob would stop me from having sex with anyone else, but he was far from my mind.

"Why don't we go into the bedroom?" he whispered, getting up.

This jolted me back to reality, and I remembered another ploy. "I'm on my period," I said, coyly.

Mike laughed. "I don't care. Come on. Let's go," as he pulled me up and led me toward the bedroom.

It wouldn't help to protest. There weren't any neighbors around. If I was going to use Bob's death as an opportunity, a second lease on life, I'd better loosen up. I took a deep breath and followed him.

⌘

The next morning, I got up early with Davey. Last night wasn't what I expected, but at least I was initiated into the post-marriage world. Downstairs in the kitchen, Mom gave me a questioning look.

"How was your date?"

I didn't tell her this was a date, so she was guessing.

"Fine."

"Who did you go out with?"

She wouldn't let this drop.

"A new reporter." I pretended I was willing to go on, divulging more. Mom let it drop.

Mike wanted to go out again tonight, but I cooled him off.

"Let's wait until you get an apartment in Akron." I was torn about seeing him again. Dating him represented a return to the adult world, ripped from me with Bob's death. But this could only be a fling. We had too many differences. In the meantime, it was thrilling. I had done something I never dreamed of. Would the rest of my life be like this?

On Monday night, Mike lurked in the shadows beyond the clump of desks, typing away. I took a break to go to the john and he intercepted me.

"I found an apartment in Stow I'm moving next weekend. Maybe I can see you Monday night."

"Whoa. That would be after eleven. Let's wait until we both have a night off."

He didn't realize I was using him to set myself free from sadness and emptiness.

The weekend arrived and Mike called, wanting to go out Sunday evening.

"We'll go to dinner then to my new place."

I relented. I dressed up. A little after 6:00, I ran out to the curb to meet him. I still tried to keep him from coming to the door, which would start an uproar with Dad. I glanced over my shoulder as we pulled away. I saw Mom watching from an upstairs window.

"Let's go to the Brown Derby in the Falls."

When we walked in, I was surprised.

"Mike!" The hostess greeted him warmly and ushered us into the main dining room. Everyone seemed to know him. He nodded to some men at a corner table.

"That's Councilmen Ferry and Theodore." He pointed discreetly to another table. "I hope they notice us."

Mike had been using me as much as I had him. He covered the lily-white Falls beat, a plum assignment, though he was new to the *Beacon*. I could only guess what politics were involved as the Falls was known jokingly as *Caucasian Falls*. No blacks allowed.

Even before the food arrived, it dawned on me—he wanted to be seen dating a white woman. Maybe he hoped I would help him fit in. I had the sinking feeling I was a pawn in his game.

While it was fine for me to use him, I didn't like him doing the same with me. But the sex was good, and I didn't have any other options for intimacy. I didn't want to break up with him.

After dinner, we drove directly to his new apartment in Stow. He showed me his new digs. I was sure he wanted sex again. This time he was a gentleman. He showed me around his three-and-a-half rooms, then enclosed me in his arms and pulled me toward him for a kiss. He led me toward the bedroom and undressed me. Things were more relaxed this time and I enjoyed his lovemaking.

"How did you like it?" he asked afterward.

"You're the best lover I've ever had," I said without hesitation.

He laughed. "How many others have you had?"

Now I was embarrassed as I realized how naïve I sounded. "Well, only one."

At this, he practically fell on the floor laughing.

"Great praise," he joked.

⌘

When I got home, there was a light in the living room. The front door was unlocked. Dad waited in one of the wingback chairs.

"Hi," was all I said. My mind raced. This was unusual. He hadn't waited up for me before, even when Bob and I were out late. *What's going on?*

"Patty," he said in his low, rumbling voice, "I want to talk to you." He held up a picture book, a little Golden Book, in his hand and it fell open to a ripped page. He shoved it towards me.

"Davey is upset lately." He pointed to the rip, making sure I understood the baby did it.

How stupid does he think I am? This is about me. It's about me dating a black man, not about Davey ripping a book that is at least 24 years old. I gathered my wits. I wouldn't let him spout off about what I was doing to Davey.

"That's not what this is about, is it? You don't like who I'm dating." *I'm no dummy. I'll show him.*

"You're right." He hesitated, then took a deep breath. "I don't want any black grandbabies."

I recoiled at his admission. My father had never said a bad word about another race to me. I was surprised.

"If you want to live in our house, you'll follow our rules," he said flatly.

What rules? They'd never been mentioned. He must have been desperate.

"You'll come in at a decent hour and you will care for your own son." I couldn't believe what I heard. None of my brothers ever had such ridiculous rules.

"If you can't follow our rules, move out," he growled.

"Fine," I yelled, as dramatically as I could, and turned on my heels to go upstairs. I felt like a ten-year-old.

64

Summer 1972

I was so angry at Dad I couldn't sleep. But this anger was working for me. What did he expect me to do, live with them forever? *I must move out. He's thrown down the gauntlet. What else could he mean when he said I must follow their rules or leave?*

My allegiance to Mike waned, especially when I suspected he used me to get in good with the Falls councilmen. That ended it for me.

This alliance was foolhardy. There are plenty of other guys. I just need to find them. In the meantime, I also needed to find Davey and me a new place to live. I lay awake all night plotting. Now that the Social Security checks were coming in, my options had broadened.

The next afternoon while I waited for Davey to wake from his nap, the phone rang. I grabbed it. I was surprised by a familiar voice on the line.

"It's Sam. Sam from Kent State."

I gasped. A chill went through me. *I'm saved.* I had fantasized a knight would come along and save me from my nightmare. Now here he was, a guy I had a secret crush on in college. He was the biker I saw turn his bike around in our driveway one day last summer. *How could I be so lucky?*

I paused to compose myself.

"Hi," I said, nonchalantly. "How are you?"

"Fine." He rushed on. "I've been working on an ore boat out on the Great Lakes. I'm just home for a couple of weeks and heard about Bob. What happened?"

I gave him the PG version of events and he seemed satisfied.

"Would you like to go out?"

He didn't realize how much I would. We agreed to meet on Saturday and he picked me up at the house. No need to hide his presence from my parents.

Sam pulled up to the curb in his beat-up Tercel and I ran out. He told me, like most of us, he couldn't find work as a journalist after graduating. He had worked on the Great Lakes during summer breaks and still had his Merchant Marine card, so he went back out.

"I make lots of money on the Lakes. I'm paying off my debts." He stayed at his parents' house between assignments.

Any thoughts I had of Mike flew out the window as we drove up to Kent. How lucky that he found me. I smiled too much and nodded at his jokes. We ended up the evening at his old rooming house.

After kissing a bit in the driveway, he guided me in through the back door.

"Don still lives here." He referred to his old roommate. He called his name as we walked into the kitchen. Don didn't answer. Taking me into the living room, he gestured for me to sit on the floor.

"They must be out." Odd his old roommates would leave the door unlocked. We resumed our kissing and embraces.

Soon, I felt passion and so did he. He left but soon returned with pillows. He tossed them on the floor and then pushed me back against them. We petted and caressed ardently. Even though the house was deserted, I couldn't help keeping an eye out for any returning roommates. Sam was attentive and soon I lost myself in the moment.

Afterward, as we smoothed our clothes back into position, we heard a noise at the back door. It was Don, home from his night out. Sam jumped up to meet him in the kitchen, leaving me alone. They chatted for a short while and then Sam came back, pulling me to my feet.

"Let's go," he said, without introducing me to Don. He drove me back to the Falls.

"I'll be out on a freighter for the next ten days, but I'll call you when I come back."

I was in heaven. My feet barely touched the ground as I walked up the front steps. Inside, everyone slept and this time no father sat up waiting for me. I breathed a sigh of relief and climbed the stairs to bed.

I lay in bed with thoughts of breaking up with Mike and looked forward to Sam's return. This was the first night since Bob's death I wasn't wracked by conflicting emotions. I slept in peace.

⌘

Things with Sam proceeded slowly. One week he was out on a boat and the next back in town. We met sporadically. He wasn't around enough to provoke any reaction from Dad. We settled into a routine of finding a place to have sex. It could be at his parents' empty house during the day or in one of his old hangouts in Kent at night. We met as often as possible.

We were meant to be. Both journalists, we were the same age and we had graduated. There was a future for us.

⌘

Things were still tense at home. Though Dad stopped waiting up for me, I still felt his steady, disapproving gaze. *What does he want me to do?* I had lost everything I worked so hard for over the years—my marriage, my husband. My dreams were wrapped up in Bob's ideas of owning and running a radio station. Those dreams died with Bob, but I couldn't get them out of my head. I saw his face as I fell asleep, in crowds, in passing cars. Davey was the very image of him. It tore at my heart to watch him.

No one understood. They said, "You're young. You'll remarry." No one fathomed that guys weren't interchangeable. I couldn't pick one randomly and continue my dreams for the future.

Though my parents provided a roof over our heads, I directed my anger at them. *How dare they try to control my social life and who I date?* The idea that I would be following their rules after living on my own for more than six years was ludicrous. I needed to save enough money for first and last month's rent and move out.

No matter I had free babysitting and almost free room and board. Moving became a symbol of independence, of leaving Bob's death and the terror that led up to it behind me. In between visits from Sam, I took to hugging my pillow again when I fell into bed at night. I checked the paper every morning for affordable apartments.

Then one spring evening as Sam drove me back from Kent; I spied a new billboard, strategically placed along the highway. *Indian Valley Townhouses*, it read, *Coming in August, Low Income Housing*, with a phone number for inquiries.

I jotted it down and early the next morning I called the rental office and found out about the rental process and a waiting list. More units would be ready by late summer. I was so excited I drove to Kent to pick up an application. It looked straight forward. They wanted to verify income. They needed to make sure I could pay the rent.

No problem. I had the Social Security payment records and my *Beacon* pay stubs, and a long sob story if they needed it. I finished the application that afternoon, even the part where they asked for references and took it back to the office. I didn't want it getting lost in the mail.

Indian Valley was beautiful, with rows of townhouses, newly-planted trees, winding drives and lots of playgrounds inviting people with kids. There were a few U-Haul trucks with young guys unloading them. I was glad I didn't have much to move, just boxes, clothes, Davey's crib, and my single bed. Of course, I also had Bob's LPs, tapes and cassettes, plus his *Playboy* collection. Most of the stuff would fit in my car.

Indian Valley sat off Sunnybrook Road on the outskirts of Kent, almost directly across from John Herning's house.

John and the rest of Bob's friends had disappeared. *What was wrong with me?* All our friends except for Chip and Mimi had abandoned me, but Sam's attention helped.

Now I just needed to wait until I reached the top of the waiting list. The nights dragged on. Work was filled with zoning board meetings and sewer district updates. I still went in from seven to eleven each morning to write obituaries.

I got less than four hours of sleep each night and looked like death during the day. I could hardly wait to tell them where to shove it, but with two months to go, I had to suck it up. It was summer so Mom cared for Davey in the morning while I worked. He played in the backyard with all his trucks.

In early August, a clerk from the rental office called. A unit would be available on August nineteenth just in time for school. I was thrilled.

"I'll take it! Thank you!"

The clerk sounded surprised. Now I needed to rent a truck and hire someone to help me move. I couldn't wait until Dad came home from work to tell him. This would fix him.

I started to rush into the kitchen to tell Mom but then sat down and calmed myself. I should conduct myself with dignity. It was the start of my new life, right?

"Who was that?" Mom asked.

"Oh, they have a townhouse ready for me," I said as coolly as I could. I picked Davey up from his high chair. "We're moving!" He squirmed out of my arms. Mom gave me a strange look, but I was used to them by now. I couldn't let her worries stop me.

"I need to find a moving truck," I told her and went looking for the phone book.

The nineteenth couldn't come soon enough for me. I wanted a couple of weeks to settle in before school started. I needed to get daycare or babysitting for Davey and contact the utility companies. I picked up the key on the evening of the eighteenth. It felt wonderful to be moving on.

Dad took the news well. He'd be glad not to be reminded of his daughter's fallen state. In fact, both my parents fell into a helpful mode now. Dad brought boxes home from work although I didn't have much to pack—mostly our clothes and Davey's toys. Everything else was in boxes in the attic. Tim and Roy agreed to help me move. Even Sam volunteered although he said he would be out on a ship that week.

Englehart didn't react when I turned in my notice. *What do I care? I'm on to bigger things.* I would get free education and be doing what Bob and I had planned. This worked out so perfectly. I couldn't foresee any pitfalls.

Saturday finally came, and Tim went for the U-Haul at 7:00. Jenny wrangled Davey. I pulled boxes out of the attic. I teetered down the stairs.

Shortly after 9:00, we'd eaten breakfast and finished loading.

I would come back for Davey after the beds were up. I planned to use Social Security money to buy furniture for the living room and my bedroom. I also had that portable TV left over from my internship days in Ashtabula. Everything was falling into place.

Indian Valley was alive with activity when we arrived. People washed cars and watered their grass. Our unit was on Sioux Place and as I looked for the street, I noticed lots of kids near Davey's age playing in front yards.

Interested onlookers gathered to see who was moving in. I met my next-door neighbors, Judy and Dave. Their baby, Heather, was a month younger than Davey.

We'd unloaded everything by 11:00. When everyone left to return the truck, I was alone for the first time in my brand-new townhouse. I loved the chalk-white walls, the smooth tile floor. An open staircase ascended to the bedrooms. Very modern.

I unpacked the kitchen things. The rest could wait until I'd gotten groceries. It was good to be on my own. I was so happy I grinned.

65

The first meeting for graduate assistants was on Monday. What would it be like to return? I refused to go back after we graduated. The anger from May 4 persisted and there was still no resolution to the many lawsuits filed against the state by the families of the dead and injured students.

The Telecommunications Department was a whole new world for me where I could control the way people saw me. No more pitiful stares at me, the helpless widow. Here I could stand on my own, but I was torn between wanting people to understand me and avoiding their pity. It wasn't that I was a widow—that was somewhat normal. It was that my husband died under unusual circumstances and people sensed it, so that aura of abnormality followed me. I didn't know how to shake it.

At twenty-five, I was the oldest. People had come from all over the country and most were experienced in radio or TV production. As the one with the least experience, I got the least-technical assignment, producing a half-hour daily talk show. Doctor Stebbing, the grad student adviser assured me I could do it.

"Don't worry. You'll be booking guests for an interview show and making sure they and the hosts show up."

The show ran on the Kent State TV station, WKSU, where I began my journey that first week of freshman year. Not exactly network news, but, it was a start. The show taped in the same studio where I first laid eyes on Bob, six years ago. I worked hard to block out the memories. The problem with this assignment was logistical. I needed to be in the studio at 6:00 P.M. for the taping and Davey's daycare closed at 5:00. I'd have to find a sitter for that hour five nights a week. Guilt rose as I thought about the number of hours I'd be away from him each day. Daycare was new for both of us.

I took Davey to try out daycare a few days early. He'd been an easy kid so far, but I wanted to make sure he adjusted. The center was in the basement of an old neighborhood elementary school five minutes away.

"He needs to be potty-trained," the director told me when I enrolled him and now a month later he was . . . almost.

I dressed him in training pants and hoped he'd copy the other kids. He had just turned two. Lots of two-year-olds have accidents. Maybe they wouldn't notice. I spent about thirty minutes sitting on the sidelines while he played and ate a snack. Miss Betsy, his teacher, gave me a high sign letting me know I could leave. I walked over and gave him a kiss on the head rather than sneaking out.

"I'll be back in a couple of hours."

He didn't burst into tears, so I kept going up the stairs and out the door. I tried to squelch the guilt pangs. There'd been a debate about whether daycare is bad for kids. But as a widow, I didn't have a choice.

"He did great," Miss Betsy said when I came back later. His pants were even dry.

"He's been playing with Ben and Tommy, from the older class," she reported.

I took his hand. "It's time to go."

He was so engrossed with the other boys he didn't hear me, so I lifted him up. We walked up the stairs. The other kids shouted a chorus of good-byes. *How nice.* Just then, a boy from the older group called out, "Good-bye, Fucker!"

Oh, my God. What had I gotten him into? Now the guilt overwhelmed me. But driving home, I started to laugh. This must be what worried Mom, the corrupting influence of daycare.

⌘

Liz, another single mother in the neighborhood, watched Davey the short time I was gone at night. Things began to settle into a routine.

I was the only graduate assistant with kids. In fact, I was the only one who'd ever been married. I focused on the opportunity I'd been given and tried to avoid thinking about the events of May 4. Many students had had to return to Kent when the school reopened and they were able to do it.

I hadn't heard from Sam who was working on a freighter. "I'll call as soon as I get into port," he'd said. But even his absences were tolerable. I liked being alone, or rather being a single parent. I could focus on my studies and my new assignment as a producer.

I did miss Bob, if only for his broadcasting expertise. It would have helped to take these classes together. He could have helped me, so I wouldn't have to struggle with technical things like splicing tape.

66

Winter 1973

With my graduate assistantship and the Social Security money, I was flush. For the first time since I graduated from high school, I had enough money to live on. But soon Social Security started sending me extra checks.

When I called to ask them to stop the checks the worker said they couldn't. "Hold on to them," she told me. "We'll notice it, eventually."

I couldn't resist spending that money. I needed furniture for the townhouse and went on a shopping spree. Determined to make my new digs vibrant, I bought a black and white checked couch and two chairs in psychedelic colors. I ordered a bedroom set for myself. Davey could use my old single bed when he outgrew the crib.

Sam showed up on Saturday morning and finished putting the bed together. My savior! He didn't come reliably, but when he did, he distracted me from my gloomy thoughts. I told him the story of Bob's death and he didn't flinch. Neither did he ask me any probing questions like *why didn't you make him go to the doctor?* I kept secret the terror of living with Bob. I didn't have a name for what I'd been through. He never hit me, so I didn't think of it as abuse, but I was happy to be free of him. I'd escaped.

Winter quarter began, and I still had my original assignment—producing *Reverb*. January 20, the anniversary of Bob's death approached. I didn't want to spend it crying and grieving, remembering my loss. The twentieth was also Inauguration Day. Nixon would be sworn in for a second term. Tim wanted to go to D.C. to protest. After the May 4 shootings I stopped going to protests, afraid someone would start shooting again. But this seemed like a good idea, a distraction. I'd be away from home and all the sad faces there. I could lose myself amid the marchers.

"I'd like to go. Would you have room for me?"

"Well, I'm driving, so yes, you can go," Tim said.

⌘

We made it to Georgetown before the snow started falling and spent the night camping out on the floor of a student crash pad there. Up early, we gorged ourselves at a local café. Who knew when we'd eat again? By 9:00 A.M. we found a group of protesters waving signs: "Stop the War," "U.S. out of Vietnam," waiting for the march to start. A frigid day—in the twenties with gales of wind—we had to keep moving to stay warm.

I didn't have delusions about making it past the guards at the Capitol, but we could at least show our disgust at Nixon for ignoring his promise to end the War. We marched and yelled for hours until the swearing-in ceremony ended. All the grief that would have paralyzed me in Ohio came out as screams of protest toward a president I didn't support.

⌘

Back in Kent, school and work continued. Happy I'd avoided the intense feelings the anniversary of Bob's death would have brought, I was desperate to just be normal—a college student, not a widow. Sam came and went but our relationship didn't seem to be advancing. One of my secret comforts after Bob's death was reassurance from the mourners that I'd be remarried soon. "Soon" to me was twenty-five and Sam wasn't acting like he wanted to get married.

One March Saturday he called late in the afternoon. "I'm going to Trey's wedding tonight. He's finally marrying Ann. Do you want to come?"

At this innocent invite, I started yelling. I couldn't find a sitter and get ready in ninety minutes.

"No. I can't. Go by yourself," I growled. I was shocked at my reaction to his invitation. What had gotten into me?

Sam acted puzzled. "What do you mean? Bring the kid along."

An evening wedding was no place for a squirmy two-year-old. "No. Go by yourself," I yelled and hung up the phone crying. That ended of our relationship. I wouldn't put up with any last-minute phone calls for dates. I'd find someone else.

I spent the rest of the weekend crying softly to myself. How could I be so upset over Sam when I'd hardly cried at the loss of Bob? I began worrying about my mental state. Maybe ignoring my emotions all these months had been a mistake.

On Monday, I started feeling better. Better that was until I picked up the mail. There was a letter from Social Security. Our checks were direct deposit, so I shouldn't be getting any mail from them.

"Dear Mrs. Turner," the letter began. "It's come to our attention that there has been an overpayment to your account."

Oh, no. The clerk warned me about this.

"Further payments will be withheld until August 1973 to recover the overpayment."

My stomach flipped. This was only March. Even though I had more money than ever, I was living payment to payment, spending most of it each month. I'd bought the furniture and car and was paying all the costs of living on my own. What would I do now? I burst into tears. Sobbing, I couldn't think my way out of this.

I started getting dizzy, shaking. I couldn't catch my breath. If I pleaded with the Social Security office, I might get them to take payments. I called and got an appointment. I hoped the worker would take pity on me.

My pleas fell on deaf ears. No way would Social Security negotiate with me. I panicked some more. How could I make it through four months living off the money in my savings account?

I couldn't think straight. I couldn't stop crying. My world fell apart. I had to pay rent, daycare, utilities, groceries. No way. I had to talk to someone. I saw an ad for free counseling in the *Stater* and called.

I got an appointment for the next day. Something to hold on to.

⌘

At the appointed hour a young guy wearing a sweater and a tie stuck his head into the waiting room.

"I'm Bill, Doctor Burns," he said and ushered me down the hallway.

His office, a converted dorm room, had been decorated to suggest a doctor's office. He gave me a kind look and asked. "What brings you in?"

The story spilled from me amid a torrent of tears—how I'd spent all the Social Security money and was cut off now. How I wouldn't get a check again until August. How I'd rejected my parents' rules and moved out of their house. How I broke up with Sam and, oh yeah, how my husband died leaving me with a toddler.

Doctor Burns eyes widened as I continued. His sympathetic looks made me cry even more. Then I told him what I thought was the worst symptom: "I'm so upset, I can't even listen to the radio. It makes me cry." I left out the part about all this stress provoking thoughts of suicide again.

"This is terrible," he said when I finished. "I want you to come to one of our groups. It meets on Thursday nights. It will help you a lot."

A group? How could that help? "I need help right now," I said, but he calmly offered the group again.

"I'd like you to try it. Just come once. It meets this Thursday at 8:00 P.M., right across the hall."

Doubtful, I shook my head. "Okay," I said hesitantly. *Couldn't they just give me some Valium?*

"If you don't like it, you can see me privately."

I was a mess. What did I have to lose?

Wary of a group knowing the sordid details of my life, I hesitated. What kind of weirdos would I meet there? I was under a lot of stress, not crazy.

⌘

I stuck my head into the group room. *Geez.* Everyone was sitting on the floor. *I was too old for this!* Sneaking in wasn't an option, as there were only eight or nine people sitting there, quietly chatting. I spotted Doctor Burns. And there was another older guy. Must be another psychologist. The rest of them? A mixture of young people, aged twenty-three, twenty-four at most. No one looked too crazy. As Bill called the group to order, I plopped myself down next to a girl with a friendly face. I would just listen.

"We're going to introduce ourselves," Bill said. "For the newcomers."

I wasn't the only new person. Jessie, the girl with the friendly face, was new too. She had just been diagnosed with a serious illness and was having trouble handling it. There were seven other students and another doctor, the old guy, Doctor Schmidt. When they got to me I told them my name and age and that I was a grad student in Telecom. No way was I spilling my guts. That first session wasn't so bad. Nobody pressured me. When my turn came again, I told a little more about myself. Well, about the money problem—nothing else.

As the weeks passed, I began to settle down. That fear of psychologists engendered by the St. Mary's nuns vanished. Listening to what the psychs said to other group members helped a lot. It didn't solve my money problem, but I learned how to calm myself down—take deep breaths, focus on the present, stop the "what ifs."

I felt like I was getting back to normal. I didn't break into sobs when something unexpected happened. I even found that I could live off the little money I had saved. Soon it would be August and my Social Security checks would resume.

There were other interesting things happening at the Counseling Center. One night I saw a flyer for a women's group. With Bill's group ending, I decided to give this new group a try.

67

Spring 1973

"You were abused."

"Me? No!" I was shocked. "He never hit me. How can that be abuse?"

Deb, one of the group leaders, explained patiently, "He controlled you, right?"

"No. I always fought back. I rebelled—until the end when he threatened to kill us. Then I knew I had to get out." The walls closed in on me. I had no place to hide after this admission and knew I had to listen to what she said.

Her eyes softened, but she persisted. "What happened when you rebelled?"

It slowly dawned on me. "Oh. He pulled his knife."

"Yes. Didn't that happen again and again?"

"I provoked him. He lost control." I didn't want to admit the humiliation his crazy actions caused.

"What do you mean, 'He lost control'?"

"Well, he never hit me. He just threatened me."

"And what happened then?"

"Nothing really. He pretended like it never happened."

"You're not getting this. Didn't you back down?"

"Yes. Right. I backed down, and he acted like nothing had happened."

"Now you're beginning to connect things."

"But what about the vacuum cleaner? He bought it even though I hadn't asked for it. How does that fit in?"

"He was buying you off. Wooing you."

I had a glimmer of recognition before slipping back into denial. *I won't be a double victim. Too unfair. A widow and an abused woman? No way. I could stand the widow part, but I cringed when I thought of myself as abused.*

I listened to the others tell their stories. My education came slowly. Angry, first at them and then at myself, I tried not to reveal too much. This new information was too overwhelming, but I kept returning to the women's group.

Rick and Deb, the leaders, had us read a book: "Your Perfect Right."[1]

I learned another way to respond. Assertiveness? I'd never heard of it.

"It means being self-assured and confident without being aggressive," Rick said. "Half of you react with fear—running away at the first sign of conflict. The other half? You strike back killing all hope of negotiating. We want to teach you to do something different."

We practiced assertiveness and stopping unassertive behavior. At the check-in which started each meeting, we reported our struggles or triumphs of the past week.

Assertiveness. The concept electrified me in a way that the therapy group hadn't. In the women's group, I was expected to solve my own problems. They cheered me on when I did.

Most were near my age. Liz, my sitter, was another single mother who was recovering from a divorce. Judy was a timid flannel-wearing business major who planned a move to Alaska with her boyfriend later in the summer. The others struggled with loss.

⌘

I tried my new skills out on Mom.

"We want you and Davey to move back home with us. You're too isolated living by yourself," she said when I dropped by for a visit.

---

1. *Your Perfect Right*, Alberti, Robert and Emmons, Michael; Impact, 2017.

"No," I said firmly and didn't apologize. That single *no* from me, stripped of theatrics and emotion, got her attention. She gasped and shut up. That wasn't the end of her antics, but it was easier to stand up to her from then on.

I slowly took control of my life, I practiced what I learned. My fear of vanishing into an abyss of emotion disappeared as I watched other group members cry and recover. My Telecom advisor's demands became a snap. I even chose a feminist theme for my thesis, "Sexism in Television Commercials."

My mother-in-law's long-ago fears of women's lib came true, not when I burned my bra but when I learned to stand up for myself. It felt good. When my new boyfriend, Josh, jealously grabbed my wrist, I broke up with him and didn't look back. I took wholeheartedly to this new approach and looked for conflicts to practice on. I got happier and discovered I could take positive actions that would improve my life.

One Saturday night in late October I went through boxes of junk that had accumulated in our moves. I came upon a pile of reel-to-reel tapes left over from Bob's days at the radio station. Must be some spots he recorded. He was famous for his puns and his sound effects and I wanted to relive old times. I popped his headphones on, threaded the first one onto the tape deck and flipped the switch.

"*Hi there!*" Bob's baritone voice boomed into my ear. Startled, I jumped as if he were right behind me. I threw the headphones across the room. My heart raced. I shook with fear. My neck prickled. *Why am I crying? Bob's dead. I lived through it. I'm okay. Stop. Focus on the present!*

This time I didn't fall apart. I took some deep breaths and told myself to settle down. I recovered my composure. As I did, the room came into view and my eyes rested on Davey's Big Wheel, his second birthday gift. He loved that trike so much, it was pure ecstasy watching him ride up and down the street. I spent a minute appreciating how far I'd come and what I had to be thankful for.

⌘

I bought a cute little rocking chair for Davey and began assembling it. I spread the parts out on the floor like Bob would have done. I lugged his heavy toolbox into the living room and tried to join the back and seat together. No matter how much I pushed and forced them, the staves wouldn't slide into their holes. After several attempts, I was frustrated. Then, to my surprise, a tear ran down my face. Soon I was overwhelmed. Davey stood there staring at me.

Why am I crying over a dumb chair?

"Goddamn it, Bob," I whispered under my breath, "why did you die and leave me alone? I can't cope with this stuff." I scared myself. This was the first time I'd cried out loud since the night Bob died.

Why did he have to die? He could have put this rocker together. I'd been afraid that if I cried and felt the depths of my emotions, I'd never be able to stop.

Now it was happening for real. Davey stared at me as I sat there, my head in my hands, sobbing. I dissolved into a heap on the floor. After what seemed like an eternity, my breathing slowed, and the tears stopped flowing. I reached out for Davey and he climbed into my lap. He tried to wipe away my tears.

"Mama," was all he said.

I calmed myself. "Come on, buddy. Let's get a snack." I took his hand and walked toward the kitchen. The rocking chair could wait.

⌘

That night I put Davey to bed early. As I sat watching *Mary Tyler Moore*, the iconic sitcom about a single TV news editor, I thought about what I had been through. I did it. I survived the abuse and the death of a husband bent on killing me. I survived the shootings at Kent State and the watchful, overprotective eyes of my parents. I didn't crack under the pressure of being penniless. I didn't succumb to thoughts of suicide that plagued the women in my family.

In the end, it wasn't one thing that saved me, but many. It was my brother, Tim, who listened when I rambled on into the night about the horrors I witnessed. It was Davey, whose growing needs gave me something to focus on outside my own misery. It was my parents, who expected me to live up to their expectations no matter how down I was. It was therapy and the women's group which taught me to handle overwhelming emotions.

The wounds are still there today but scarred over, protected. Whoever said, "Time heals," was only half-right. Time plus learning new skills so that I could experience the world differently were the key to my healing.

I glanced at the rocking chair still strewn about the floor in front of me. Slowly I rose and grabbed a stave. I knelt and shoved it into its hole. I could do this.

AFTERWORD

June 10, 1970, Arthur Krause, father of Allison Krause, one of the four students killed, filed a $6 million suit in federal court against Gov. James A. Rhodes and two Ohio National Guard commanders. His suit stated the defendants "intentionally and maliciously disregarded the lives and safety of students, spectators and passersby, including Allison Krause." Krause also filed a $2 million suit in Portage County Court of Common Pleas against the state of Ohio.

July 23, 1970, A Justice Department report on the Kent shootings is revealed in an article published in the Akron Beacon Journal." Details in a 10-page Justice Department memo summarize the reports of 100 FBI agents. The article quotes Jerris Leonard, chief of the civil rights division for the Justice Department, who said that the shootings "were not necessary and not in order" and that about 200 demonstrators heckling the guardsmen could have been repulsed by more tear gas and arrests, there was no hail of rocks thrown before the shooting, no guardsmen were hit by rocks or other projectiles, and no guardsmen were in danger of losing their lives. The statements in the memo and report differ greatly from accounts provided previously by Ohio officials and Guard officers . . .

July 23, 1971, A $4 million lawsuit against the state of Ohio filed by Louis Schroeder in connection with the death of his son William is dismissed by U.S. District Court Judge James C. Connell in Cleveland. As in three previous suits filed by the parents of the dead students, his ruling is the same: The state has sovereign immunity and cannot be sued unless it consents.

May 4, 1972, The American Civil Liberties Union files damage suits totaling $12.1 million in Cleveland against Ohio and the Ohio National Guard in connection with the 1970 shootings at Kent . . .

August 3, 1973, The Justice Department announces it will reopen the May 4, 1970 case. The announcement is made almost two years after the department rejected further federal inquiries into the case.

December 4, 1973, Attorneys for parents of three slain students ask the Supreme Court to allow the parents to sue former Ohio Gov. James Rhodes and National Guardsmen as individuals after suits against the state and Guard had been dismissed under the doctrine of sovereign immunity.

April 17, 1974, The Supreme Court rules that parents of three students allegedly killed by National Guardsmen at Kent can sue Ohio officials and officers of the guard . . .

October 21, 1974, The federal trial of eight former National Guardsmen accused of violating civil rights of the four slain students opens in Cleveland before U.S. District Court Judge Frank J. Battisti . . .

November 8, 1974, U.S. District Court Judge Frank J. Battisti acquits eight former guardsmen in Cleveland . . .

May–August 1975, Civil trials begin in Cleveland before a federal jury in which the wounded students and parents of the dead students had filed civil suits seeking a total of $46 million in damages from Rhodes, former Kent president Robert I. White and 27 former and current guardsmen. All individual suits are consolidated into one case, Krause vs. Rhodes . . .

August 27, 1975, The federal court jury meeting in Cleveland exonerates Ohio Gov. James Rhodes and 28 other defendants from any financial or personal responsibility in connection with the shootings . . .

June 1977, An appeal of the federal court jury on the civil cases is underway.

September 12, 1977, In a reversal of the 1975 lower court ruling which had cleared those defendants charged in a damage suit resulting from the shootings, the U.S. Court of Appeals for the Sixth Circuit Court orders a retrial.

January 24, 1979, An out-of-court settlement is reached in the civil cases and approved by the State Controlling Board with a vote of 6-to-1. The board is required to approve all state expenditures.

Shortly after the board announces its decision, the judge in the U.S. District Court in Cleveland dismisses a jury that had been called to hear testimony in a second trial against the state.

The plaintiffs receive $675,000 for injuries received in 1970 and this compensation is accompanied by a statement from the defendants, which reads in part, "In retrospect the tragedy of May 4, 1970, should not have occurred . . . We deeply regret those events and are profoundly saddened by the deaths of four students and the wounding of nine others which resulted."[1]

---

1. Kent State University, University Libraries: Special Collections and Archives: *Legal Chronology May 5, 1970–January 4, 1979*, compiled and edited by Margaret Ann Garmon; prepared for the Internet by Jennifer Schrager.

DISCUSSION QUESTIONS

1. What led up to the events of May 4?

2. What are the limits of free speech?

3. Have you ever been in a situation that risked your life?

4. What types of resources are available to abused women today?

5. What resources are available to grieving spouses?

6. What parallels do you see between the country's atmosphere in 1970 and today?

7. What lessons can we take away from Kent State/May 4?

8. What lessons from the Seventies can be applied to our lives today?

ABOUT THE AUTHOR

Paula Stone Tucker was a witness to the May 4, 1970 shootings at Kent State University. A retired clinical psychologist, she worked with survivors of trauma and abuse. In her younger days she was a reporter for the *Akron Beacon Journal* and the *Daily Kent Stater*. She grew up in Cuyahoga Falls, Ohio and graduated from Kent State. She splits her time between northeast Ohio and The Villages, Florida. This is her first book. She is available for  interviews. You can contact her at paulastonetucker.com or on Facebook at Paula Stone Tucker, Author. She looks forward to hearing from you and reading your reviews.